A Fireside Book · Published by Simon & Schuster

BEATLESONGS

WILLIAM J. DOWLDING

New York London Toronto Sydney Tokyo Singapore

**FIRESIDE**

Rockefeller Center
1230 Avenue of the Americas
New York, New York 10020

FIRESIDE and colophon are registered trademarks of Simon & Schuster Inc.

Designed by Bonni Leon
Manufactured in the United States of America

9   10

Library of Congress Cataloging in Publication Data
Dowlding, William J.
Beatlesongs/William J. Dowlding.
p.   cm.
"A Fireside book."
Bibliography: p.
Includes index.
1. Beatles.   2. Rock music—England—History and criticism.
I. Title.

ML421.B4D7   1989                                          89-33032
                                                                CIP
                                                                 MN

ISBN 0-671-68229-6

Excerpts from *The Playboy Interviews with John Lennon and Yoko Ono*
by David Sheff © 1981 Playboy Press. Reprinted with permission. All rights
reserved.

Excerpts from *John Lennon In My Life* © 1983 Pete Shotton and
Nicholas Schaffner. Reprinted with permission of Stein and Day Publishers.

Excerpts from *All You Need Is Ears* by George Martin with
Jeremy Hornsby, © 1979 in the United States by St. Martin's Press Inc., New York.
Published in England by Macmillan, London. Reprinted with permission.

All references to U.S. chart positions in this book are based on *Billboard*
magazine's Hot 100 chart surveys, as researched and compiled by Joel Whitburn.

●

## ACKNOWLEDGMENTS

This book could not have been possible without the numerous authors and interviewers who did the original research and asked the right questions of the various Beatles. I recommend that the reader wanting more information about the Fab Four go directly to the sources listed in the bibliography at the back of the book.

On a more personal level, I'd like to thank Linda Potter for her support and understanding; Steve Ostermann for his good suggestions and friendship; John Morris and Michele Thompson for their support; Rachel Anastasi, Bob Helf, and Jim Cieslewicz for information; Jim Kates and Dave Hendrickson for suggestions; Patty Romanowski for copy editing and tough questions; Bill Hathaway and Joel Whitburn for their understanding and permission; and the staff of *The Milwaukee Journal* newspaper, where I work in real life.

At Fireside Books, I'd like to thank Cynthia Lao, my editor; Marcia Peterson and Melissa Johnson, who copy edited the words; Bonni Leon, who designed the pages; and the other people who made this book a reality.

Special thanks go to my agent, Sandy Hintz, and the late Tim McGinnis, for sensing this book's potential.

DEDICATED
TO MY PARENTS
WILLIAM F. S. AND MARY DOWLDING
WHOSE LOVE SHAPED ME

## CONTENTS

*"Forms and rhythms in music are never changed without producing changes in the most important political forms and ways."*

—Plato

Twenty-five years after the Beatles invaded America, the effect of their conquest still reverberates.

The Beatles changed just about everything: hairstyles, clothing, lifestyles, perceptions, and most importantly, music. They took music from the tinny, formularized pop of the early '60s to the full-bodied, innovative rock of 1969's *Abbey Road,* which still sounds fresh today. They took control of the music away from producers and professional songwriters and made it the responsibility of the individual performing artists.

The Beatles were the sociological and cultural phenomenon of the 1960s. They succeeded on so many levels—as concert performers, recording artists, songwriters, and actors. John Lennon even added author to his list of credits. Their wit mesmerized us. Never before had rock performers been so much more than *rock performers.*

The huge baby-boom generation ate them up, buying millions and millions of their records and standing in line to see their films. The Beatles were more popular than any other group—*ever.* But the most distinctive thing about them was their constant growth. The Beatles became gurus to many people—they were looked to for answers because they always seemed to be one step ahead. Their fame was so huge that they assumed mythic proportions. When a rumor—based on alleged clues found in lyrics and album art—spread in the fall of 1969 that Paul McCartney was dead, the radio airwaves were full of speculation for weeks.

Even today, the Beatles' massive success is felt. Musicians are still generally required to create music with their minds as well as their fingers, and rock music now continues to echo the Beatles.

To question the impact of the Beatles is to question the reality of the shelf-loads of books already written about them. It is turning a blind eye to the front covers of magazines—to this day—that feature a Beatle face each time one of them releases a successful album. Their influence endures.

What this book attempts to do is to bring together all the information available about every song recorded and officially released by the Beatles. Source material includes some of that shelf-load of books, newswire and magazine articles, films and documentaries, as well as my own observations.

Many print sources have used previously published material, often misquoting or misinterpreting crucial information, so I've attempted to use original sources whenever possible. Unfortunately, there are as many myths about the Beatles as there are facts, and it's difficult to winnow falsehoods from the truth. I have spent hundreds of hours trying to do so. Nevertheless, there is still disagreement on many points. For example, key sources disagree widely on how long it took to record the *Please Please Me* album:

11 hours   Coleman
12 hours   *Diary* and Salewicz
13 hours (probably the most accurate)   *Live* and *Ears* and *Record*
14 hours (which McCartney says)   *Trouser Press* (February 1978) and *RS* (July 12, 1979)
16 hours   *Road*
53 hours (undoubtedly a typographical error)   *Love*
585 minutes (9¾ hours)   *Abbey*

As above, abbreviated references to sources appear in small type after individual items, and, in some cases, after parts of sentences. Agreements and disagreements between sources are also noted. Information about the sources can be found by looking for the source name in the Bibliography at the end of the book.

When the source is a periodical, I have given a date. If the date precedes the name of the periodical, it refers to the date the quote was spoken; if the date follows the name of the periodical, it refers to the publication date.

The song entries are arranged chronologically, generally by release date in the United Kingdom. The U.S. releases were haphazardly issued— often, songs from one project appear with others that were recorded for a different project many months before. By following the U.K. release dates —and the songs the Beatles themselves intended for the albums—the reader can better sense the Beatles' growing experimentation in the studio. There *are* exceptions to this: The album *Let It Be* sat on the shelf for more than a year before release. Accordingly, here it precedes *Abbey Road,* as it would have had the Beatles not lost heart in the project. The new songs used on *Yellow Submarine* were recorded at least eleven months before the LP was issued, so those are placed before *The Beatles* (the so-called White Album). And finally, the singles used to fill up the U.S. version of *Magical Mystery Tour* are presented as they were issued—as singles. Singles that appeared on albums—the title songs from *A Hard Day's Night* and *Help!,* for example—are listed with the albums.

This format allows the reader to listen to an album and read along, song by song.

Readers wishing to find a particular song can find its page number by consulting the alphabetical song index at the back of the book.

The U.K. chart positions are taken from the *New Musical Express* sales chart. This chart only tracks the A sides of singles, so the names of A sides are noted in the Chart Action sections of B side entries. The U.S. chart referred to here is the Top 40 of *Billboard*'s Hot 100, which tracks both sides.

The true authors of the songs—not those credited officially on the album and single labels—are noted in the Authorship sections of the entries. Most Lennon-McCartney songs were actually written by one or the other, not both. In two cases, in fact, Lennon wrote songs with Yoko Ono, so she is properly credited in both entries. Credit for each song's creation is apportioned based on all the information that could be amassed. In many cases, unfortunately, this comes down to an offhand remark by John Lennon or Paul McCartney on how they helped each other write songs. Still, this book is the first to attempt to *quantify* the contributions they made. (See Appendix 1, "The Great Songwriting Contest," for a more detailed explanation of this point and an actual count of who wrote the most songs the Beatles recorded and released.)

This is the book I always wanted to find in a book store. I hope you enjoy learning more about the most important music in rock history.

William J. Dowlding
*May 1989*

# PLEASE PLEASE ME
## *ALBUM*

○

Though the Beatles' debut single, "Love Me Do," was a moderate success, their second release, "Please Please Me," was a huge hit. As it neared the top of the charts, the Beatles took one night off from touring to rush to London to record most of this album in one daylong session. The following night they were back on tour and performed in both Yorkshire and Lancashire. *Live*

## CHART ACTION

UNITED KINGDOM: Rush-released March 22, 1963, shortly after the title song fell from its No. 1 position. The album entered the chart March 27 at No. 9 and in seven weeks was No. 1, where it stayed for twenty-nine weeks. It set a record for the longest continuous run at No. 1 in the *NME (New Musical Express)* album chart. *Road*

UNITED STATES: Capitol refused to release the album. It was released in a different form by the little Vee Jay record label as *Introducing the Beatles,* which failed to place in the charts. It differed from the U.K. version by not including "Please Please Me" and "Ask Me Why." *Road*

## RECORDED

February 11, 1963, except for the title song and "Ask Me Why" (since both were previously released as a single) and "Love Me Do" and "P.S. I Love You" (another single), at Abbey Road. *ATN; Live* and Salewicz agree on date.

Sources disagree significantly on how long it took to record this album —anywhere from 9¾ hours to 16 hours—but it probably took about 13. About the only thing the sources agree on is that it required just one session to complete. various

GEORGE MARTIN, producer: "All we did really was to reproduce the Cavern performance in the comparative calm of the studio.

"At the beginning [of the Beatles' recording career], my specialty was the introductions and the endings, and any instrumental passages in the middle. I might say, for instance: ' "Please Please Me" only lasts a minute and 10 seconds, so you'll have to do two choruses, and in the second chorus we'll have to do such-and-such.' That was the extent of the arranging." *Ears*

► ## PAUL AS THE BUDDING MUSICAL DIRECTOR

*McCARTNEY: ". . . Then [Martin] had a lot of control—we used to record the stuff, and leave him to mix it, pick a single, everything. After a while though, we got so into recording we'd stay behind while he mixed it, watching what he was doing."* Jamming! (June 1982)

*NORMAN SMITH, engineer: "[It was] nearly always Paul who was the MD, the musical director, as early as this. Obviously John would have quite a lot to say, but overall it was always Paul who was the guv'nor. Which is fair, because he was the natural musician, and even at this stage, the natural producer. On this session he was trying to figure out everything we were doing with the controls."*
Salewicz

A two-track tape machine was used, and the recording was entirely live. None of the vocals was overdubbed, and no more than four takes were made of any song. Salewicz

NORMAN SMITH: "I kept the sound relatively 'dry.' I hated all that echo that everyone was using back then. And I placed the singers' microphones right there with the rest of the band, although singers were usually hidden away in a separate recording booth. I thought that was a bad idea, because you lost the live feel of the session." *Diary*

At the Beatles' request, a large candy jar of cough lozenges and two new packs of Peter Stuyvesant cigarettes were placed on the piano for the session. So began a tradition that lasted for years. Salewicz

**INSTRUMENTATION**
McCARTNEY: bass                    HARRISON: lead guitar
LENNON: rhythm guitar              STARR: drums
*Road*

**ALBUM PACKAGE**
The cover photograph was taken on the staircase of EMI House in Manchester Square, London, by Angus McBean. *Road* McBean shot a similarly

staged photo six years later, to adorn the *Get Back* album (which later became *Let It Be*). It wasn't used for that but later appeared on *The Beatles 1967–1970* compilation album. A photo from the original shoot was used for the cover of *The Beatles 1962–1966.*  Road

## MISCELLANEOUS
McCartney had designed a cover for the album with the name *Off the Beatle Track.* The title was later used for producer George Martin's album of orchestrated Beatles hits.  Road

## COMMENTS BY BEATLES
LENNON: "We were just writing songs à la Everly Brothers, à la Buddy Holly, pop songs with no more thought to them than that—to create a sound. And the words were almost irrelevant."  September 1980, *Playboy Interviews*

●

# "I SAW HER STANDING THERE"

## CHART ACTION
UNITED STATES: Released as a single January 13, 1964 (the B side of "I Want to Hold Your Hand"), this song entered the Top 40 in January 1964, hitting No. 14 during its eight-week stay.  Road and *Billboard*

## AUTHORSHIP McCartney (.8) and Lennon (.2)
LENNON: "That's Paul doing his usual good job of producing what George Martin used to call a 'potboiler.' I helped with a couple of the lyrics." September 1980, *Playboy Interviews*

McCartney and Lennon wrote the song in Paul's living room while playing hooky from school.  Coleman

## RECORDED
February 11, 1963, at Abbey Road  *Day* and *Abbey* and *Road*

## INSTRUMENTATION
McCARTNEY: bass, lead vocal  
LENNON: rhythm guitar, harmony vocal  
HARRISON: lead guitar  
STARR: drums

*Record; Road* agrees on vocals.

**MISCELLANEOUS**
This song was part of the Beatles' repertoire for concerts from 1962 to 1964. *Live* It was one of six songs performed during the Beatles' second appearance on *The Ed Sullivan Show,* February 16, 1964. *Forever, Live* says it was also one of five on first show. It also was played at the Washington Coliseum and Carnegie Hall concerts in February 1964 and on the 1964 North American tour (some shows). *Forever*

On November 28, 1974, Lennon joined Elton John on the Madison Square Garden stage and performed the song. Elton John released the recorded performance in the United States on March 1, 1975, as the B side of "Philadelphia Freedom." *A-Z and Road* It was the A side of a single in the United Kingdom.

McCartney performed this song at the Prince's Trust Concert (1986) with several rock luminaries. *Prince's*

●

# "MISERY"

**AUTHORSHIP** Lennon (.6) and McCartney (.4)
Written mainly by Lennon with an assist from McCartney.
*Road* and *ATN* and *Hit Parader* (April 1972)

This was written originally for singer Helen Shapiro during the Beatles' tour of Britain with her in February and March 1963. *A-Z and Road and Day; Live* agrees for Shapiro. Her management, however, rejected the song. At the time Shapiro was sixteen years old and the most popular singer in Britain.

SHAPIRO: "We were leaning out of hotel windows, throwing photographs of ourselves at fans, and it was an incredible period, looking back." *Coleman*

**RECORDED**
February 11, 1963, at Abbey Road   *Day* and *Abbey* and *Road*

**INSTRUMENTATION**
McCARTNEY: bass, lead vocal          HARRISON: lead guitar
LENNON: rhythm guitar, lead vocal    STARR: drums
*Record; Road* and *ATN* agree on double lead vocals.
George Martin: piano
*Shout*

**MISCELLANEOUS**
This song was part of the Beatles' live repertoire in 1963. *Live*

●

# "ANNA (GO TO HIM)"

**AUTHORSHIP** Arthur Alexander (1.00)

**RECORDED**
February 11, 1963, at Abbey Road   *ATN* and *Day* and *Abbey* and *Road*

**INSTRUMENTATION**
McCARTNEY: bass, backing vocal        HARRISON: lead guitar, backing
LENNON: rhythm guitar, lead vocal     vocal
                                      STARR: drums

*Record; Road* says McCartney and Harrison provided harmony vocals.

**MISCELLANEOUS**
Arthur Alexander's original recording was released as a single September 17, 1962, on Dot. It didn't crack the Top 40.   *Road*
    This song was part of the Beatles' live repertoire in 1962 and 1963.
*Live*

●

# "CHAINS"

**AUTHORSHIP** Gerry Goffin (.5) and Carole King (.5)

**RECORDED**
February 11, 1963, at Abbey Road   *Day* and *Abbey* and *Road*

**INSTRUMENTATION**
McCARTNEY: bass, harmony vocal       HARRISON: lead guitar, lead vocal
LENNON: rhythm guitar,               STARR: drums
harmonica, harmony vocal

*Record; Road* says McCartney and Lennon contributed backing vocals; *ATN* says all three shared lead vocals.

**MISCELLANEOUS**
Original recording artist: the Cookies. Their version was released October 2, 1962, and entered the Top 40 in early December. It hit No. 17 during its eight-week stay there.   *Lists* and *Road*
    This song was part of the Beatles' concert repertoire in 1963, and Harrison, Lennon, and McCartney shared lead vocals live.   *Live*

●

# "BOYS"

**AUTHORSHIP** Luther Dixon (.5) and Wes Farrell (.5)  *Road*

**RECORDED**
February 11, 1963, at Abbey Road  *Day* and *Abbey* and *Road*   in one take  *Abbey*

**INSTRUMENTATION**
McCARTNEY: bass, backing vocal
LENNON: rhythm guitar, backing vocal

HARRISON: lead guitar, backing vocal
STARR: drums, lead vocal

*Record* and *Road*

**MISCELLANEOUS**
Original recording artist: the Shirelles. Used as the B side of their big hit "Will You Love Me Tomorrow?" which was released November 7, 1960, it entered the Top 40 in December, and held the No. 1 position for two weeks.  *Lists* and *Road*

This song was part of the Beatles' live repertoire from 1961 to 1964 (Pete Best sang lead until he was fired in August 1962).  *Live*  It was performed during the group's 1964 North American tour.  *Forever*

●

# "ASK ME WHY"

**CHART ACTION**
UNITED KINGDOM: Previously released as a single January 11, 1963, as the B side of "Please Please Me."  *Road*

UNITED STATES: Capitol refused to release this, but Vee Jay did February 25, 1963, as the B side to "Please Please Me," the Beatles' first U.S. single. It was not a Top 40 hit.  *Road*

**AUTHORSHIP** Lennon (.7) and McCartney (.3)  *Road; ATN* says Lennon.

**RECORDED**
November 26, 1962, at Abbey Road  *Abbey* and *Day* and *Road* and *ATN*

## INSTRUMENTATION

McCARTNEY: bass, harmony vocal
LENNON: rhythm guitar, lead vocal

HARRISON: lead guitar, harmony vocal
STARR: drums

*Record* and *Road*

## MISCELLANEOUS

This song was part of the Beatles' live repertoire in 1962 and 1963. *Live* It was performed at the Parlophone Records audition in 1962. *A-Z*

The public first heard this song on the BBC radio program *Teenager's Turn,* June 11, 1962, exactly seven months before it was released as a single. *Live*

●

# "PLEASE PLEASE ME"

## CHART ACTION

UNITED KINGDOM: Originally released as the Beatles' second single, January 11, 1963, it entered the chart January 30, and by February 22 was No. 1, where it stayed for two weeks. It was the group's first U.K. No. 1 record. The success of this caused the hurried recording and release of the *Please Please Me* album. *Road*

UNITED STATES: Capitol and several other U.S. record firms passed when it was originally offered to them. *various* It was later released as a single three times. When it was issued February 25, 1963, by Vee Jay it failed to chart. *Road*

Years later, star record producer Phil Spector blamed the initial commercial failure of this song not on the music, but on the backwardness of the American public. *RS* (November 1, 1969) The Beatles' sound had been ignored, but it was only a matter of time before the U.S. would come around.

Nearly a year later, on January 30, 1964, about two weeks after the release of "I Want to Hold Your Hand," Vee Jay released "Please Please Me" again. It entered the Top 40 February 22, hit No. 3, and spent ten weeks on the chart. *Road* and *Billboard*

Vee Jay rereleased it on August 10, 1964, but it didn't chart. *Road*

## AUTHORSHIP Lennon (1.00)

LENNON: " 'Please Please Me' is my song completely. It was my attempt at writing a Roy Orbison song, would you believe it? I wrote it in the bedroom in my house at Menlove Avenue, which was my auntie's place . . . I remem-

ber the day and the pink eyelet on the bed, and I heard Roy Orbison doing 'Only the Lonely' or something. That's where that came from. And also I was always intrigued by the words of 'Please, lend your little ears to my pleas'—a Bing Crosby song. I was always intrigued by the double use of the word 'please.' So it was a combination of Bing Crosby and Roy Orbison."
September 1980, *Playboy Interviews*

Lennon grew to love Bing Crosby records in the late 1970s.  Coleman

## RECORDED

The original, slow version was recorded September 11, 1962, at the second session for "Love Me Do." It was not released.  *Day* and *Abbey*

The Beatles recorded the second, faster version on November 26, 1962, at Abbey Road. George Martin almost refused to allow them to rerecord this song because he was not happy with the first version. He recommended that they record "How Do You Do It," a song written by a professional songwriter (and later a No. 1 U.K. hit for Gerry and the Pacemakers) and make that their second single. The Beatles refused.  *Day; Live* says Beatles recorded "How Do You Do It" September 4.  Martin agreed that if they recorded "How Do You Do It" first, they could record the revamped "Please Please Me." They played "How Do You Do It" without much effort and then tore into "Please Please Me."  *Road*

MARTIN: "I listened. It was great. . . . I told them what beginning and what ending to put on it, and they went into No. 2 studio to record. It went beautifully. The whole session was a joy. At the end of it, I pressed the intercom button in the control room and said, 'Gentlemen, you've just made your first No. 1 record.' "  *Ears*

After a break the band then recorded "Ask Me Why."  *Diary* and *Abbey*

McCARTNEY: "George Martin's contribution was quite a big one, actually. The first time he really ever showed that he could see beyond what we were offering him was 'Please Please Me.' It was originally conceived as a Roy Orbison–type thing, you know. George said, 'Well, we'll put the tempo up.' He lifted the tempo, and we all thought that was much better, and that was a big hit."  *Own Words*

Lennon and McCartney sing different lyrics on one line of the last verse. This was not intended but was kept in anyway.  *Musician* (July 1987)

## INSTRUMENTATION

McCARTNEY: bass, harmony vocal
LENNON: rhythm guitar,
harmonica, lead vocal

HARRISON: lead guitar, harmony vocal
STARR: drums

*Record; Road* omits harmonica; *ATN* says Lennon and McCartney shared lead vocal with Harrison in the background.

## MISCELLANEOUS

This song was part of the Beatles' concert repertoire from 1962 to 1964. *Live*  It was one of six songs performed during the Beatles' second appearance on *The Ed Sullivan Show,* February 16, 1964. It was also performed at the Washington Coliseum and Carnegie Hall concerts in February 1964. *Forever*

Song publisher Dick James was so impressed by this song that he offered Beatles manager Brian Epstein and the Beatles a deal to set up their own publishing company, Northern Songs, so they could retain control over the copyrights of their own songs.  *Salewicz*  The Beatles later sold part of the company for tax reasons and then lost control over their copyrights completely in 1969.

The "Please Please Me" single was one of the first two records Elvis Costello owned. (The other was "The Folksinger" by John Leyton.) Costello was in the Beatles fan club when he was eleven years old.

*RS* (September 2, 1982)

GEORGE MARTIN: ". . . A super record, a super tune."   *Musician* (February 1985)

●

# "LOVE ME DO"

## CHART ACTION

UNITED KINGDOM: The Beatles' first single on Parlophone, released October 5, 1962, this had a very erratic run on the chart. It entered the Top 30 at No. 27 on October 24, immediately dropped off, and later peaked at No. 17 on December 27.  *Road* with *Live*

Brian Epstein ordered ten thousand copies for his record store, hoping that would be enough to automatically land it on the British charts. He also conducted a letter-writing campaign to Radio Luxembourg and the BBC to force more airplay.  *Love;* Salewicz and other sources agree on ten thousand as number.  Epstein always denied ordering the copies, but close business associates and friends said it was almost certain he did.  *Live*

EMI promoted the single in the United Kingdom with a full-page ad in

*Record Retailer* a week before release. It was the only time that year EMI did so for any artist.   *Live*

Brian Epstein's NEMS Enterprises promoted the single with a press release that included a biography and pen portraits and suggested jokes on the Beatles' name.   *Live*

UNITED STATES: Capitol refused to release this as a single. It was later released on Tollie April 27, 1964, after Beatlemania erupted, entered the Top 40 May 2, held the No. 1 spot for one week, and stayed in the Top 40 for eleven weeks. Vee Jay released it August 10, 1964, but it didn't chart. *Road*

**AUTHORSHIP** McCartney (.7) and Lennon (.3)
McCartney played hooky from school one day in 1958 to write this song with Lennon.   *Day; Love* says it was written in the back of a van on the way to a gig.

LENNON: "Paul wrote the main structure of this when he was sixteen, or even earlier. I think I had something to do with the middle."
*Hit Parader* (April 1972); *Road* says Lennon wrote the middle-eight; *Love* supports sixteen.

It was extremely rare in 1962 for recording artists to write their own songs, especially their debut singles.

**RECORDED**
VERSION ONE: Recorded September 4, 1962, during the Beatles' first Parlophone session, at EMI's Abbey Road studio. Seventeen takes were needed before George Martin was satisfied, and even then he wanted a different drummer on the track.   *Road*

VERSION TWO: Recorded September 11, 1962. Studio drummer Andy White replaced Starr, who played tambourine.
*Road* and *ATN; Abbey* and *Live* agree on dates and drummers; *Diary* says White sat in on September 4.

Martin chose the September 4 version for the single, although later pressings substituted the Andy White version, which was also used for the album. You can tell the difference between the two versions by noting whether a tambourine is being used; their lengths also differ.
*Live* and *Abbey* and *Road*

NORMAN SMITH: "After the first take we listened to the tape. It was horrible. Their equipment wasn't good enough. We hooked Paul's guitar up to our own bass amplifier, and we had to tie John's amplifier together because it was rattling so loud."   *Diary*

"They were very much in awe of the studio. Also, they didn't realize the disparity between what they could play on the studio floor and how it would come out sounding in the control room. They refused to wear headphones, I remember. In fact, subsequently they hardly ever wore them." Salewicz

McCARTNEY: "I was very nervous, I remember. John was supposed to sing the lead, but they changed their minds and asked me to sing lead at the last minute, because they wanted John to play harmonica. Until then, we hadn't rehearsed with a harmonica; George Martin started arranging it on the spot. It was very nerve-wracking." *Playboy* (December 1984)

Harrison had a black eye at the sessions. The Beatles and Brian Epstein had been attacked at the Cavern Club by ex-Beatles drummer Pete Best's fans, angry over his firing the month before. Salewicz and *Musician* (November 1987)

## INSTRUMENTATION
The album version:

| | |
|---|---|
| McCARTNEY: bass, lead vocal | STARR: tambourine |
| LENNON: harmonica, Rickenbacker | Andy White: drums |
| Capri 325 guitar, lead vocal | |
| HARRISON: acoustic guitar, | |
| harmony vocal | |

*Record* (but omits Lennon's guitar); *Road* agrees on double lead vocal and Harrison's harmony but says Lennon played guitar; guitar from *Guitar* (November 1987)

Starr's drum kit on his first Beatles sessions was the Premier set he got at the age of nineteen as a Christmas present from his parents. It was his first drum kit. *Diary*

Lennon shoplifted the harmonica he played on this song in Arnheim, Holland. *Love*

During this period, Bruce Channel's "Hey! Baby!"—with Delbert McClinton playing harmonica *Live*—was one of the Beatles' favorite songs. On June 21, 1962, Channel and McClinton headlined a show that included the Beatles; "Hey! Baby!" had become a Top 10 hit five weeks earlier, so Lennon probably saw it performed live that night. *Live* A harmonica player himself, Lennon liked McClinton's style and tried to imitate it. Coleman and *Shout* The Beatles added Lennon's harmonica to "Love Me Do," then "Please Please Me," "From Me to You," and several other early songs until they recognized their own overenthusiasm and stopped using the harmonica altogether. December 1970; *Remembers*

Lennon was later kidded about this harmonica solo by Rolling Stone Brian Jones. Jones said he wondered how Lennon got such a deep bottom note from just a harmonica; Jones thought it might be a blues harp. Coleman

## MISCELLANEOUS
This song was part of the Beatles' concert repertoire in 1962 and 1963. *Live*

This was one of the songs the Beatles performed during their audition with George Martin June 6, 1962. *A-Z* and *Diary*

Martin didn't like Pete Best's drumming. On August 16 Epstein told Best that Ringo Starr would replace him. Ringo's first live performance as a Beatle was August 18 at the Cavern. (On that date, the Beatles were recorded at the Cavern performing "Some Other Guy.") *Day*; *Diary* says another drummer filled in until Starr was available August 28. While all this was going on, Lennon married Cynthia Powell August 23. *Diary*

Martin decided to have Andy White sit in on drums.

STARR: "I was shattered. What a drag. How phony the record business was, I thought." *Compleat*(b)

▶ **RINGO AS A DRUMMER**

MARTIN: *"[Ringo] hit good and hard, and used the tom-tom well, even though he couldn't do a roll to save his life."* Shout
*". . . He's got tremendous feel. He always helped us to hit the right tempo for a song, and gave it that support—that rock-solid backbeat—that made the recording of all the Beatles' songs that much easier. He was sympathetic. His tempos used to go up and down, but up and down in the right way to help the song."*
Musician (July 1987)

HARRISON: *"He could be the best rock 'n' roll drummer—or at least one of the best rock 'n' roll drummers. . . . He does fills which crack up people like Jim Keltner. He's just amazed because Ringo starts them in the wrong place and all that, but that is brilliant. That's pure feel. . . . You know, he does everything back to front."*
Guitar (November 1987)

McCARTNEY: *". . . Ringo is right down the center, never over-plays."* Musician (February 1988)
*"We always gave Ringo direction—on every single number. It was usually very controlled. Whoever had written the song, John for instance, would say, 'I want this.' Obviously, a lot of the stuff came out of what Ringo was playing, but we would always control it."* May 1980, Musician (August 1980)

LENNON: "Ringo's a damn good drummer. He was always a good drummer. He's not technically good, but I think Ringo's drumming is underrated the same way as Paul's bass playing is underrated." September 1980, *Playboy Interviews*

STARR, on getting his first drum set: "I banged me thumb the very first day. I became a drummer because it was the only thing I could do!" Compleat(b)

"But whenever I hear another drummer I know I'm no good. ...I'm no good on the technical things but I'm good with all the motions, swinging my head, like. That's because I love to dance but you can't do that on drums." Own Words

"...I'm your basic offbeat drummer with funny fills. The fills were funny because I'm really left-handed playing a right-handed kit.... I can't roll around the drums because of that. I have to start with my left hand. If I come off the snare onto the tom-tom, I can't go on to the other tom, to the floor tom. That's why we used to call them funny fills." Big Beat

Completion of recording was celebrated by the Beatles and George Martin at Swiss Cottage, a London steak house. A-Z

The song was recorded on single-track tape, so no true stereo version exists. Road

A performance video tape aired November 7, 1962, on *People and Places,* a show on Granada TV in England. Day

George Martin hated the lyrics. Love

MARTIN: "That was the best of the stuff they had, and I thought it pretty poor." Coleman

Three days before the release of this single, the Beatles signed a binding five-year management contract with Epstein. Live

## COMMENTS BY BEATLES

McCARTNEY: "You get to the bit where you think, if we're going to write great philosophy it isn't worth it. 'Love Me Do' was our greatest philosoph-

ical song. . . . For it to be simple, and true, means that it's incredibly simple."
*Own Words*

Lennon later said this song was "pretty funky."   December 1970, *Remembers*

McCARTNEY: ". . . In Hamburg we clicked, at the Cavern we clicked, but if you want to know when we *knew* we'd arrived, it was getting in the charts with 'Love Me Do.' That was the one—it gave us somewhere to go."   *Jamming!* (June 1982)

## COMMENTS BY OTHERS
Leonard Bernstein said on CBS-TV that the song included a drone effect that foretold later use of Indian ragas as source material.   *Compleat*(b)

Recording artist Sting vividly remembers his discovery of the Beatles. He was eleven years old when "Love Me Do"—with its vocal braids and haunting harmonica—captured his attention. He was swimming with friends at a public pool when he heard it. The music had an overwhelming, almost spiritual impact on the boys: they were up in an instant, dancing naked and twirling and singing. It was at that moment, so moved by the Beatles' song, that Sting knew he would devote his life to music.
*RS* (February 16, 1984)

MIMI SMITH, John's aunt, after listening to a demonstration disc of this song: "If you think you're going to make your fortune with that, you've got another think coming." She liked "Please Please Me" much more.   *Coleman*

●

# "P.S. I LOVE YOU"

## CHART ACTION
UNITED KINGDOM: Released originally as a single, the B side to "Love Me Do," on October 5, 1962.   *Road*

UNITED STATES: Released as a single April 27, 1964, on Tollie. It entered the Top 40 May 16, climbed to No. 10, and stayed in the Top 40 for seven weeks.   *Road* and *Billboard*   Vee Jay released it August 10, 1964, but it didn't chart.   *Road*

## AUTHORSHIP McCartney (.8) and Lennon (.2)   *Road*
The song was written in Hamburg during May 1962.

*Day; A-Z* says McCartney wrote it like a letter first and then put music to it, but McCartney quote in *Playboy* (December 1984) contradicts that.

## RECORDED
September 11, 1962, at Abbey Road    *Day* and *Road* and *Live*    It was the Beatles' second recording of the song. It was recorded the week before, on September 4, with Starr on drums, but George Martin found it unsatisfactory.    *Road;*

*Live* doesn't mention it for September 4.

## INSTRUMENTATION

McCARTNEY: bass, lead vocal
LENNON: acoustic guitar
(electrified Gibson J-160E), lead vocal

HARRISON: lead guitar (electrified Gibson J-160E)
STARR: maracas
Andy White: drums

*Record* (except vocals); *Road* provides vocals; *Record* and *ATN* say McCartney and Lennon both sing lead vocals; guitars from *Guitar* (November 1987).

## MISCELLANEOUS
This song was part of the Beatles' concert repertoire in 1962 and 1963.
*Live*

This song was performed at the audition for Parlophone Records on June 6, 1962, at Abbey Road.    *Diary*

MARTIN: "Frankly, the material didn't impress me, least of all their own songs. I felt that I was going to have to find suitable material for them, and was quite certain that their songwriting ability had no saleable future!"    *Ears*

NORMAN SMITH: "Their sound didn't impress me much. Actually they were pretty bad. We even had to adjust their amplifiers for them! They played for about twenty minutes, songs like 'Besame Mucho.' But afterwards they came into the control booth and we got to talking with them—and really, *that* was fascinating. I really think the Beatles got their recording contract because of that conversation. Let's be honest: they got that contract because of their enthusiasm, their presence, not because of their music. During that one conversation, we realized that they were something special."    *Diary*

MARTIN, to the band during the recording session: ". . . If there's anything you don't like, tell me, and we'll try and do something about it."
HARRISON: "Well, for a start, I don't like your tie."    *Ears*

●

# "BABY IT'S YOU"

**AUTHORSHIP** Hal David (.33), Barney Williams (.33), and Burt Bacharach (.33)   *Compleat*(b); *Road* and *Live* say Mack David instead of Hal David.

**RECORDED**
February 11, 1963, at Abbey Road   *Day* and *Abbey*

**INSTRUMENTATION**

McCARTNEY: bass, backing vocal
LENNON: rhythm guitar, lead vocal

HARRISON: lead guitar, backing vocal
STARR: drums
George Martin: piano

*Record; Road* omits piano; *ATN* agrees with Martin piano.

**MISCELLANEOUS**
Original recording artist: the Shirelles. Their version was released December 4, 1961, on the Scepter label.   *Lists* and *Road*   It was very successful, hitting No. 8 and staying in the Top 40 for eleven weeks, beginning in early January 1962.   *Billboard*
　　This song was part of the Beatles' concert repertoire in 1962 and 1963.
*Live*

●

# "DO YOU WANT TO KNOW A SECRET"

**CHART ACTION**
UNITED STATES: Also issued as a single more than a year after it was recorded, during the frenzied days of Beatlemania in the United States. The song, on Vee Jay, entered the Top 40 in mid-April 1964, hitting No. 2 during its nine-week run. Vee Jay rereleased it August 10, 1964, but it didn't chart.
*Road*

**AUTHORSHIP** Lennon (1.00)
Lennon got the idea for the song from a Walt Disney film, probably the song "Wishing Well" in *Snow White and the Seven Dwarfs.*

*A-Z* and *Own Words* and Coleman and *Compleat*(b); *Road* says either *Cinderella* or *Fantasia; Love* says title was from a line Lennon remembered Jiminy Cricket asking Pinocchio in *Pinocchio.*

LENNON: "[My mother] used to do this little tune when I was just a one-
or two-year-old. . . . The tune was from the Disney movie. . . . So, I had this
sort of thing in my head and I wrote it and just gave it to George to sing."
September 1980, *Playboy Interviews*

Harrison said this song (or its recording) was inspired, to some extent,
by "I Really Love You," a rhythm and blues hit for the Stereos in 1961.
*Musician* (November 1987)

**RECORDED** February 11, 1963, at Abbey Road   *Day* and *Road* and *Abbey*

**INSTRUMENTATION**

McCARTNEY: bass, backing vocal         HARRISON: lead guitar, lead vocal
LENNON: rhythm guitar, backing         STARR: drums
vocal

*Record; Road* agrees on vocals.

**MISCELLANEOUS**
This song was part of the Beatles' concert repertoire in 1963.  *Live*
    Billy J. Kramer and the Dakotas, also managed by Brian Epstein, re-
corded a version of this song. It was released in Britain on April 26, 1963
(backed with a McCartney song, "I'll Be on My Way"), and was a big hit:
No. 1 for two weeks. Although it bombed in the United States, Kramer's
U.K. success proved for the first time that Lennon-McCartney songs could
be hits for other artists. That began a long and fruitful career for the pair as
songwriters for other artists.  *Road*
    Lennon, solo on acoustic guitar, recorded the demo of this song for
Billy J. Kramer in a lavatory. The toilet was flushed at the end of the tape.
Lennon told Kramer that the lavatory was the quietest place he could find
to make the recording.  Coleman; supported by *RS* (August 25, 1988).

●

# "A TASTE OF HONEY"

**AUTHORSHIP** Ric Marlow (.5) and Bobby Scott (.5) for the play *A Taste
of Honey* (1960).  *Road*

**RECORDED**
February 11, 1963, at Abbey Road  *Day* and *Abbey* and *Road;* some sources say March.

**INSTRUMENTATION**

McCARTNEY: bass, lead vocal (double-tracked)
LENNON: rhythm guitar, harmony vocal

HARRISON: lead guitar, harmony vocal
STARR: drums

*Record; Road* and *Shout* contribute double-tracking; *ATN* says McCartney sang lead vocal.

**MISCELLANEOUS**

This song was part of the Beatles' repertoire for concerts in 1962 and 1963. *Live* The studio version is similar to the Beatles' live rendition, as *Live at the Star-Club* shows.

The original recording artist was Bobby Scott and Combo, whose 1960 version appeared on the soundtrack album of the movie of the same name. *Lists* Other versions were also recorded before the Beatles': the Victor Feldman Quartet (released June 4, 1962) and Martin Denny (June 18, 1962) versions were instrumentals. Lenny Welch released the first vocal version September 17, 1962. *Road*

●

# "THERE'S A PLACE"

**CHART ACTION**

UNITED STATES: Released by Vee Jay August 10, 1964, but it didn't crack the Top 40. *Road*

**AUTHORSHIP** Lennon (1.00)

LENNON: " 'There's a Place' was my attempt at a sort of Motown, black thing." September 1980, *Playboy Interviews*

**RECORDED**

February 11, 1963, at Abbey Road    *Day* and *Abbey* and *Road*

**INSTRUMENTATION**

McCARTNEY: bass, harmony vocal
LENNON: rhythm guitar, harmonica, lead vocal

HARRISON: lead guitar
STARR: drums

*Record; Road* and *ATN* say Lennon and McCartney shared lead vocals.

**MISCELLANEOUS**

This song was part of the Beatles' concert repertoire in 1963. *Live*

●

# "TWIST AND SHOUT"

## CHART ACTION
UNITED STATES: Also released as a single, March 2, 1964, on the Tollie label. Entered the Top 40 March 21 and during its nine weeks there rose to No. 2 for four weeks. *Road* with *Billboard* Vee Jay released it again August 10, 1964, but it didn't chart. *Road*

**AUTHORSHIP** Bert Berns (1.00) under the pseudonym "Medley/Russell" *Road*

## RECORDED
February 11, 1963, at Abbey Road  *Day* and *Road* and *Abbey*
The Beatles were tired by the time they recorded this, the last song of the long album session. One more song was needed, so the Beatles and George Martin chose this. Lennon's voice was almost gone and his throat was sore. Two takes were recorded but the first was used. *Abbey* and *Compleat; Road* and Salewicz say one take was recorded.

MARTIN: "... There was one number which always caused a furor in the Cavern—'Twist and Shout.' John absolutely screamed it. God alone knows what he did to his larynx each time he performed it, because he made a sound rather like tearing flesh. That *had* to be right on the first take, because I knew perfectly well that if we had to do it a second time it would never be as good." *Ears*
    Lennon later agreed that he was only screaming the lyrics.
December 1970, *Remembers*

## INSTRUMENTATION
McCARTNEY: bass, backing vocal  
LENNON: rhythm guitar, lead vocal

HARRISON: lead guitar, backing vocal  
STARR: drums

*Record; ATN* agrees on vocals.

## MISCELLANEOUS
Original recording artist: the Isley Brothers. Their version, released May 7, 1962, was their first Top 40 hit in the United States, entering the charts in June 1962 and hitting No. 17 during its eleven-week run. *Road* and *Billboard*
    This song was a perennial favorite in concert. The Beatles performed it regularly from 1962 to 1965, as the closing number for a long time and then as the opener in many 1964 performances when McCartney's show-

case, "Long Tall Sally," got the final spot. *Live* and *Forever*  It was one of five songs performed during the famous London Palladium show (which revealed Beatlemania for the first time to millions across the United Kingdom and from which the term "Beatlemania" was coined) on October 13, 1963, and one of four songs at the Royal Command performance, November 4. *Live*  One of six songs played during the Beatles' second appearance on *The Ed Sullivan Show,* February 16, 1964, it was also performed at the Washington Coliseum and Carnegie Hall concerts in February 1964 and during the 1964 North American tour, 1964 London Christmas concerts, 1965 European tour, and the 1965 North American tour. *Forever*

LENNON, circa 1964: "I hate singing 'Twist and Shout' when there's a colored artist on the bill. It doesn't seem right, you know. It seems to be their music, and I feel sort of embarrassed. Makes me curl up. . . . They can do these songs much better than us." Coleman

LENNON: ". . . The more interesting [songs] to me were the black ones because they were more simple. They sort of said shake your arse, or your prick, which was an innovation really. . . . The blacks were singing directly and immediately about their pain and also about sex, which is why I like it." *Red Mole* (March 8–22, 1971) via *Companion*

The Beatles' recording was used in the 1986 film *Ferris Bueller's Day Off* and charted again. Capitol
McCARTNEY: ". . . I saw 'Twist and Shout' in *Ferris Bueller's Day Off,* which I liked as a film, but they'd overdubbed some lousy brass on the stuff! If it had needed brass, we'd have stuck it on it ourselves." *Musician* (February 1988)

●

# "FROM ME TO YOU"

**CHART ACTION**
UNITED KINGDOM: Released on April 11, 1963, as the A side of the Beatles' third single. It entered the pop chart one week later at No. 6 and a week later was at No. 1, where it stayed for five more weeks. *Road*

UNITED STATES: Released as a single May 27, 1963, on Vee Jay. It failed to break into the Top 40. Vee Jay released it again August 10, 1964, but it didn't chart. *Road*

**AUTHORSHIP** Lennon (.5) and McCartney (.5)
Lennon and McCartney wrote this together on February 28, 1963, while on a bus traveling from York to Shrewsbury during a tour with headliner Helen Shapiro.

*Day* and *Diary* and *Love* and others agree; *Live* says February 27 and agrees on bus and route (they played York on February 27 and Shrewsbury on February 28); *Forever* says in back of "their van on the way to work"; Shotton says in a van; Lennon quote in *Own Words* says he and McCartney wrote this together on tour.

LENNON: ". . . I think the first line was mine. I mean, I know it was mine. And then after that we took it from there. It was far bluesier than that when we wrote it." September 1980, *Playboy Interviews*

The title of the song was taken from a letters column called "From You to Us" in the *New Musical Express*.
*Road* and *Diary; A-Z* and *Compleat(b)* say "From Us to You."

**RECORDED**
March 5, 1963, at Abbey Road *Live* and *Abbey; Day* and *Diary* say March 4.

LENNON: "We nearly didn't record it because we thought it was too bluesy at first, but when we'd finished it and George Martin had scored it with harmonica, it was alright." *Own Words*

**INSTRUMENTATION**
McCARTNEY: bass, lead vocal
LENNON: rhythm guitar,
harmonica, lead vocal
*Record* and *Road*

HARRISON: lead guitar, harmony vocal
STARR: drums

Lennon told singer Helen Shapiro that he sang the high falsetto part on this song and that "I can do the high stuff better than Paul." Coleman He apparently changed his opinion in the next year. (*See:* "A Hard Day's Night.")

## MISCELLANEOUS

This song was part of the Beatles' concert repertoire in 1963 and 1964. It was one of four songs performed at the Royal Command performance, November 4, 1963. Live It was also one of six songs performed during the Beatles' second appearance on *The Ed Sullivan Show,* February 16, 1964, and one of twelve performed at the Washington Coliseum and Carnegie Hall concerts the same month. Forever

This song introduced a Beatle trademark—a falsetto "whoooooo." It was so successful that it was used liberally in the next single, "She Loves You." Forever

The harmonica beginning of the British single differs from the opening of all other versions. A-Z

This song was used as the theme song for a radio series in England called *From Us to You* that starred the Beatles and consisted of five two-hour programs, from December 1963 through June 1965. For the program, the Beatles performed "From Me to You" but changed the lyrics to "From us to you." A-Z

Del Shannon recorded this song, releasing it as a single in the United States on June 3, 1963, about a week after the Beatles' version was released there. Shannon's version did not break into the Top 40. Shannon had performed on the same bill as the Beatles earlier in the year in Britain and undoubtedly heard the song in performance. A-Z and Day

Three days before this song was released in the United Kingdom, John's son Julian Lennon was born, April 8, 1963.

Day; Salewicz says four days before "it went into the shops."

●

# "THANK YOU GIRL"

## CHART ACTION

UNITED KINGDOM: Released as a single April 11, 1963, the B side to "From Me to You." Road

UNITED STATES: Released as a single three times on Vee Jay. The first time, May 27, 1963, it was the B side to "From Me to You" and failed to chart. The second time, March 23, 1964, it backed "Do You Want to Know a

Secret" and became a moderate hit. It entered the Top 40 April 25, hit No. 35, and charted for three weeks.  *Road* with *Billboard*  Vee Jay released it again August 10, 1964, but it didn't chart.  *Road*

**AUTHORSHIP**  Lennon (.5) and McCartney (.5)
LENNON: "[This was written by] Paul and me. This was just a silly song we knocked off."  *Hit Parader* (April 1972)

**RECORDED**
March 5, 1963, at Abbey Road, with harmonica overdubbed on March 13
*Abbey; Day* and *Diary* say it was recorded March 4.

**INSTRUMENTATION**
McCARTNEY: bass, lead vocal          HARRISON: lead guitar
LENNON: acoustic guitar,             STARR: drums
harmonica, lead vocal
*Record* and *Road; ATN* omits harmonica.

**MISCELLANEOUS**
This song was part of the Beatles' live repertoire in 1963.  *Live*

**COMMENTS BY BEATLES**
LENNON: " 'Thank You Girl' was one of our efforts at writing a single that didn't work. So it became a B side."  September 1980, *Playboy Interviews*

●

# "SHE LOVES YOU"

**CHART ACTION**
UNITED KINGDOM: Released as a single August 23, 1963. The Beatles' fourth single entered the pop chart at No. 2 five days after release and by September 4 was No. 1, where it stayed for four weeks. Seven weeks after relinquishing the top spot, it returned to No. 1 on November 20 and stayed there for two more weeks. The single sold 1.3 million copies in Great Britain by the end of the year, making it the year's best-selling single. It remained the biggest seller in the United Kingdom until McCartney and Wings' "Mull of Kintyre" in 1978.  *Road*

UNITED STATES: Not only did Capitol Records refuse to release this as a single, but even Vee Jay passed on it, after the failure of the previous two singles. Brian Epstein was finally able to talk the small Swan label into releasing it Stateside.  *Record2*

Released as a single September 16, 1963. It was not an immediate hit but sold heavily once "I Want to Hold Your Hand" ushered Beatlemania into the United States. It entered the Top 40 February 1, 1964, and rose quickly to No. 1, where it stayed for two weeks. It spent fourteen weeks in the Top 40.  *Road*

The week "She Loves You" hit No. 1, the Beatles had five songs in the *Billboard* Top 20. The others were: "I Want to Hold Your Hand" (No. 2), "Please Please Me" (No. 3), "Twist and Shout" (No. 7), and "I Saw Her Standing There" (No. 14).  *Road*

## AUTHORSHIP Lennon (.5) and McCartney (.5)
Lennon and McCartney wrote this song together in a Newcastle hotel room after performing June 26, 1963.

*Live; Road* and *Day* say it was written on tour with headliner Helen Shapiro (February 2 to March 3); *Playboy Interviews* says in a van en route to Newcastle; *Love* says lyrics were written in a hotel room three nights before it was recorded.

LENNON: "It was written together . . . I remember it was Paul's idea: Instead of singing 'I love you' again, we'd have a third party."

September 1980, *Playboy Interviews*

## RECORDED
July 1, 1963, at Abbey Road  *Day* and *Road* and *Abbey* and *Live; Diary* says both July 1 and July 29 and 30.

McCARTNEY: "Occasionally, we'd overrule [George Martin], like on 'She Loves You,' we end on a 6th chord, a very jazzy sort of thing, and he said, 'Oh! You *can't* do that! A 6th chord? It's too jazzy.' We just said, 'No, it's a great hook, we've got to do it.' "  *Jamming!* (June 1982)

McCartney credited Harrison with the idea for the jazzy chord.

*Compleat*(b)

GEORGE MARTIN: "Glenn Miller was doing it twenty years ago." But he liked it and let the Beatles have their way.  *Compleat*(b)

## INSTRUMENTATION
McCARTNEY: bass, lead vocal
LENNON: rhythm guitar, lead vocal

HARRISON: lead guitar (Gretsch Country Gentleman, model PX6122)
STARR: drums

*Record; Road* agrees with double lead vocals but says Harrison provided harmony vocal; guitar from *Guitar* (November 1987); *ATN* omits Harrison vocal.

**MISCELLANEOUS**

This song was part of the Beatles' concert repertoire in 1963 and 1964. It was one of four songs performed at the Royal Command performance, November 4, 1963. A film clip of the Beatles performing the song was aired in the United States on NBC's *Jack Paar Show,* January 3, 1964. *Live; Compleat*(b) agrees on Paar. This was the only song to be played by the Beatles during both of their appearances on *The Ed Sullivan Show,* February 9 and 16, 1964. *Forever; Live* says two others were also performed on both: "I Saw Her Standing There" and "I Want to Hold Your Hand." It was also performed at the Washington Coliseum and Carnegie Hall concerts in February 1964 and at some shows during the Beatles' 1964 North American tour. *Forever*

A German version—"Sie Liebt Dich"—was recorded January 29, 1964, in the Pathé Marconi Studios in Paris. *Road* and *Live* and *Abbey; Diary* says January 18. (*See:* "I Want to Hold Your Hand.") The German version was also released as a single in the United States on Swan May 21, 1964. It hit No. 97. *Road*

> ▶ **THE "WOO WOO" AND THE "YEAH, YEAH, YEAH"**
>
> *The "yeah, yeah, yeah" phrase that is featured so prominently in this song quickly became one of the Beatles' trademarks. In fact, in Southeast Asia, the Beatles' music was known as "yeah, yeah, yeah music" in government decrees.* Forever *McCartney's father had suggested using "yes, yes, yes" instead because it was more dignified.* A-Z
>
> *KENNY LYNCH, singer who toured with the Beatles and Helen Shapiro in early 1963: "I remember John and Paul saying they were thinking of running up to the microphone together and shaking their heads and singing, 'whoooooooo.' It later became a very important, terrifically popular part of their act when they sang 'She Loves You.' But at the time they were planning it, even before the song was written, I remember everybody on the coach fell about laughing. I said, 'You can't do that. They'll think you're a bunch of poofs.' I remember John saying to me he thought it sounded great and they were having it in their act."* Coleman
>
> *LENNON: "The 'woo woo' was taken from the Isley Brothers' 'Twist and Shout,' which we stuck into everything—'From Me to You,' 'She Loves You,' they all had that 'woo woo.' "*
> September 1980, *Playboy Interviews*

**COMMENTS BY BEATLES**
McCARTNEY: "Nearly everything I've ever done or been involved in has received some negative critical reaction. You'd think the response to something like 'She Loves You' with the Beatles would have been pretty positive. It wasn't. The very first week that came out it was supposed to be the *worst* song the Beatles had ever thought of." *Musician* (August 1980)

●

# "I'LL GET YOU"

**CHART ACTION**
UNITED KINGDOM: Released as a single August 23, 1963, the B side to "She Loves You." *Road*

UNITED STATES: Released as a single September 16, 1963, on the Swan label. It was not a hit. It was rereleased May 21, 1964, and again was not a hit. *Road*

**AUTHORSHIP** Lennon (.5) and McCartney (.5)

**RECORDED**
July 1, 1963, at Abbey Road
*Day* and *Abbey* and *Live; Road* says both July 1 and July 7; *Diary* says both July 1 and July 29 and 30.

**INSTRUMENTATION**
McCARTNEY: bass, harmony vocal     HARRISON: lead guitar, harmony
LENNON: rhythm guitar,             vocal
harmonica, lead vocal              STARR: drums
*Record; Road* omits Harrison vocal; *ATN* omits Harrison vocal and harmonica.

# WITH THE BEATLES
## *ALBUM*

○

With *Please Please Me* out for less than four months, the Beatles began recording songs for their next long-player in mid-July 1963. The band's intent was to release two albums and four double-backed singles each year. They were generally able to maintain this exhausting recording schedule through 1965.

Instead of trying to record all of *With the Beatles* in one day à la *Please Please Me*, however, the sessions were extended over three months, during which time the Beatles also kept up their grueling tour schedule and recorded parts of several BBC radio and TV shows.

**CHART ACTION**
UNITED KINGDOM: Released November 22, 1963. It entered the album chart five days later at No. 1, taking over the top spot from *Please Please Me*, and staying there for twenty-one weeks. (It was the longest continuous stay at the top by any artist—fifty weeks.) *With the Beatles* was the second album (the first being the *South Pacific* soundtrack) to sell a million copies in Britain, meaning that 2 percent of the population bought the record.
*Road* with *Forever*

UNITED STATES: The U.S. equivalent, *Meet the Beatles*, excluded five tracks and added three others. It was released January 20, 1964, as Beatlemania was about to erupt. In its first week, it sold 750,000 copies, and by mid-March it had sold 3.65 million. *Road*

**RECORDED**
Between July 18 and October 23, 1963, at Abbey Road
*Abbey; Road* and *ATN* and *Record* and *Compleat*(b) *say all of it was recorded on July 15.*

**INSTRUMENTATION**
Basic instrumentation was used.

McCARTNEY: bass

LENNON: rhythm guitar

HARRISON: lead guitar (including Gretsch Country Gentleman, model PX6122)

STARR: drums

*Road;* guitar from *Guitar* (November 1987).

With their second album, the Beatles began to experiment with studio technology. They took advantage of a new option for vocals: double-tracking. But, according to Lennon, they went too far and used that trick too often on the album. December 1970, *Remembers*

## ALBUM PACKAGE

The cover photo, with the Beatles in black turtlenecks against a black background and lit from the side in the style of Richard Avedon, was shot by Robert Freeman, a London fashion photographer. He was also a friend of John and Cynthia Lennon, who lived in a flat above Freeman at about that time. The cover photo was so successful that Freeman became the group's official photographer on their 1964 America tour.  *Diary*

Freeman used the same technique· Astrid Kichener had used three years before in photographing Stu Sutcliffe in Hamburg.

*Shout;* "Kichener" spelling from *Forever*

## COMMENTS BY OTHERS

PETE THOMAS, drummer for Elvis Costello's Attractions: "When I was nine, I got *With the Beatles,* and my grandma bought me a honky old drum and an old cymbal. That's it isn't it; what more is there? A drum, a cymbal and *With the Beatles.* Has the world really come on much further?"

*Musician* (June 1988)

●

# "IT WON'T BE LONG"

## AUTHORSHIP  Lennon (1.00)

## RECORDED

July 30, 1963, at Abbey Road   *Abbey; Road* says July 15.

## INSTRUMENTATION

McCARTNEY, bass, backing vocal      HARRISON: lead guitar, backing
LENNON: rhythm guitar, lead vocal    vocal
                                     STARR: drums

*Record; Road* says backing consists of harmony vocals; *ATN* omits backing vocals.

## MISCELLANEOUS

Lennon, and his interviewers, would often confuse this song with the one that supposedly had an "Aeolian cadence"—"Not a Second Time."

## COMMENTS BY OTHERS

"It Won't Be Long" was the first song Neil Young performed for an audience. The high school cafeteria concert also included "Money (That's What I Want)," another song featured on *With the Beatles.*  *RS* (August 14, 1975)

●

# "ALL I'VE GOT TO DO"

**AUTHORSHIP** Lennon (1.00)
LENNON: "That's me trying to do Smokey Robinson again."
September 1980, *Playboy Interviews*

Copyrighted in 1961 in the United Kingdom, the song was later recopyrighted when Lennon and McCartney had their own music publishing company in 1964.

**RECORDED**
September 11, 1963, at Abbey Road   *Abbey; Road* says July 15.

**INSTRUMENTATION**

McCARTNEY: bass, harmony vocal        HARRISON: lead guitar
LENNON: rhythm guitar, lead vocal     STARR: drums

*Record; Road* says McCartney's vocal is backing.

●

# "ALL MY LOVING"

**AUTHORSHIP** McCartney (1.00)
LENNON: "This was one of his first biggies."   *Hit Parader* (April 1972)

McCARTNEY: "It was the first song I ever wrote where I had the words before the music. I wrote the words on a bus on tour, then we got the tune when I arrived there."
*Playboy* (December 1984); *A-Z* says the lyrics came to McCartney while he was shaving one morning.

**RECORDED**
July 30, 1963, at Abbey Road   *Abbey; Road* and *Diary* say July 15.

**INSTRUMENTATION**

McCARTNEY: bass, lead vocal          HARRISON: lead guitar, harmony
LENNON: rhythm guitar, harmony       vocal
vocal                                STARR: drums

*Record; Road* says harmony vocals are backing.

**MISCELLANEOUS**
This song was part of the Beatles' repertoire for concerts in 1963 and 1964. It was one of five songs performed during the London Palladium show on October 13, 1963. *Live* It was one of four songs performed during the Beatles' first appearance on *The Ed Sullivan Show,* February 9, 1964, and included in the Washington Coliseum and Carnegie Hall concerts in February 1964 and during the Beatles' 1964 North American tour. *Forever*

This was the first Beatles composition to become a standard. *Forever*

**COMMENTS BY BEATLES**
LENNON: " 'All My Loving' is Paul, I regret to say. . . . Because it's a damn good piece of work. . . . But I play a pretty mean guitar in back."
September 1980, *Playboy Interviews*

●

# "DON'T BOTHER ME"

**AUTHORSHIP** Harrison (1.00)
Harrison's first recorded song. *Beatles*

HARRISON: "The first song that I wrote—as an exercise to see if I *could* write a song. I wrote it in a hotel in Bournemouth, England, where we were playing a summer season in 1963. I was sick in bed—maybe that's why it turned out to be 'Don't Bother Me.'

"I don't think it's a particularly good song, it mightn't even be a song at all, but at least it showed me that all I needed to do was keep on writing and then maybe eventually I would write something good." *I Me Mine*

Bill Harry, then editor of *Mersey Beat,* disagrees with Harrison's story. He said he pestered Harrison to write a song other than the instrumental, "Cry for a Shadow," and that finally Harrison did just to stop Harry from bothering him. *Road* and *Record*

**RECORDED**
September 11 and 12, 1963, at Abbey Road  *Abbey; Road* and *ATN* say July 15.

**INSTRUMENTATION**
McCARTNEY; bass, claves
LENNON: rhythm guitar,
tambourine

HARRISON: lead guitar, vocal
(double-tracked)
STARR: drums, bongos, loose-skinned Arabian bongo

*Record* and *Road* and *ATN* and *Compleat*(b); *Road* supplies double-tracking.

## COMMENTS BY BEATLES

LENNON, replying to Harrison's complaints of mistreatment of his songs, autumn 1969: "We put a lot of work in your songs, even down to 'Don't Bother Me'; we spent a lot of time doing all that and we grooved—I can remember the riff you were playing."   Fawcett

HARRISON: "To write a song . . . even one like 'Don't Bother Me,' helps to get rid of some subconscious burden. Writing a song is like going to confession."   *I Me Mine*

●

# "LITTLE CHILD"

**AUTHORSHIP** Lennon (.5) and McCartney (.5)
LENNON: "Both of us [wrote this]. This was a knock-off between Paul and me."   *Hit Parader* (April 1972)

## RECORDED
September 11 and 12 and October 3, 1963, at Abbey Road
*Abbey; Road* says July 15.

## INSTRUMENTATION
McCARTNEY: bass, piano, lead vocal
LENNON: rhythm guitar, harmonica, lead vocal

HARRISON: lead guitar
STARR: drums

*Record* and *Road* and *ATN*

●

# "TILL THERE WAS YOU"

**AUTHORSHIP** Meredith Willson (1.00)
The song was written for the 1957 Broadway musical *The Music Man*, in which it was originally sung by Robert Preston and Barbara Cook. Their version appeared on the original cast album.   *Road*

## RECORDED
July 18 and 30, 1963, at Abbey Road   *Abbey; Road* says July 15.

**INSTRUMENTATION**

McCARTNEY: bass, vocal

LENNON: acoustic guitar

HARRISON: acoustic guitar

STARR: bongos

*Record* and *Road* and *ATN*

**MISCELLANEOUS**

The Beatles played this song in concert for several years, particularly on their early tours of England and the Hamburg stands. McCartney liked Peggy Lee's version so much that he wanted it included in the Beatles' act. *A-Z*

This was one of the songs performed during the Beatles' unsuccessful audition for Decca in 1962. *A-Z*

This song was part of the Beatles' repertoire for concerts from 1961 to 1964. It was one of four songs performed at the Royal Command performance, November 4, 1963. *Live* It was one of four songs performed during the Beatles' first appearance on *The Ed Sullivan Show,* February 9, 1964. They also performed it at the Washington Coliseum and Carnegie Hall concerts in February 1964. *Forever*

●

# "PLEASE MISTER POSTMAN"

**AUTHORSHIP** William Garrett (.2), Robert Bateman (.2), Georgia Dobbins (.2), Brian Holland (.2), and Freddie Gorman (.2)

There is some confusion on who wrote this song. The credit above is from the sheet music in *The Compleat Beatles. People* (March 7, 1988) says Freddie Gorman and four friends. Other sources *Road* and *A-Z* and *Live* and *ATN* say the songwriters were Brian Holland, Robert Bateman, and Berry Gordy. The compact disc credits Dobbins, Garrett, Garman, and Brianbert.

**RECORDED**

July 30, 1963, at Abbey Road   *Abbey; Road* says July 15.

**INSTRUMENTATION**

McCARTNEY: bass, harmony vocal

LENNON: rhythm guitar, lead vocal (double-tracked)

HARRISON: lead guitar, harmony vocal

STARR: drums

*Record; Road* contributes double-tracking, says harmony is backing.

## MISCELLANEOUS

This was originally recorded by the Marvelettes, a female recording group. Their version, released as a single August 7, 1961, became a No. 1 hit. It was the Marvelettes' first single and the biggest hit of their ten Top 40 singles.   *Road* and *Billboard*

This song was part of the Beatles' concert repertoire in 1961 and 1962. *Live*

This was performed during an unsuccessful audition for Decca in 1962. *A-Z*

## COMMENTS BY BEATLES

McCARTNEY: "[Our recording was] influenced by the Marvelettes, who did the original version. We got it from our fans, who would write PLEASE MR. POSTMAN on the back of the envelopes. 'POSTY, POSTY, DON'T BE SLOW, BE LIKE THE BEATLES AND GO, MAN, GO!' That sort of stuff."   *Playboy* (December 1984)

●

# "ROLL OVER BEETHOVEN"

**AUTHORSHIP** Chuck Berry (1.00)

**RECORDED**

July 30, 1963, at Abbey Road.   *Abbey; Road* says July 15.

**INSTRUMENTATION**

McCARTNEY: bass, handclaps

LENNON: rhythm guitar, handclaps

HARRISON: lead guitar, vocal (double-tracked), handclaps

STARR: drums, handclaps

*Record; Road* provides double-tracking and handclaps; *ATN* omits handclaps.

## MISCELLANEOUS

Originally recorded by Chuck Berry and released as a single May 14, 1956, on Chess. Now considered a rock classic, Berry's version spent only *one* week in the Top 40, peaking at No. 29.   *Road* and *Billboard*

This song was part of the Beatles' repertoire for concerts from the late 1950s into 1964. Lennon sang lead into 1961.   *Live*   It was also performed at the Washington Coliseum and Carnegie Hall concerts in February 1964 and during the 1964 North American tour.   *Forever*

●

# "HOLD ME TIGHT"

**AUTHORSHIP** McCartney (.8) and Lennon (.2)
LENNON: "Both of us [wrote this], but mainly Paul."
*Hit Parader* (April 1972); *Road* supports.

**RECORDED**
September 12, 1963, at Abbey Road    *Abbey; Road* says July 15.

**INSTRUMENTATION**

McCARTNEY: bass, lead vocal
LENNON: rhythm guitar, backing vocal

HARRISON: lead guitar, backing vocal
STARR: drums

*Record* and *Road*

**MISCELLANEOUS**
This song was part of the Beatles' concert repertoire from 1961 to 1963.
*Live*

A version of this song was recorded February 11, 1963, during the *Please Please Me* session but not released.    *Diary* and *Day* and *Abbey*

**COMMENTS BY BEATLES**
McCARTNEY: "I can't remember much about that one. Certain songs were just 'work' songs, you haven't got much memory of them. That's one of them. . . . It was a bit Shirelles."    *Abbey*

LENNON: "It was a pretty poor song."    September 1980, *Playboy Interviews*

●

# "YOU REALLY GOT A HOLD ON ME"

**AUTHORSHIP** William (Smokey) Robinson (1.00)

**RECORDED**
July 18, 1963, at Abbey Road    *Abbey; Road* and *ATN* say July 15.

## INSTRUMENTATION

McCARTNEY: bass, backing vocal    STARR: drums
LENNON: rhythm guitar, lead vocal    George Martin: piano
HARRISON: lead guitar, lead vocal

*Record* and *Road*

## MISCELLANEOUS

This song was originally recorded by Smokey Robinson and the Miracles. Their version, released as a single November 19, 1962, was the Miracles' second Top 10 hit. In its ten weeks in the Top 40, it reached No. 8.

*Road* and *Billboard*

This song was part of the Beatles' live repertoire in late 1962 and 1963.

*Live*

The Beatles later performed a version of this song in the film *Let It Be.*

●

# "I WANNA BE YOUR MAN"

**AUTHORSHIP** McCartney (.7) and Lennon (.3)

LENNON: "Both of us [wrote this] but mainly Paul. . . . I helped him finish it." *Hit Parader* (April 1972)

The Rolling Stones recorded their version of "I Wanna Be Your Man" in October of 1963, *Day* hoping it would succeed as a commercial single. They'd first heard the song at a rehearsal when Stones manager Andrew Oldham invited Lennon and McCartney in to peddle their wares. *RS* (October 12, 1968) The two Beatles actually finished writing the song for the Stones, providing them with their first big hit.

*A-Z* says Lennon and McCartney wrote it in ten minutes.

LENNON: " 'I Wanna Be Your Man' was a kind of lick Paul had. . . . It was a throwaway. The only two versions of the song were Ringo and the Rolling Stones. That shows how much importance we put on it: We weren't going to give them anything *great,* right?" September 1980, *Playboy Interviews*

## RECORDED

September 11 and 12 and October 3 and 23, 1963, at Abbey Road

*Abbey; Road* says July 15.

## INSTRUMENTATION

McCARTNEY: bass, harmony vocal    HARRISON: lead guitar
LENNON: rhythm guitar, Hammond    STARR: drums, maracas, lead vocal
organ, harmony vocal

*Record; Road* says Harrison also sang harmony vocals.

**MISCELLANEOUS**

This was the only song released by both the Beatles and the Rolling Stones. It was answered by Bob Dylan with his "I Wanna Be Your Lover," unreleased until his *Biograph* album (1985).

This song was part of the Beatles' repertoire for concerts from 1963 through 1966 as Ringo's showpiece. *Live* It was also performed at the Washington Coliseum and Carnegie Hall concerts in February 1964, and during the Beatles' 1964 North American tour, 1965 European tour, 1965 North American tour (alternating with "Act Naturally"), and 1966 world tour. *Forever*

●

# "DEVIL IN HER HEART"

**AUTHORSHIP** Richard P. Drapkin (1.00)

**RECORDED**
July 18, 1963, at Abbey Road   *Abbey; Road* says July 15.

**INSTRUMENTATION**

McCARTNEY: bass, harmony vocal
LENNON: rhythm guitar, harmony vocal

HARRISON: lead guitar, lead vocal
STARR: drums, maracas

*Record* and *Road*

**MISCELLANEOUS**

The original recording artist was the Donays, who released it as a single August 6, 1962. It did not crack the Top 40. *Road* Because the Donays were female, the original title was "Devil in *His* Heart." *Live*

This song was part of the Beatles' repertoire for concerts in 1962 and 1963. *Live*

●

# "NOT A SECOND TIME"

**AUTHORSHIP** Lennon (1.00)
Lennon attributed authorship to himself.
*Hit Parader* (April 1972); *ATN* and *Road* support.

McCartney said the song was influenced by Smokey Robinson and the Miracles. *Playboy* (December 1984)

## RECORDED
September 11, 1963, at Abbey Road   *Abbey; Road* says July 15.

## INSTRUMENTATION
LENNON: acoustic guitar, vocal          STARR: drums
(double-tracked)                              George Martin: piano

*Record,* which says McCartney and Harrison were not present; *Road* and *Abbey* agree on Martin piano.

## MISCELLANEOUS
WILLIAM MANN, London *Times* critic: ". . . But harmonic interest is typical of their quicker songs too, and one gets the impression that they think simultaneously of harmony and melody, so firmly are the major tonic sevenths and ninths built into their tunes, and the flat-submediant key-switches, so natural is the Aeolian cadence at the end of 'Not a Second Time' (the chord progression which ends Mahler's 'Song of the Earth') . . ."

The London *Times* (December 27, 1963), via *Companion*

LENNON: "To this day I don't have *any* idea what [Aeolian cadences] are. They sound like exotic birds."   September 1980, *Playboy Interviews*

LENNON: ". . . Really, it was just chords like any other chords. That was the first time anyone had written anything like that about us."   *Own Words*

●

# "MONEY (THAT'S WHAT I WANT)"

**AUTHORSHIP** Janie Bradford (.5) and Berry Gordy (.5)
To the original lyrics, Lennon added the line "I want to be free."   *A-Z*

## RECORDED
July 18, 1963, at Abbey Road, with an overdub on July 30
*Abbey; Road* and *ATN* say July 15.

**INSTRUMENTATION**
McCARTNEY: bass, backing vocal     STARR: drums
LENNON: rhythm guitar, lead vocal     George Martin: piano
HARRISON: lead guitar, backing
vocal

*Record* and *Road* and *ATN*

**MISCELLANEOUS**
Originally recorded by Barrett Strong and released December 10, 1959, this peaked at No. 23 and stayed in the Top 40 for eight weeks.

*Road* and *Billboard*

This song was part of the Beatles' live repertoire from 1960 to 1964. It was one of five songs performed during the London Palladium show, October 13, 1963. *Live*

This was one of the songs performed during an unsuccessful audition for Decca in 1962. *A-Z*

Playing this song at high volume approximates the Beatles' sound at the Cavern, according to Mike Evans, author of *The Art of the Beatles.*

via Salewicz

•

# "I WANT TO HOLD YOUR HAND"

**CHART ACTION**
UNITED KINGDOM: Released as a single November 29, 1963, the Beatles' fifth single entered the chart at No. 1 a week later and stayed there for six weeks. By January 17, it had sold 1.5 million copies in the United Kingdom alone. *Road*

UNITED STATES: Released as a single January 13, 1964, it was the group's first U.S. Top 40 hit. Entering the Top 40 January 25, it held the No. 1 position for seven weeks and remained in the Top 40 for fourteen weeks. The single sold better in its first ten days than any previous British single released in the United States.

*Road* and Salewicz and *Billboard; ATN* and *Compleat*(b) agree on release date; *Forever* says January; *Live* says January 13 was original release date but it was rush-released December 26; *Love* says originally scheduled for January release, but released December 26.

Capitol Records had refused to release the first several Beatles singles in the United States. In his attempt to convince them this time, Brian Epstein told Capitol that "I Want to Hold Your Hand" was produced specifically with the "American sound" in mind. Capitol finally agreed to release it. Its surprisingly huge success prompted Capitol to spend the unprecedented amount of $50,000 on an advertising blitz to break the group in the United States. *Love; Diary* says campaign was launched January 1. Epstein never had to beg Capitol to release another Beatles single.

The Beatles celebrated their first No. 1 hit record on the U.S. *Cashbox* chart January 15, 1964, *Live* says January 16; *Diary* says January 17. at the George V Hotel in Paris, where they were staying. The group had a celebration dinner with Brian Epstein, George Martin, and others. *Day* The Beatles were in Paris for their French debut at the Paris Olympia and to make a recording at EMI's Paris studio.

**AUTHORSHIP** Lennon (.5) and McCartney (.5)
LENNON: "We wrote a *lot* of stuff together, one on one, eyeball to eyeball. Like in 'I Want to Hold Your Hand,' I remember when we got the chord that made the song. We were in Jane Asher's house, downstairs in the cellar playing on the piano at the same time. And we had 'oh, you-u-u . . . got that something . . .' And Paul hits this chord and I turn to him and say, 'That's *it!*' I said, 'Do that again!' In those days, we really used to absolutely write like that—both playing into each other's noses."

September 1980, *Playboy Interviews; Compleat*(b) agrees on location—Jane Asher's basement den.

## RECORDED

October 17, 1963, at Abbey Road   *Abbey; Day* and *Road* and *Diary* say October 19.

This was the first Beatles recording for which four-track recording equipment was used.   *Abbey*

## INSTRUMENTATION

McCARTNEY: bass, lead vocal  
LENNON: rhythm guitar, lead vocal

HARRISON: lead guitar, harmony vocal  
STARR: drums

*Record* and *Road; ATN* omits Harrison's vocals.

## MISCELLANEOUS

This song was part of the Beatles' repertoire for concerts in 1963 and 1964. It was one of five songs performed during the London Palladium show, October 13, 1963.   *Forever; Live*   It was one of six songs performed during the Beatles' second appearance on *The Ed Sullivan Show,* February 16, 1964.   *Forever; Live* says it was performed on both shows.   It was also performed at the Carnegie Hall and Washington, D.C., concerts in February 1964 and during the Beatles' 1964 North American tour.   *Forever*

EMI in Germany insisted that the Beatles record German versions of their songs for sales there. The German rendition of this song, "Komm, Gib Mir Deine Hand," was recorded January 29, 1964, at the Pathé Marconi studio in Paris.   *Live* and *Road; Diary* says January 18.   It appeared on the *Something New* LP in the United States, on the U.K. *Rarities* LP, and on the *Past Masters, Volume 1* compact disc.

## COMMENTS BY BEATLES

This song was of special and lasting interest to Lennon; the melody stayed with him. Even seven years after he and Paul had written the tune, Lennon entertained the possibility of recording it again.   December 1970, *Remembers*

## COMMENTS BY OTHERS

Poet Allen Ginsberg had a revelation of sorts when he first heard "I Want to Hold Your Hand" in a New York City nightclub. He was so carried away by the Beatles' music and its revolutionary style that he got up and danced —Ginsberg had never before danced in public.   *RS* (February 16, 1984)

Bob Dylan thought there was a reference to marijuana in this song. On August 28, 1964, in the Beatles' suite at the Delmonico Hotel in New York, Dylan offered them a joint and was shocked when Brian Epstein said they had never smoked pot. Dylan had misinterpreted the line "I can't hide" for "I get high."   Salewicz

Singer Teddy Pendergrass was a junior high school student when "I

Want to Hold Your Hand" brought the Beatles into the black community. As a musician, Pendergrass looked beyond the group's media trademarks— the hair and style of dress—and heard the originality in their music. He credits the Beatles with inspiring his own musical development and independent growth as a performer.  *RS* (February 16, 1984)

•

# "THIS BOY"

## CHART ACTION
UNITED KINGDOM: Released as a single November 29, 1963, as the B side of "I Want to Hold Your Hand."  *Road* and *Abbey*

UNITED STATES: This was not released as a single, but instead appeared on Capitol's *Meet the Beatles* album, issued January 20, 1964.  *Road*

## AUTHORSHIP Lennon (1.00)
LENNON: "Just my attempt at writing one of those three-part-harmony/ Smokey Robinson songs. Nothing in the lyrics; just a sound and harmony." September 1980, *Playboy Interviews*

HARRISON: "If you listen to the middle-eight of 'This Boy,' it was John trying to *do* Smokey."  *Musician* (November 1987)

## RECORDED
October 17, 1963, at Abbey Road
*Abbey* and *Live; Day* and *Road* and *Diary* say October 19.

## INSTRUMENTATION
McCARTNEY: bass, harmony vocal
LENNON: acoustic guitar, lead vocal

HARRISON: lead guitar, harmony vocal
STARR: drums

*Record* and *Abbey; Road* and *ATN* omit Harrison's vocal.

## MISCELLANEOUS
This song was part of the Beatles' repertoire for concerts in 1963 and 1964. It was one of five songs performed during the London Palladium show, October 13, 1963.  *Live*  It was one of four songs performed during the Beatles' first appearance on *The Ed Sullivan Show,* February 9, 1964.  *Forever; Live* says five and excludes this one.  It was also performed at the Washington Coliseum and Carnegie Hall concerts in February 1964.  *Forever*

An instrumental version was recorded as "Ringo's Theme" by the George Martin Orchestra and used during Ringo's big scene in *A Hard Day's Night.* Road

William Mann, of the London *Times,* wrote that this song contained "chains of pandiatonic clusters." London *Times* (December 27, 1963) via *Companion*

## COMMENTS BY BEATLES
LENNON: "There was a period when I thought I didn't write melodies, that Paul wrote those and I just wrote straight, shouting rock 'n' roll. But of course, when I think of some of my own songs—'In My Life,' or some of the early stuff, 'This Boy'—I was writing melody with the best of them." September 1980, *Playboy Interviews*

●

# "LONG TALL SALLY"

## CHART ACTION
UNITED KINGDOM: Released on the *Long Tall Sally* EP June 19, 1964. The disc was No. 1 on the EP chart for seven weeks. Road

**AUTHORSHIP** Enotris Johnson (.33), Richard Penniman (Little Richard) (.33) and Robert Blackwell (.33)
The composition was originally called "The Thing" and later "Bald Headed Sally." Road

## RECORDED
March 1, 1964, at Abbey Road
*Abbey; Day* says February 25; *Road* and *ATN* and *Compleat*(b) say late February.
Only one take was needed. Abbey

## INSTRUMENTATION
McCARTNEY: bass, piano, vocal          HARRISON: lead guitar
LENNON: rhythm guitar                  STARR: drums
*Record; Road* says McCartney probably played piano; *ATN* omits piano.

## MISCELLANEOUS
This was originally recorded in New Orleans as "The Thing" by Little Richard. He recorded it again and released it as a single March 12, 1956, under the title "Long Tall Sally." It was a No. 6 hit in the United States and No. 3 in the United Kingdom. Road

McCartney sang this song during his first public performance at the age of fifteen at a holiday camp with his family. *Salewicz and Macs* One other song was performed: the Everly Brothers' "Bye Bye Love," with his brother, Mike. *Macs*

This song was performed many times by the Beatles. It was part of their repertoire from the late 1950s through 1966 and was often the show's finale. *Live* It was performed at the Washington Coliseum and Carnegie Hall concerts in February 1964 and during the 1964 North American tour, the 1964 London Christmas shows, and the 1965 European tour. *Forever* This was the last song the Beatles performed on a paid concert stage, at San Francisco's Candlestick Park, August 29, 1966, after more than 1,400 concert appearances. *Live*

McCartney performed this song at the Prince's Trust Concert (1986) with several rock luminaries. *Prince's*

●

## "SLOW DOWN"

**CHART ACTION**
UNITED KINGDOM: Released on the *Long Tall Sally* EP June 19, 1964. *Road*

UNITED STATES: Released as a single August 24, 1964. Entered the Top 40 September 26, 1964, climbed to No. 25, and stayed in the Top 40 for four weeks. *Road* with *Billboard*

**AUTHORSHIP** Larry Williams (1.00)

**RECORDED**
June 1, 1964, at Abbey Road, with the piano overdubbed June 4
*Abbey; Day* says February 25; *Road* and *ATN* and *Compleat*(b) say late February; *Live* says June 1 and 2.

**INSTRUMENTATION**

| | |
|---|---|
| McCARTNEY: bass | HARRISON: lead guitar |
| LENNON: rhythm guitar, vocal | STARR: drums |
| (double-tracked) | George Martin: piano |

*Record; Road* provides double-tracking and says McCartney probably played piano; *ATN* omits piano.

**MISCELLANEOUS**
This was originally recorded by Larry Williams, who released it as a single February 24, 1958. It was not a Top 40 hit. *Road*

This song was part of the Beatles' live repertoire from 1960 to 1962.
*Live*

●

# "MATCHBOX"

**CHART ACTION**
UNITED KINGDOM: Released on the *Long Tall Sally* EP June 19, 1964.
*Road*

UNITED STATES: Released as a single August 24, 1964. Entered the Top 40 September 19, where it remained for five weeks, climbing as high as No. 17.   *Road* and *Billboard*

**AUTHORSHIP** Carl Perkins (1.00)

**RECORDED**
June 1, 1964, at Abbey Road
*Abbey; Day* says February 25; *Road* and *ATN* and *Compleat*(b) say late February.

**INSTRUMENTATION**
McCARTNEY: bass                     STARR: drums, vocal
LENNON: rhythm guitar          George Martin: piano
HARRISON: lead guitar
*Record; Road* and *ATN* agree on Starr's vocal.

**MISCELLANEOUS**
This song was originally recorded by Carl Perkins, who released it as a single February 11, 1957. It was not a Top 40 hit.   *Road*
     This song was part of the Beatles' repertoire for concerts in 1961 and 1962. Drummer Pete Best sang lead vocal until August 1962; Lennon sang lead from then on.   *Live*

●

# "I CALL YOUR NAME"

**CHART ACTION**
UNITED KINGDOM: Released on the *Long Tall Sally* EP June 19, 1964.
*Road*

**AUTHORSHIP** Lennon (1.00)
LENNON: "That was my song. When there was no Beatles and no group . . .
It was my effort as a kind of blues originally, and then I wrote the middle-
eight just to stick it in the album when it came out years later. . . . It was
one of my *first* attempts at a song."

September 1980, *Playboy Interviews;* Lennon quote in *Own Words* supports.

**RECORDED**
March 1, 1964, at Abbey Road

*Abbey; Day* says February 25; *Road* and *ATN* and *Compleat*(b) say late February.

**INSTRUMENTATION**
McCARTNEY: bass                           HARRISON: lead guitar
LENNON: rhythm guitar, vocal      STARR: drums
(occasionally double-tracked)

*Record; Road* provides double-tracking information; *Road* and *ATN* agree on vocals.

**MISCELLANEOUS**
This song was originally given to Billy J. Kramer and the Dakotas, who
released their version as a B side to "Bad to Me" on July 26, 1963, in the
United Kingdom and on September 23 in the United States.   *Road*

Lennon later said that the unusual guitar solo in the bridge was an early
attempt at ska, the reggae beat of Jamaica that gained popularity in the
1970s.   *Abbey*

**COMMENTS BY BEATLES**
LENNON: "I like this one."   *Own Words*

▲ ▼ ▲

●

# A HARD DAY'S NIGHT
## ALBUM

○

Back from their triumphant first visit to the United States, the Beatles faced a deadline for producing another album, this time a tie-in with a feature film. This necessitated immediate recording of some songs for the soundtrack, followed by filming for the movie and more recording to fill out the album. Despite the harsh time pressures, the Beatles even found time for a few live gigs and several BBC-TV and radio appearances. This album, the only one that exclusively featured Lennon and McCartney originals, proved a huge success. It was in fact a tour de force for Lennon since he wrote the vast majority of the songs. In addition, *A Hard Day's Night* heralded the Beatles' increasingly more sophisticated use of the studio.

## CHART ACTION
UNITED KINGDOM: Released July 10, 1964, it was No. 1 five days later, and remained so for twenty-one weeks, until it was knocked off by *Beatles for Sale.* Road

UNITED STATES: A version of the album was released June 26, 1964. By late July it was No. 1 on the album chart, where it stayed for fourteen weeks. It was one of the fastest-selling albums in history, and sold two million copies by October.

The U.S. version, released on United Artists, contained only eight Beatles performances—the seven used in the film (the first seven on the U.K. release) and "I'll Cry Instead" (with an extra verse), which was dropped from the film. The other four selections were George Martin orchestrations of Beatles songs. The U.K. version contained another five Beatles performances instead of the orchestrations; in the United States Capitol used three of them on *Something New.* Road

## RECORDED
The songs were basically recorded in two batches: songs for the film, February 25 through March 1, and most of the rest June 1 and 2. Exceptions are noted under individual song entries.

*Abbey; Road* says the two periods were March-April and June 1 to 3; *Day* says March 2 to April 27.

Starr collapsed on the morning of June 3 after the busy sessions. He was admitted to a hospital suffering from exhaustion. He was discharged June 11, after missing performances in Denmark, the Netherlands, Hong Kong, and Australia.

*Diary; Live* agrees on date, provides "morning," and says collapse occurred during a photo session and that the problems were tonsillitis and pharyngitis.

Harrison used a Rickenbacker 360/12 (12-string) guitar throughout most of the sessions. *Guitar* (November 1987)

## MISCELLANEOUS

The title came from something Ringo said to describe a particularly heavy night. *Beatles Monthly* (February 1965) via *Day,* and Coleman  Lennon had also used the phrase in his short story "Sad Michael," part of the *In His Own Write* collection of writings. The story contains the line: "He'd had a hard day's night that day, for Michael was a Cocky Watchtower."

Filming of the movie began March 2, 1964, at Twickenham Studios. George met Patti Boyd, his future wife, on the first day; she was an extra in the film and can be seen in the dining car scene. Filming ended April 24. *Day*

This was the first album to consist entirely of self-composed Beatles compositions.

●

## "A HARD DAY'S NIGHT"

### CHART ACTION

UNITED KINGDOM: Released as a single July 10, 1964. In five days it went to No. 1, where it stayed for four weeks. *Road*

UNITED STATES: Released as a single July 13, 1964, more than two weeks after the album debuted in the United States. Entered the Top 40 July 18, stayed twelve weeks, and held the No. 1 spot for two. *Road* and *Billboard*

### AUTHORSHIP Lennon (1.00)

LENNON: "I was going home in the car and Dick Lester suggested the title *Hard Day's Night* [for the movie] from something Ringo'd said. I had used it in *In His Own Write,* but it was an off-the-cuff remark by Ringo. You know, one of those malapropisms. A Ringoism, where he said it not to be funny, just said it. So Dick Lester said we are going to use that title, and the next morning I brought in the song. 'Cause there was a little competition between Paul and I as to who got the A side, who got the hit singles." September 1980, *Playboy Interviews*

### RECORDED

April 16, 1964, at Abbey Road  *Abbey* and *Day* and *Diary* and *ATN* and *Road*

This song was written, arranged, rehearsed, and recorded in a little more than twenty-four hours. *Compleat*(b)

## INSTRUMENTATION

McCARTNEY: bass, harmony vocal  
LENNON: rhythm guitar, lead vocal  
(double-tracked)  
HARRISON: lead guitar  
(Rickenbacker 360/12 [12-string])

STARR: drums  
George Martin: piano

*Record; Road* provides double-tracking information, says Harrison sang harmony too, and agrees on Martin's piano; *ATN* omits Harrison vocal; guitar from *Guitar* (November 1987).

LENNON: "The only reason [Paul] sang on 'Hard Day's Night' was because I couldn't reach the notes." September 1980, *Playboy Interviews*

## MISCELLANEOUS

This song was part of the Beatles' repertoire for concerts in 1964 and 1965. *Live* It was performed on their 1964 North American tour, in their 1964 London Christmas shows, and on their 1965 European and North American tours. *Forever*

●

# "I SHOULD HAVE KNOWN BETTER"

## CHART ACTION

UNITED STATES: Released as a single July 13, 1964. It did not crack the Top 40, but its A side, "A Hard Day's Night," hit No. 1. *Road*

## AUTHORSHIP Lennon (1.00)

## RECORDED

February 25 and remade February 26, 1964, at Abbey Road

*Abbey; Road* and *ATN* say March or April; *Day* says March 2 to April 27.

## INSTRUMENTATION

McCARTNEY: bass  
LENNON: acoustic guitar,  
harmonica, vocal (double-tracked)

HARRISON: lead guitar  
(Rickenbacker 360/12 [12-string])  
STARR: drums

*Record; Road* agrees and provides double-tracking; *ATN* omits mouth organ; guitar from *Road* and *Guitar* (November 1987).

## MISCELLANEOUS

This song was performed in the film *A Hard Day's Night* in the train compartment scene. It was actually filmed in a van, with crew members rocking the vehicle to fake the action of a train in motion. *A-Z*

A George Martin—orchestrated instrumental version of this appears on the U.S. soundtrack LP. *ATN*

This song was part of the Beatles' repertoire for concerts in 1964. *Live*

●

# "IF I FELL"

## CHART ACTION
UNITED STATES: Also released as a single, July 20, 1964. It did not crack the *Billboard* Top 40, although its A side ("And I Love Her") hit No. 12. *Road*

## AUTHORSHIP Lennon (1.00)
LENNON: "That's my first attempt at a ballad proper. That was the precursor to 'In My Life.' It has the same chord sequences as 'In My Life': D and B minor and E minor, those kind of things. And it's semiautobiographical, but not consciously." September 1980, *Playboy Interviews*

## RECORDED
February 27, 1964, at Abbey Road

*Abbey; Road* and *ATN* say March or April; *Day* says March 2 to April 27.

## INSTRUMENTATION
McCARTNEY: bass, lead vocal          HARRISON: lead guitar
LENNON: acoustic guitar, lead        STARR: drums
vocal

*Record; Road* and *ATN* agree on double lead vocals.

## MISCELLANEOUS
This song was part of the Beatles' repertoire for concerts in 1964, *Live* including the North American tour. *Forever*

Lennon's manuscript of the lyrics was auctioned for £7,800 at Sotheby's, London, in early April 1988. AP (April 8, 1988)

## COMMENTS BY BEATLES
McCARTNEY: "This was our close-harmony period. We did a few songs— 'This Boy,' 'If I Fell,' 'Yes It Is'—in the same vein." *Playboy* (December 1984)

●

# "I'M HAPPY JUST TO DANCE WITH YOU"

## CHART ACTION
UNITED STATES: Also released as a single July 20, 1964. It didn't make the *Billboard* Top 40.  *Road*

## AUTHORSHIP Lennon (1.00)
LENNON: "That was written *for* George to give him a piece of the action. . . . I couldn'ta sung it."  September 1980, *Playboy Interviews*

## RECORDED
March 1, 1964, at Abbey Road

*Abbey; Road* and *ATN* say March or April; *Day* says March 2 to April 27.

## INSTRUMENTATION
McCARTNEY: bass, backing vocal
LENNON: rhythm guitar, backing vocal

HARRISON: lead guitar, lead vocal
STARR: drums, loose-skinned Arabian bongo

*Record; Road* agrees on vocals; *ATN* omits backing vocals.

## MISCELLANEOUS
This song was part of the Beatles' repertoire for concerts in 1964.  *Live*
    Performed in the film *A Hard Day's Night.*

●

# "AND I LOVE HER"

## CHART ACTION
UNITED STATES: Also released as a single, July 20, 1964. It entered the Top 40 on August 8, spent seven weeks there, and peaked at No. 12.
*Road* and *Billboard*

## AUTHORSHIP McCartney (.65) and Lennon (.35)
McCartney had the original idea, and Lennon helped to write it.  *Road*

LENNON: "Both of us [wrote this]. The first half was Paul's and the middle-eight is mine."  *Hit Parader* (April 1972)

## RECORDED
February 25, remade February 26 and again February 27, 1964, at Abbey
Road   *Abbey; Road* and *ATN* say March or April; *Day* says March 2 to April 27.

## INSTRUMENTATION
McCARTNEY: acoustic guitar, vocal      HARRISON: acoustic guitar solo,
(occasionally double-tracked)          claves
LENNON: acoustic guitar                STARR: bongos

*Record; Road* provides double-tracking only; *ATN* agrees on Harrison solo but adds that Harrison and Starr
played claves and bongos; *Compleat*(b) agrees on Harrison solo.

## MISCELLANEOUS
This song was one of the most-covered Beatles compositions, with 372
different versions recorded by October 1972.   *Road*

## COMMENTS BY BEATLES
McCARTNEY: "It's just a love song; no, it wasn't for anyone. Having the title
start in midsentence, I thought that was clever. Well, Perry Como did 'And
I Love You So' many years later. Tried to nick the idea. I like that—it was a
nice tune, that one. I still like it."   *Playboy* (December 1984)

●

# "TELL ME WHY"

**AUTHORSHIP** Lennon (1.00)
LENNON: "They needed another upbeat song, and I just knocked it off. It
was like a black-New York-girl-group song."   September 1980, *Playboy Interviews*

## RECORDED
February 27, 1964, at Abbey Road
*Abbey; Road* and *ATN* say March or April; *Day* says March 2 to April 27.

## INSTRUMENTATION
McCARTNEY: bass, harmony vocal      HARRISON: lead guitar
LENNON: rhythm guitar, lead vocal   STARR: drums

*Record; Road* and *ATN* say Lennon and McCartney shared lead vocals; *Road* also says Harrison sang backing
vocal.

## MISCELLANEOUS
Performed in the film *A Hard Day's Night.*

•

# "CAN'T BUY ME LOVE"

**CHART ACTION**
UNITED KINGDOM: Originally released as a single, March 20, 1964. It had huge advance sales and entered the chart at No. 1 on March 24.  *Road*

UNITED STATES: Originally released as a single, March 16, 1964. Entered the *Billboard* Top 40 March 28 and stayed nine weeks, five at No. 1.  *Road*
There were advance orders of 2.1 million copies.  *Transcriptions*

▶ **RULING THE CHARTS**

*This song headed the largest monopoly of the U.S. charts by any group or individual in recording history. The Beatles' positions on the* Billboard *Hot 100 chart of April 4, 1964:*
  *No. 1: "Can't Buy Me Love"*
  *No. 2: "Twist and Shout"*
  *No. 3: "She Loves You"*
  *No. 4: "I Want to Hold Your Hand"*
  *No. 5: "Please Please Me"*
  *No. 31: "I Saw Her Standing There"*
  *No. 41: "From Me to You"*
  *No. 46: "Do You Want to Know a Secret"*
  *No. 58: "All My Loving"*
  *No. 65: "You Can't Do That"*
  *No. 68: "Roll Over Beethoven"*
  *No. 79: "Thank You Girl"*
  *At the same time, the Beatles also occupied the top two positions on the album chart, with* Meet the Beatles *and* Introducing the Beatles.  *Road*

**AUTHORSHIP** McCartney (.9) and Lennon (.1)

LENNON, 1972: "John and Paul, but mainly Paul."    *Hit Parader* (April 1972)

LENNON, 1980: "That's Paul's completely. Maybe I had something to do with the chorus, but I don't know. I always considered it his song."    September 1980, *Playboy Interviews*

Sources differ on when and where this was written. Assuming EMI's own written records are accurate for when the song was recorded, it was probably written in Paris in mid-January.

*Day; Beatles* via *Day* says February 13 en route to Miami, Florida, during the Beatles' first visit to the United States; *A-Z* says in Miami; *Compleat*(b) and *Transcriptions* say in February in Miami while en route to tape an *Ed Sullivan* appearance; *Diary* says February 14 on a yacht.

## RECORDED
January 29, 1964, at Pathé Marconi Studios, Paris

*Abbey* and *Road* and *Live; Diary* says Harrison changed his lead guitar part on February 25; *ATN* and *Compleat*(b) say it was recorded entirely on February 25.

## INSTRUMENTATION

McCARTNEY: bass, vocal             HARRISON: lead guitar
LENNON: rhythm guitar              (Rickenbacker 360/12 [12-string])
                                   STARR: drums

*Record; Road* and *Transcriptions* say Lennon shared vocals; *ATN* omits Lennon's vocal; guitar from *Guitar* (November 1987), supported by *Transcriptions.*

## MISCELLANEOUS
It was George Martin's idea to start the song with the chorus.

*Musician* (July 1987) and *Compleat*(b)
MARTIN: "The way they first sang 'Can't Buy Me Love' was by starting on the verse, but I said: 'We've got to have an introduction, something that catches the ear immediately, a hook. So let's start off with the chorus.' "
*Ears*

"Can't Buy Me Love" was used for a pivotal scene in *A Hard Day's Night.* In the early scenes director Richard Lester had developed the feeling of confinement by shooting most scenes in enclosed spaces. (The idea had been spurred when Lennon replied to Lester's question of how he had liked Sweden on a recent tour: "It was a room and a room and a car and a room and a room and a car . . .") The movie led up to the point where the Beatles rebelled.

RICHARD LESTER: "We see them break out. We needed a visual example of that escape. Suddenly, the film opens up, and that's really the point of 'Can't Buy Me Love.' "    *Compleat*(b)

This song was part of the Beatles' repertoire for concerts in 1964 and 1965. *Live* It was performed on their 1964 North American tour, in their 1964 London Christmas shows, and on their 1965 European and North American tours. *Forever*

This song was played as a march by a military band as the Beatles received their MBEs in the Great Throne Room at Buckingham Palace, October 26, 1965. Before the ceremony Lennon smoked pot while sitting on a palace bathroom toilet. *Diary*

McCARTNEY: "[We] felt proud because Ella Fitzgerald recorded it, too, though we didn't realize what it meant that she was doing it." *Playboy* (December 1984) The version by jazz singer Fitzgerald was a minor hit in May 1964. *Road*

**COMMENTS BY BEATLES**
McCARTNEY: "Personally, I think you can put any interpretation you want on anything, but when someone suggests that 'Can't Buy Me Love' is about a prostitute, I draw the line. That's going too far." *Own Words*

●

# "ANY TIME AT ALL"

**AUTHORSHIP** Lennon (1.00)
LENNON: "[This was] an effort at writing 'It Won't Be Long.' Same ilk: C to A minor, C to A minor—with me shouting."
September 1980, *Playboy Interviews; Road* agrees Lennon wrote it.

**RECORDED**
June 2, 1964, at Abbey Road
*Abbey; Day* and *Road* and *ATN* and *Compleat*(b) say during sessions June 1 to 3.

**INSTRUMENTATION**
McCARTNEY: bass, piano          HARRISON: lead guitar
LENNON: acoustic guitar, vocal          STARR: drums
*Record; Road* and *ATN* say McCartney and Harrison sang backing vocals.

**MISCELLANEOUS**
Lennon's manuscript of the lyrics sold for £6,000 at an auction at Sotheby's, London, in early April 1988. AP (April 8, 1988)

●

# "I'LL CRY INSTEAD"

## CHART ACTION
UNITED STATES: Also released as a single, July 20, 1964. Entered the Top 40 August 15 and rose to No. 25 before dropping out of the Top 40 five weeks after entering.   *Road* with *Billboard*

## AUTHORSHIP Lennon (1.00)
Lennon later said the line "A chip on my shoulder that's bigger than my feet" was an accurate indication of his feelings at the time.   *Compleat*(b)

## RECORDED
June 1, 1964, at Abbey Road, in two sections later edited together
*Abbey; Road* and *ATN* say March or April; *Day* says March 2 to April 27.

## INSTRUMENTATION
McCARTNEY: bass, lead vocal            HARRISON: lead guitar
LENNON: acoustic guitar,               STARR: drums
tambourine, lead vocal
*Record; Road* and *ATN* agree on double lead vocals.

## MISCELLANEOUS
There is an extra verse in the U.S. version on the *A Hard Day's Night* LP.
*A-Z*

## COMMENTS BY BEATLES
LENNON: "I wrote that for *A Hard Day's Night,* but Dick Lester didn't even want it. He resurrected 'Can't Buy Me Love' for that sequence instead. I like the middle-eight to that song, though."
September 1980, *Playboy Interviews; Road* supports refusal by Lester.

●

# "THINGS WE SAID TODAY"

## CHART ACTION
UNITED KINGDOM: Also released as a single July 10, 1964, as the B side to "A Hard Day's Night."   *Road*

**AUTHORSHIP** McCartney (1.00)
McCartney wrote this while vacationing in the Bahamas with Jane Asher, Starr, and Maureen Starkey in May 1964. *A-Z*

**RECORDED**
June 2, 1964, at Abbey Road
*Abbey; Day* and *Road* and *ATN* and *Compleat*(b) say during sessions June 1 to 3.

**INSTRUMENTATION**

McCARTNEY: bass, lead vocal          HARRISON: lead guitar
LENNON: acoustic guitar, ·           STARR: drums
tambourine, harmony vocal
*Record; Road* agrees on vocals; *ATN* omits backing vocal.

**MISCELLANEOUS**
This song was part of the Beatles repertoire for concerts in 1964, including their 1964 North American tour. *Forever*

**COMMENTS BY BEATLES**
LENNON: "Good song." September 1980, *Playboy Interviews*

●

## "WHEN I GET HOME"

**AUTHORSHIP** Lennon (1.00)
LENNON: "That's me again, another Wilson Pickett, Motown sound, a four-in-the-bar cowbell song." September 1980, *Playboy Interviews*

**RECORDED**
June 2, 1964, at Abbey Road
*Abbey; Day* and *Road* and *ATN* and *Compleat*(b) say during sessions June 1 to 3.

**INSTRUMENTATION**

McCARTNEY: bass, harmony vocal     HARRISON: lead guitar
LENNON: rhythm guitar, lead vocal  STARR: drums
*Record; Road* and *ATN* say Harrison also sang harmony.

●

# "YOU CAN'T DO THAT"

**CHART ACTION**
UNITED KINGDOM: Originally released as a single, March 20, 1964, as the B side to "Can't Buy Me Love." *Road*

UNITED STATES: Released as a single March 16, 1964. It did not crack the *Billboard* Top 40, but its A side, "Can't Buy Me Love," hit No. 1. *Road*

**AUTHORSHIP** Lennon (1.00)
LENNON: "That's me doing Wilson Pickett." September 1980, *Playboy Interviews*

**RECORDED**
February 25, 1964, at Abbey Road

*Abbey; Road* and *ATN* say instrumental track was recorded January 29 at Pathé Marconi Studios, Paris, and that vocals were added February 25 at Abbey Road; *Diary* says date for instrumental track was January 18 and that vocals were added February 25.

**INSTRUMENTATION**

McCARTNEY: bass, harmony vocal
LENNON: lead guitar, lead vocal

HARRISON: 12-string guitar, harmony vocal
STARR: drums, cowbells, bongos

*Record* (but has lead guitar switched between Harrison and Lennon); *A-Z* and Coleman and *Guitar* (November 1987) say Lennon played lead guitar; *Road* agrees on harmony vocals and Harrison's 12-string; *ATN* omits lead guitar.

LENNON: "I'd find it a drag to play rhythm [guitar] all the time so I always work myself out something interesting to play. The best example I can think of is like I did on 'You Can't Do That.' There wasn't really a lead guitarist and a rhythm guitarist on that because I feel that the rhythm guitarist role sounds too thin for records. Anyway, it'd drive me potty to play *chunk-chunk* rhythm all the time. I never play anything as lead guitarist that George couldn't do better. But I like playing lead sometimes, so I do it." 1964, on a British concert tour, Coleman

Lennon's guitar on this song was a highly prized possession. It was a Rickenbacker model No. 1996, slimline, and had cost a lot—159 guineas—at the start of 1964. You can hear it during his solo. Coleman

Harrison played a 12-string guitar for the first time on a Beatles recording. *Diary* and *A-Z*

**MISCELLANEOUS**
This song was part of the Beatles' repertoire for concerts in 1964. *Live* A performance of this song aired on *The Ed Sullivan Show,* May 24, 1964. It

and an accompanying interview were filmed during the making of the film *A Hard Day's Night.*  Day  The song was performed during the Beatles' 1964 North American tour.  Forever

▶ **JOHN HATED HIS VOICE**

*RAY COLEMAN, Lennon biographer: "John was genuinely bashful about his voice. I remember telling him how much I liked it on one particular track, 'You Can't Do That,' and he was astonished that anyone should single out his vocal work for any praise. 'You really mean it?' he asked incredulously. 'I can't say I ever liked hearing myself.' "*  Coleman

*MARTIN: "[John] had an inborn dislike of his own voice which I could never understand, as it was one of the best voices I've heard. He was always saying to me: 'Do something with my voice! You know, put something on it. Smother it with tomato ketchup or something. Make it different.'...As long as it wasn't his natural voice coming through, he was reasonably happy. But he'd always want his vocals to get special treatment."*  Coleman

●

## "I'LL BE BACK"

**AUTHORSHIP** Lennon (1.00)

**RECORDED**

June 1, 1964, at Abbey Road

*Abbey; Day* and *Road* and *ATN* and *Compleat*(b) say during sessions June 1 to 3.

## INSTRUMENTATION

McCARTNEY: bass, acoustic guitar, harmony vocal

LENNON: acoustic guitar, lead vocal

HARRISON: acoustic guitar

STARR: drums

*Record; Road* and *ATN* say McCartney and Harrison sang backing vocals.

## COMMENTS BY BEATLES

Lennon called this song an "early favorite."    *Own Words*

LENNON: "A nice tune, though the middle is a bit tatty."    *Hit Parader* (April 1972)

▲ ▼ ▲

●

# "I FEEL FINE"

## CHART ACTION
UNITED KINGDOM: Released as a single November 27, 1964. It entered the chart at No. 1 and stayed there for six weeks, selling a million copies by December 11 and making it one of the fastest-selling singles ever in the United Kingdom. *Road*

UNITED STATES: Released as a single November 23, 1964. It entered the Top 40 December 5 at No. 22. By December 26 it was No. 1 where it stayed for three weeks. It was Top 40 for eleven weeks. *Road* with *Billboard*

## AUTHORSHIP Lennon (1.00)
LENNON: "I wrote this at a recording session. It was tied together around the guitar riff that opens it." *Own Words*

## RECORDED
October 18, 1964, at Abbey Road

*Abbey; Day* and *ATN* and *Road* say early October near the end of the *Beatles for Sale* sessions or shortly afterward.

LENNON: "This was the first time feedback was used on a record. It's right at the beginning." *Hit Parader* (April 1972)

The buzz from the amplifier was accidental, but the Beatles liked the effect and decided to use it. *A-Z; Abbey* says it was intentional.

## INSTRUMENTATION
McCARTNEY: bass, backing vocal  HARRISON: lead guitar, backing
LENNON: rhythm guitar, lead  vocal
guitar, lead vocal  STARR: drums

*Record; Road* says Lennon and Harrison played guitar duet and all sang harmony; *ATN* omits backing vocal.

## MISCELLANEOUS
This song was part of the Beatles' repertoire for concerts from 1964 to 1966. *Live* It was performed during their 1964 London Christmas shows, 1965 North American tour, 1965 U.K. tour, and 1966 world tour. It was also performed on *The Ed Sullivan Show,* September 12, 1965. *Forever*

●

# "SHE'S A WOMAN"

## CHART ACTION
UNITED KINGDOM: Released November 27, 1964, as the B side to "I Feel Fine." *Road*

UNITED STATES: Released as a single November 23, 1964. It entered the Top 40 December 12, climbed to No. 4, and was Top 40 for eight weeks. *Road*

## AUTHORSHIP McCartney (.9) and Lennon (.1)
LENNON: "That's Paul with some contribution from me on lines, probably. We put in the words 'turns me on.' We were so excited to say 'turn me on' —you know, about marijuana and all that, using it as an expression."

September 1980, *Playboy Interviews;* Lennon quote in *Hit Parader* (April 1972) says he probably helped with the middle-eight.

The song was written in the studio and recorded the same day. *Road*

## RECORDED
October 8, 1964, at Abbey Road

*Abbey; Day* and *Road* and *ATN* say early October near the end of the *Beatles for Sale* sessions or shortly afterward.

## INSTRUMENTATION
McCARTNEY: bass, piano, vocal        HARRISON: lead guitar
LENNON: rhythm guitar                STARR: drums, maracas

*Record; Road* agrees on McCartney's piano but says Lennon and Harrison join chorus; *ATN* omits Lennon and Harrison on chorus.

## MISCELLANEOUS
This song was part of the Beatles' repertoire for concerts from 1964 to 1966. *Live*  It was performed during their 1964 London Christmas shows, 1965 European tour, 1965 North American tour, 1965 U.K. tour, and 1966 world tour. *Forever*

Part of this song is heard during the film *Help!*

●

# BEATLES FOR SALE
### *ALBUM*

○

*A Hard Day's Night,* composed of all Lennon and McCartney orginals, had been out for only two months when the Beatles began recording this album. Although some of its songs were more sophisticated—"I'm a Loser," "No Reply"—Lennon and McCartney were just not able to write a whole album's worth. They did come up with eight originals, however, and padded out the album with Beatles versions of six of their stage favorites.

## CHART ACTION
UNITED KINGDOM: Released December 4, 1964, and five days later it was No. 1, replacing *A Hard Day's Night.* It was No. 1 for nine weeks.  *Road*

UNITED STATES: The U.S. equivalent, *Beatles '65,* was released December 15, 1964. It contained eight songs from the U.K. album, one from *A Hard Day's Night,* and both sides of a single. It sold more than a million copies in its first week of release.  *Road*

## RECORDED
August 11 to October 26, 1964, at Abbey Road

*Road* and *ATN* say late September to mid-October; *Day* says September 21 to October 8.

## ALBUM PACKAGE
The cover photograph shows the Beatles with weary faces. Was Beatle-mania taking its toll?

MARTIN: "They were rather war-weary during *Beatles for Sale.* One must remember that they'd been battered like mad throughout 1964, and much of 1963. Success is a wonderful thing but it is very, very tiring. They were always on the go. *Beatles for Sale* doesn't appeal to me very much now, it's not one of their most memorable ones. They perked up again after that." *Abbey*

●

# "NO REPLY"

**AUTHORSHIP** Lennon ( 1.00)
LENNON: "That's my song. . . . It was sort of my version of 'Silhouettes.' . . .

I had that image of walking down the street and seeing her silhouetted in the window and not answering the phone." September 1980, *Playboy Interviews*

LENNON: "I remember [music publisher] Dick James coming to me after we did this one and saying, 'You're getting much better now—that was a complete story.' Apparently before that he thought my songs tended to sort of wander off." *Hit Parader* (April 1972)

**RECORDED**
September 30, 1964, at Abbey Road *Abbey*

**INSTRUMENTATION**
McCARTNEY: bass, harmony vocal
LENNON: acoustic guitar, lead vocal (double-tracked)
HARRISON: lead guitar, harmony vocal
STARR: drums
George Martin: piano

*Record; Road* provides double-tracking; *Road* and *ATN* agree on vocals.

●

# "I'M A LOSER"

**AUTHORSHIP** Lennon (1.00)
LENNON: "That's me in my Dylan period. . . . Part of me suspects I'm a loser and part of me thinks I'm God almighty." September 1980, *Playboy Interviews*

Singer Jackie DeShannon was on the Beatles' summer 1964 North American tour. She recalled that Lennon was writing this song on the plane during the tour. *RS* (February 16, 1984)

**RECORDED**
August 14, 1964, at Abbey Road *Abbey*

**INSTRUMENTATION**
McCARTNEY: bass, harmony vocal
LENNON: acoustic guitar, harmonica, lead vocal
HARRISON: lead guitar (Gretsch Tennessean [model PX6119])
STARR: drums, tambourine

*Record; Road* and *ATN* agree on vocals; guitar from *Guitar* (November 1987).

**MISCELLANEOUS**
This was once considered for release as a single in the United Kingdom until Lennon wrote "I Feel Fine." *Road*

This was in the Beatles' live repertoire in 1964 and 1965. *Live* It was performed during their 1964 London Christmas shows and their 1965 European tour. *Forever*

**COMMENTS BY BEATLES**
Lennon thought this was one of his best early songs. *A-Z*

●

## "BABY'S IN BLACK"

**AUTHORSHIP** Lennon (.5) and McCartney (.5)
LENNON: "[We wrote it] together, in the same room."
September 1980, *Playboy Interviews*

**RECORDED**
August 11, 1964, at Abbey Road. It was the first song recorded for the album. *Abbey*

**INSTRUMENTATION**
McCARTNEY: bass, lead vocal          HARRISON: lead guitar
LENNON: acoustic guitar, lead        STARR: drums, tambourine
vocal
*Record; Road* and *ATN* agree on double lead vocals.

**MISCELLANEOUS**
This song was in the Beatles' live repertoire from 1964 to 1966. *Live* It was also performed during their 1964 London Christmas shows, 1965 European tour, 1965 North American tour, 1965 U.K. tour, and 1966 world tour. *Forever*

●

## "ROCK AND ROLL MUSIC"

**AUTHORSHIP** Chuck Berry (1.00)

**RECORDED**
October 18, 1964, at Abbey Road in one take *Abbey*

**INSTRUMENTATION**

McCARTNEY: bass

LENNON: rhythm guitar, vocal

HARRISON: acoustic guitar

STARR: drums

Lennon, McCartney, George Martin: same piano

Record; Road and ATN agree on vocal and same piano by Lennon, McCartney, and Martin.

**MISCELLANEOUS**

Chuck Berry's original recording was released as a single September 30, 1957, and hit No. 8.  *Road*

This song was a staple of the Beatles' concerts, and remained part of the group's repertoire from 1960 through 1966.  *Live*  It was performed during their 1964 London Christmas shows, 1965 European tour, and 1966 world tour.  *Forever*

●

# "I'LL FOLLOW THE SUN"

**AUTHORSHIP** McCartney (1.00)

LENNON: "That's Paul again. Can't you tell? I mean—'Tomorrow may rain so I'll follow the sun.' That's another early McCartney, you know, written almost before Beatles, I think. He had a *lot* of stuff. . ."

September 1980, *Playboy Interviews*

**RECORDED**

October 18, 1964, at Abbey Road  *Abbey*

**INSTRUMENTATION**

McCARTNEY: acoustic guitar, lead vocal (occasionally double-tracked)

LENNON: acoustic guitar, harmony vocal

HARRISON: lead guitar

STARR: bongos

Record; Road provides double-tracking information.

**COMMENTS BY BEATLES**

LENNON: "A nice one."  *Hit Parader* (April 1972)

●

# "MR. MOONLIGHT"

**AUTHORSHIP** Roy Lee Johnson (1.00)

CD and ATN and Compleat(b) and Record; Road says Jackson.

**RECORDED**
August 14 but remade October 18, 1964, at Abbey Road  *Abbey*

**INSTRUMENTATION**

McCARTNEY: bass, Hammond organ, harmony vocal
LENNON: acoustic guitar, lead vocal

HARRISON: lead guitar, African drum
STARR: bongos

*Record; Road* and *ATN* agree on McCartney's organ and Harrison's African drum; *Road* agrees on McCartney harmony vocal; *ATN* omits harmony vocal.

**MISCELLANEOUS**
The original recording, by Dr. Feelgood and the Interns, was released as a single January 15, 1962. It was not a Top 40 hit.  *Road* and *Billboard*

This song was part of the Beatles' live repertoire in 1962 and 1963.
*Live*

●

# "KANSAS CITY/HEY, HEY, HEY, HEY"

**AUTHORSHIP** Jerry Leiber (.25) and Mike Stoller (.25) / Richard Penniman (.5)

**RECORDED**
October 18, 1964, at Abbey Road  *Abbey*

McCARTNEY: "John always used to egg me on. He used to say, 'Come on, Paul, knock the shit out of "Kansas City," ' just when the engineers thought they had a vocal they could handle."  *Time Out* via *Musician* (February 1985)

"It requires a great deal of nerve to just jump up and scream like an . . . idiot, you know? Anyway, I would often fall a little bit short, not have that little kick, that soul, and it would be John who would go, 'Come on, you can sing it better than that, man! Come on, come on! Really throw it!' All right, John, okay . . ."  *Playboy* (December 1984)

**INSTRUMENTATION**

McCARTNEY: bass, lead vocal
LENNON: rhythm guitar, backing vocal

HARRISON: lead guitar, backing vocal
STARR: drums
George Martin: piano

*Record; Road* and *ATN* agree on vocals.

## MISCELLANEOUS

The original recording artist of "Kansas City," then known as "K.C. Loving," was Little Willie Littlefield, who released it as a single December 29, 1952. But the Beatles' version was styled after Little Richard (Richard Penniman), who recorded the two songs as a medley in 1959 and sang them as a medley on stage.  *Road*  The Beatles toured with Little Richard in the early 1960s, so they undoubtedly saw this arrangement performed live several times. *Compleat* (Billy Preston said 1962).

"Kansas City/Hey, Hey, Hey" was also recorded by Tony Sheridan and the Beat Brothers (the Beatles) in May 1961 in Hamburg for Polydor Records, but apparently was not released.  *Day;* some sources say April.

This song was part of the Beatles' live repertoire in 1961 and 1962 and again in 1964.  *Live*

The Beatles performed this on the U.S. television show *Shindig* in January 1965. *A-Z*

●

# "EIGHT DAYS A WEEK"

## CHART ACTION
UNITED STATES: Also released as a single, February 15, 1965. It entered the Top 40 February 27 and stayed at No. 1 for two weeks. It spent nine weeks in the Top 40.  *Road* and *Billboard*

This song was originally one of those on the album being considered for release as a single in the United Kingdom before Lennon composed "I Feel Fine."  *Road*

## AUTHORSHIP McCartney (.7) and Lennon (.3)
LENNON: "Both of us [wrote this]. I think we wrote this when we were trying to write the title song for *Help!* because there was at one time the thought of calling the film *Eight Arms to Hold You . . .*"  *Hit Parader* (April 1972)

LENNON: "It was Paul's effort at getting a single for the movie. That luckily turned to 'Help!' which I wrote, bam! bam! like that and got the single." September 1980, *Playboy Interviews*

The title came from something Ringo said.
McCARTNEY: "He said it as though he were an overworked chauffeur: [Heavy accent] 'Eight days a week.' When we heard it, we said, 'Really? Bing! Got it!' "  *Playboy* (December 1984)

**RECORDED**
October 6, 1964, at Abbey Road, with an outro edit piece taped October 18  *Abbey*

**INSTRUMENTATION**
McCARTNEY: bass, harmony vocal
LENNON: rhythm guitar, acoustic
guitar, lead vocal

HARRISON: lead guitar
STARR: drums

*Record; Road* and *ATN* say Lennon and McCartney shared lead vocal and Harrison sang backing vocal.

**MISCELLANEOUS**
A promotional film was made.  *A-Z*
This song may be the first to begin with a fade-in.  *Road*

**COMMENTS BY BEATLES**
LENNON: " 'Eight Days a Week' was never a good song. We struggled to record it and struggled to make it into a song. It was [Paul's] initial effort, but I think we both worked on it. I'm not sure. But it was lousy anyway."
September 1980, *Playboy Interviews*


●


# "WORDS OF LOVE"

**AUTHORSHIP** Buddy Holly (1.00)

**RECORDED**
October 18, 1964, at Abbey Road  *Abbey*

**INSTRUMENTATION**
McCARTNEY: bass, lead vocal
LENNON: rhythm guitar, lead vocal

HARRISON: lead guitar (Gretsch
Tennessean [model PX6119])
STARR: drums, packing case

*Record; Road* agrees on vocals, packing case; *ATN* says Harrison shared vocals; guitar from *Guitar* (November 1987).

**MISCELLANEOUS**
The original version was recorded by Buddy Holly and released as a single June 17, 1957. It was not a hit.  *Road*
This song was part of the Beatles' live repertoire from the late 1950s to 1962. Lennon and Harrison shared the lead vocals in concert.

●

# "HONEY DON'T"

**AUTHORSHIP** Carl Perkins (1.00)

**RECORDED**
October 26, 1964, at Abbey Road, during the last session for the album
*Abbey*

**INSTRUMENTATION**

McCARTNEY: bass
LENNON: acoustic guitar,
tambourine

HARRISON: lead guitar (Gretsch
Tennessean [model PX6119])
STARR: drums, vocal

*Record; Road* and *ATN* agree on Starr vocal; guitar from *Guitar* (November 1987)

**MISCELLANEOUS**
The original recording artist was Carl Perkins, who released it January 2,
1956, as the B side of "Blue Suede Shoes."  *Road*
    This song was part of the Beatles' live repertoire from 1962 to 1965
(Lennon sang lead until about August 1963).  *Live*  It was performed during
their 1964 London Christmas shows.  *Forever*

●

# "EVERY LITTLE THING"

**AUTHORSHIP** McCartney (.9) and Lennon (.1)

**RECORDED**
September 29 and 30, 1964, at Abbey Road  *Abbey*
    The second night's session was fun. One take was ended when Mc-
Cartney burped his vocal, and the next take, although complete, ended in
loud laughter.  *Abbey*

**INSTRUMENTATION**

McCARTNEY: bass, piano, lead
vocal
LENNON: acoustic guitar, lead
vocal

HARRISON: lead guitar
STARR: drums, tympani

*Record; Road* agrees with double lead vocals and Starr's tympani; *ATN* says McCartney's vocals were backing and omits tympani; *B-Lists* says that Harrison was not present and that Lennon provided lead guitar and vocal, McCartney provided bass and vocal, and Starr played tympani.

•

# "I DON'T WANT TO SPOIL THE PARTY"

**AUTHORSHIP** Lennon (1.00)

**RECORDED**
September 29, 1964, at Abbey Road   *Abbey*

**INSTRUMENTATION**

| | |
|---|---|
| McCARTNEY: bass, lead vocal | HARRISON: lead guitar (Gretsch |
| LENNON: acoustic guitar, lead | Tennessean [model PX6119]) |
| vocal | STARR: drums, tambourine |

*Record; Road* agrees on double lead vocals, but adds Harrison's harmony vocal; *ATN* omits harmony vocal; guitar from *Guitar* (November 1987).

**COMMENTS BY BEATLES**
LENNON: "That was a very personal one of mine."   *Own Words*

•

# "WHAT YOU'RE DOING"

**AUTHORSHIP** McCartney (.9) and Lennon (.1)

**RECORDED**
September 29 and 30, but remade October 26, 1964, at Abbey Road   *Abbey*

**INSTRUMENTATION**

| | |
|---|---|
| McCARTNEY: bass, lead vocal | HARRISON: lead guitar |
| LENNON: acoustic guitar, backing | STARR: drums |
| vocal | George Martin: piano |

*Record; Road* says Lennon and McCartney provided harmony vocals; *ATN* omits harmony vocals.

•

# "EVERYBODY'S TRYING TO BE MY BABY"

**AUTHORSHIP** Carl Perkins (1.00)

**RECORDED**
October 18, 1964, at Abbey Road, in just one take   *Abbey*

**INSTRUMENTATION**

McCARTNEY: bass

LENNON: acoustic guitar, tambourine

HARRISON: lead guitar, vocal (occasionally double-tracked)

STARR: drums

*Record; Road* provides double-tracking; *ATN* says McCartney sang backing vocals.

**MISCELLANEOUS**
The original recording artist was Carl Perkins, who issued it on his *Teen Beat* LP, released August 18, 1958. The LP also included two other songs covered by the Beatles: "Matchbox" and "Honey Don't."   *Road*

This song was part of the Beatles' live repertoire in 1961 and 1962 and again in 1964 and 1965.   *Live*   It was performed during their 1964 London Christmas shows, 1965 European tour, and 1965 North American tour. After that, Harrison's spotlight vocal number became "If I Needed Someone."   *Forever*

▲ ▼ ▲

•

# "YES IT IS"

**CHART ACTION**
UNITED KINGDOM: Released as a single April 9, 1965, as the B side to "Ticket to Ride." *Road*

UNITED STATES: Released as a single April 14, 1965. It was not a Top 40 hit. *Road*

**AUTHORSHIP** Lennon (1.00)
LENNON: "That's me trying a rewrite of 'This Boy,' but it didn't work."
September 1980, *Playboy Interviews*

**RECORDED**
February 16, 1965, at Abbey Road
*Abbey; Day* says February 12; *Road* and *ATN* say February.

**INSTRUMENTATION**
McCARTNEY: bass, backing vocal
LENNON: acoustic guitar, lead vocal

HARRISON: lead guitar, backing vocal
STARR: drums

*Record; Road* and *ATN* agree on vocals.

•

# "BAD BOY"

**RELEASED**
This song was recorded mainly for the U.S. market, so it was released there first.

UNITED KINGDOM: Unreleased in Britain until the *Collection of Beatles Oldies* album was issued December 9, 1966. *Abbey; Road* says December 10.

UNITED STATES: Originally released on the *Beatles VI* LP June 14, 1965.
*Road* and *ATN* and *Abbey*

**AUTHORSHIP** Larry Williams (1.00)

## RECORDED

May 10, 1965, at Abbey Road, between sessions for the *Help!* LP

*Abbey; Day* and *Road* and *Compleat*(b) say during an overnight session held May 10 and 11; *Abbey* says session ended before midnight.

The session lasted three and a half hours and yielded several songs.

*Abbey*

## INSTRUMENTATION

McCARTNEY: bass

LENNON: rhythm guitar, Hammond organ, vocal

HARRISON: lead guitar

STARR: drums, tambourine

*Record; Road* and *ATN* agree on Lennon's vocal.

## MISCELLANEOUS

This song was originally recorded by Larry Williams, who released it as a single January 19, 1959. It was not a Top 40 hit.  *Road* and *Billboard*

This song was part of the Beatles' live repertoire from 1960 to 1962.

*Live*

●

# "I'M DOWN"

## CHART ACTION

UNITED KINGDOM: Released as a single July 23, 1965, as the B side to "Help!"  *Road* and *ATN* and *Abbey*

UNITED STATES: Released as a single July 19, 1965. It did not crack the Hot 100.  *Road*

## AUTHORSHIP McCartney (.9) and Lennon (.1)

LENNON: "That's Paul, with a little help from me, I think."  September 1980,

*Playboy Interviews*

## RECORDED

June 14, 1965, at Abbey Road

*Abbey; Road* and *ATN* say late May; *Day* says two versions were recorded during sessions between late May and early June.

## INSTRUMENTATION

McCARTNEY: bass, lead vocal

LENNON: Hammond organ, backing vocal

HARRISON: lead guitar, backing vocal

STARR: drums, bongos

*Record; Road* agrees on vocals and Lennon's Hammond organ; *ATN* omits all backing vocals.

**MISCELLANEOUS**
This song was part of the Beatles' live repertoire in 1965 and 1966. *Live* It was performed as the closing number on the 1965 North American tour, 1965 United Kingdom tour, and 1966 world tour. It was also performed on *The Ed Sullivan Show,* September 12, 1965. *Forever*

**COMMENTS BY OTHERS**
STEVE TYLER, of Aerosmith: ". . . The first song we ever recorded was 'I'm Down.' It was something like eighteen years ago (1969), five years before Aerosmith was even formed. We needed a demo to present to MGM Records. So we went to this Beatles memorabilia store, got the tape, listened to it three times, ran back to the studio and put it down live. . . . " ENS (November 8, 1987)

▲ ▼ ▲

# HELP!
*ALBUM*

○

Half of *Help!* is composed of songs from the Beatles' second film, while the other half consists of tracks recorded a couple of months later. The album is basically a transitional one, with elements of both the group's raucous past and its experimental future. It is heavily influenced by the then-pervasive folk-rock sound, particularly as embodied by Bob Dylan.

The introspective glimpses provided by the previous *Beatles for Sale* grew deeper on *Help!* According to author John Lennon, the title song is an honest cry for help. "You've Got to Hide Your Love Away" invokes a melancholy mood. And while not autobiographical, Paul McCartney's "Yesterday" fits with the album's tamer tone.

## CHART ACTION

UNITED KINGDOM: Released August 6, 1965. It entered the album chart August 11 at No. 1, where it stayed for eleven weeks. *Road*

UNITED STATES: Released August 13, 1965. The original American LP was significantly different from the U.K. version. It featured only the seven Beatles songs from the film and six orchestral cuts from the soundtrack. *Road*

▶ ## THE HATED U.S. REPACKAGING

*McCartney was frustrated by the group's lack of control over the American repackaging of their British releases. On a trip to California, they came across the U.S. version of* Help! *Hearing it for the first time, they discovered that parts of Ken Thorne's film score had been added to the album, despite the Beatles' decision to keep it off the British release.* RS (July 12, 1979)

*HARRISON, on U.S. repackagings: "...They'd make new packages like* Yesterday and Today, *just awful packages."*
*Crawdaddy* (February 1977)

Despite the repackaging, the U.S. album immediately qualified as a gold record because of advance orders of a million copies—the first time this occurred in the recording industry. *Help!* reached No. 1 on the album chart on September 11 and stayed there for nine weeks.   *Road*

In 1982 world sales were estimated to have been 2.3 million.   *Road*

## RECORDED
Most of the songs were recorded during two time periods: February 15 to 19 and June 14 to 17. Exceptions are noted within individual song entries. *Abbey*

During the recording of instrumentals for the movie soundtrack, a twenty-one-string sitar was used to create exotic effects. Harrison was fascinated with the instrument, bought one for himself, and studied Indian music and, later, religion. This had a major effect on the Beatles' music and activities months later.   *Forever*

McCartney was heard on lead guitar for the first time on this album. He played it on two songs, "Another Girl" and "Ticket to Ride."   *Record*

While in the studios on February 18, the Beatles' song publishing company, Northern Songs Ltd., went public.   *Diary*   The action, taken for tax reasons, would later prevent Lennon and McCartney from controlling the rights to their songs.

## ALBUM PACKAGE
On the cover, the Beatles signal "Help us" in semaphore, but the photo was reverse-printed. Holding it up to a mirror reveals the letters LPUS—"Help us."   *Diary*

## MISCELLANEOUS
The movie *Help!* was filmed from February 22 to May 12, 1965.   *Diary; Day* is more general; *Live* says shooting was February 22 to March 10 in the Bahamas, March 13 to 22 in Austria, and then at Twickenham afterward until May 12.   The Beatles generally didn't like the finished film. McCartney said it was "a bit wrong for us. We were sort of guest stars."   *Compleat*(b)   Lennon went so far as to call it "crap" and say that director Richard Lester "forgot about who and what we were. And that's why the film didn't work. It was like having clams in a movie about frogs." *Forever*

The songs that were included in the film make up the first half of the album, up to and including "Ticket to Ride."

●

## "HELP!"

### CHART ACTION
UNITED KINGDOM: Also released as a single, July 23, 1965. It became a No. 1 hit immediately and held that position for four weeks. Final sales totaled 900,000. *Road*

UNITED STATES: Also released as a single, July 19, 1965. It entered the Top 40 August 14, remained on the chart for twelve weeks, and held the No. 1 position for three. *Road* and *Billboard*

### AUTHORSHIP Lennon (.9) and McCartney (.1)
The song was written on April 4, 1965. *Day* and *Diary*

McCARTNEY: "John wrote that—well, John and I wrote it at his house in Weybridge for the film. I think the title was out of desperation."
*Playboy* (December 1984)

LENNON: "Later, I knew I really was crying out for help. So it was my fat Elvis period. You see the movie: He—I—is very fat, very insecure, and he's completely lost himself." September 1980, *Playboy Interviews*

### RECORDED
April 13, 1965, at Abbey Road *Abbey* and *Day* and *Diary*
   The album and single versions have different lyrics. *A-Z*

### INSTRUMENTATION
McCARTNEY: bass, backing vocal
LENNON: acoustic guitar, lead vocal

HARRISON: lead guitar, backing vocal
STARR: drums, tambourine

*Record; Road* says backing vocals are harmony.

### MISCELLANEOUS
On the single's first pressing the label caption says: "From the United Artists screenplay, *Eight Arms to Hold You.*" That was the original title for *Help!*
Various
   This song was part of the Beatles' live repertoire in 1965. *Live* It was performed during the Beatles' North American tour in summer 1965 and their U.K. tour that December. It was also performed on *The Ed Sullivan Show,* September 12, 1965. *Forever*
   In the mid-'80s, the Ford Motor Company paid a reported $100,000 to

use this song in a TV ad for its Lincoln-Mercury division. But, unlike Nike's later use of the actual Beatles' performance of "Revolution," this song was performed by a sound-alike group. Los Angeles *Times* (May 1987); *B-Lists* agrees on product.

## COMMENTS BY BEATLES

Lennon was proud of the lyrics and the self-awareness they expressed. He maintained that the words were true—he *was* asking for help. But the Beatles quickened the tempo to make the song more commercial, which Lennon later regretted. December 1970, *Remembers*

●

# "THE NIGHT BEFORE"

**AUTHORSHIP** McCartney (1.00)

**RECORDED**
February 17, 1965, at Abbey Road
*Abbey; Day* says during sessions between early February and early March.

**INSTRUMENTATION**
McCARTNEY: bass, lead vocal
LENNON: electric piano, backing vocal
*Record* and *Road* and *ATN*

HARRISON: lead guitar, backing vocal
STARR: drums

**MISCELLANEOUS**
Performed on the Salisbury Plains in the film *Help!* A-Z

●

# "YOU'VE GOT TO HIDE YOUR LOVE AWAY"

**AUTHORSHIP** Lennon (1.00)
LENNON: "That's me in my Dylan period. . . . I am like a chameleon, influenced by whatever is going on." September 1980, *Playboy Interviews*

PETE SHOTTON, longtime friend of Lennon: "The first Beatles song composed in my presence was 'You've Got to Hide Your Love Away,' to which I myself contributed the sustained 'hey's that introduce the main chorus.

This Dylan-inspired number originally included the line 'I can't go on, feeling two foot tall'; when he first performed it for Paul McCartney, however, John accidentally sang 'two foot *small.*' He paused to correct himself, then burst into laughter. 'Let's leave that in, actually,' he exclaimed. 'All those pseuds will really love it.' " Shotton

(Several Beatles songs were improved by similar accidents. *See:* "Ob-La-Di, Ob-La-Da" and "Hey Bulldog.")

## RECORDED
February 18, 1965, at Abbey Road   Abbey; Day says between early February and early March.

## INSTRUMENTATION
McCARTNEY: acoustic guitar   HARRISON: acoustic guitar
LENNON: acoustic guitar, vocal   STARR: tambourine
Session musicians: flutes

*Record* and *Road* and *ATN*
This was the first time the Beatles called in outside musicians to play instruments that they themselves could not play. Many people consider "Yesterday" the first, because its strings are so obvious and because it was on the same album, but "Yesterday" was recorded nearly four months later.

## MISCELLANEOUS
Performed in the film *Help!*

Paul played rhythm guitar and George played tambourine during the recording of this song by the folk group Silkie in early August 1965 in London. Day The session was produced by Lennon and McCartney. The single hit No. 29 on the *New Musical Express* chart in England for one week in September 1965. Road

## COMMENTS BY OTHERS
TOM ROBINSON, homosexual musician/singer, said that the first gay rock song was "You've Got to Hide Your Love Away." He said the lyrics were a message to Brian Epstein, who was gay. Coleman

●

# "I NEED YOU"

**AUTHORSHIP** Harrison (1.00)
Harrison wrote the song for Patti Boyd, from whom he was separated while filming *Help!* in the Bahamas. A-Z

**RECORDED**
February 15, 1965, at Abbey Road, with overdubs February 16
*Abbey; Day* says between early February and early March.

**INSTRUMENTATION**
McCARTNEY: bass, backing vocal
LENNON: acoustic guitar, backing vocal

HARRISON: lead guitar, lead vocal (double-tracked)
STARR: drums

*Record* and *ATN; Road* says backing vocals are harmony.

**MISCELLANEOUS**
Performed in the film *Help!*

●

# "ANOTHER GIRL"

**AUTHORSHIP** McCartney (1.00)

**RECORDED**
February 15, 1965, at Abbey Road, with McCartney overdubbing lead guitar on February 16   *Abbey; Day* says between early February and early March.

**INSTRUMENTATION**
McCARTNEY: bass, lead guitar (solo at end), lead vocal
LENNON: acoustic guitar, backing vocal

HARRISON: lead guitar, backing vocal
STARR: drums

*Record; Road* and *ATN* agree on vocals and McCartney's lead guitar.

**MISCELLANEOUS**
Performed in the film *Help!*

●

# "YOU'RE GOING TO LOSE THAT GIRL"

**AUTHORSHIP** Lennon (1.00)

**RECORDED**
February 19, 1965, at Abbey Road   *Abbey; Day* says between early February and early March.

## INSTRUMENTATION

McCARTNEY: bass, piano, backing vocal
LENNON: acoustic guitar, lead vocal

HARRISON: lead guitar (Fender Stratocaster, Sonic Blue tremolo), backing vocal
STARR: drums, bongos

*Record* and *Road;* guitar from *Guitar* (November 1987).

## MISCELLANEOUS

Performed in the film *Help!*

•

# "TICKET TO RIDE"

## CHART ACTION

UNITED KINGDOM: Originally released as a single on April 9, 1965. It was a No. 1 hit within a week and held that position for five weeks.  *Road*

UNITED STATES: Also released as a single on April 14, 1965. Entered the Top 40 May 1, stayed nine weeks, and rose to No. 1 for one week.
*Road* with *Billboard*

## AUTHORSHIP Lennon (1.00)

## RECORDED

February 15, 1965, at Abbey Road

*Abbey; Day* says February 12; *Diary* says session was on February 9 although it also has Beatles out of the country that day.

## INSTRUMENTATION

McCARTNEY: bass, lead guitar (Sunburst Epiphone Casino), harmony vocal
LENNON: rhythm guitar, tambourine, lead vocal

HARRISON: lead guitar
STARR: drums

*Record; Road* agrees on McCartney's lead guitar, but says Harrison sang backing vocal; *ATN* omits Harrison's vocal; guitar from *Guitar* (November 1987).

## MISCELLANEOUS

As with "Help!," the first pressing's label caption read: "From the United Artists screenplay, *Eight Arms to Hold You.*"  A-Z

This song is heard during *Help!*'s skiing sequence, which was largely spontaneous because the Beatles were all amateur skiers and fell down a lot. *A-Z*

This song was part of the Beatles' live repertoire in 1965. *Live* It was performed on their European tour in early summer 1965, the North American tour that summer, and the British tour that December. It was also performed on *The Ed Sullivan Show,* September 12, 1965. *Forever*

## COMMENTS BY BEATLES
LENNON: "That was one of the earliest heavy-metal records made. Paul's contribution was the way Ringo played the drums."

September 1980, *Playboy Interviews*

•

# "ACT NATURALLY"

## CHART ACTION
UNITED STATES: Also released as a single September 13, 1965, as the B side to "Yesterday." It missed the Top 40 by seven positions, peaking at No. 47.

## AUTHORSHIP Johnny Russell (.5) and Vonie Morrison (.5)
Russell later said he wrote the song in half an hour in 1961. He spent two years trying to get the song recorded. In 1988 he was a singer and humorist at the Grand Ole Opry. AP (July 11, 1988)

## RECORDED
June 17, 1965, at Abbey Road. It was the last song recorded for the album and was chosen specifically for Ringo to sing.

*Abbey; Day* and *ATN* say between late May and early June.

The session was shortly after filming for *Help!* was completed, so this song's lyrics about appearing in movies may have been of interest to the Beatles.

## INSTRUMENTATION
McCARTNEY: bass, harmony vocal    HARRISON: lead guitar
LENNON: acoustic guitar           STARR: drums, lead vocal

*Record; Road* says McCartney's vocal was backing.

**MISCELLANEOUS**

This song's original recording artist was Buck Owens. *Lists* His version, released March 11, 1963, became a No. 1 country and western hit in the United States. *Road*

    This song was part of the Beatles' live repertoire in 1965. *Live* It was performed on the summer 1965 North American tour (only some shows) and on the British tour that December. It was also performed on *The Ed Sullivan Show,* September 12, 1965. *Forever*

    The song was prophetic in a way. Starr later acted in many films—more than any other Beatle—and always played a Ringoesque character.

●

# "IT'S ONLY LOVE"

**AUTHORSHIP** Lennon (1.00)

**RECORDED**

June 15, 1965, at Abbey Road   *Abbey; Day* and *ATN* say between late May and early June.

**INSTRUMENTATION**

McCARTNEY: bass            HARRISON: lead guitar

LENNON: acoustic guitar,      STARR: drums

tambourine, vocal

*Record; Road* and *ATN* say McCartney added backing vocal.

**MISCELLANEOUS**

The original title was "That's a Nice Hat (Cap)." The tune was later recorded as an instrumental by George Martin and his orchestra under that name. *B-Lists* and *A-Z* (but "... Hat-Cap").

**COMMENTS BY BEATLES**

LENNON: "That's the one song I really hate of mine. Terrible lyric." *Hit Parader* (April 1972)

●

# "YOU LIKE ME TOO MUCH"

**AUTHORSHIP** Harrison (1.00)

**RECORDED**
February 17, 1965, at Abbey Road   *Abbey; Day* and *Compleat*(b) say May 10 to 11.

**INSTRUMENTATION**

McCARTNEY: Steinway piano, harmony vocal
LENNON: acoustic guitar, electric piano
HARRISON: lead guitar, lead vocal

STARR: drums, tambourine
George Martin: Steinway piano
McCartney and Martin play the same acoustic piano

*Record; Road* and *ATN* agree on vocals and pianos; *Compleat*(b) agrees on pianos.

●

# "TELL ME WHAT YOU SEE"

**AUTHORSHIP** McCartney (1.00)

**RECORDED**
February 18, 1965, at Abbey Road   *Abbey; Day* and *Compleat*(b) say May 10 to 11.

**INSTRUMENTATION**

McCARTNEY: bass, electric piano, lead vocal
LENNON: washboard guitar, lead vocal

HARRISON: lead guitar, tambourine
STARR: drums, claves

*Record; Road* and *ATN* agree on lead vocals and electric piano.

●

# "I'VE JUST SEEN A FACE"

**AUTHORSHIP** McCartney (1.00)

**RECORDED**
June 14, 1965, at Abbey Road   *Abbey; Day* and *ATN* say between late May and early June.

**INSTRUMENTATION**

McCARTNEY: acoustic guitar, vocal      HARRISON: acoustic lead guitar
LENNON: acoustic guitar                STARR: drums, maracas

*Record; Road* agrees on McCartney's vocal.

**MISCELLANEOUS**

McCartney's Aunt Gin liked this tune, so its working title was "Auntie Gin's Theme." Later the George Martin Orchestra recorded the song as an instrumental with that title.   *A-Z* and *B-Lists*

This was one of five Beatles songs performed during McCartney's Wings over America tour in 1976.

●

# "YESTERDAY"

**CHART ACTION**

UNITED STATES: Also released as a single, September 13, 1965. It entered the Top 40 October 2, stayed for nine weeks, and held the No. 1 position for four. (Despite the song's massive popular success in the United States, it wasn't released as a single in the United Kingdom until February 1976.)
*Road*

McCARTNEY: "The hits are always the ones that you thought wouldn't be hits, like 'Yesterday' or 'Mull of Kintyre.' I didn't want to put them out. We didn't put 'Yesterday' out in England, it was only [in the United States] it was a single. We didn't think it was going to be a good idea, so it's crazy how it goes."   *Rock Express* (November–December 1986)

**AUTHORSHIP** McCartney (1.00)

McCARTNEY: "It fell out of bed. I had a piano by my bedside and I . . . must have dreamed it, because I tumbled out of bed and put my hands on the piano keys and I had a tune in my head. It [the music] was just all there, a complete thing. I couldn't believe it. It came too easy. In fact, I didn't believe I'd written it. I thought maybe I'd heard it before, it was some other tune, and I went around for weeks playing the chords of the song for people, asking them, 'Is this *like* something? I *think* I've written it.' And people would say, 'No, it's not like anything else, but it's good.' "
*Playboy* (December 1984)

Paul used the working title of "Scrambled Eggs" until he could figure out real lyrics. *Love* Among the lines he played with at first were: "Scrambled eggs / Oh, how I loved your legs." *Salewicz*

LENNON: "[Paul] wrote the lyrics to 'Yesterday.' Although the lyrics don't resolve into any sense, they're *good* lines. They certainly work. You know what I mean? They're good—but if you read the whole song, it doesn't *say* anything; you don't know what happened. She left and he wishes it were yesterday—that much you get—but it doesn't really resolve. So, mine didn't used to resolve, either . . ."   September 1980, *Playboy Interviews*

## RECORDED
June 14, 1965, at Abbey Road
*Abbey; Day* and *Road* and *ATN* say between late May and early June.

McCartney sang this sweet, melancholy song a couple of hours after he shouted/sang the raucous, larynx-tearing "I'm Down."   *Abbey*

MARTIN, after using the master tapes to produce the compact disc version of the album: "Originally, I recorded Paul singing and playing at the same time, miking up both guitar and voice. Then later on I wrote and over-dubbed the strings, and on my fourth track I got Paul to have another go at recording the voice, just in case we got a better performance. Well, we didn't—not in my opinion anyway—except in one particular part which was at the end of the first section: ('I said something wrong'). So I used that as an alternative voice, and during the past twenty years I've forgotten about it and have always thought that is where I decided to double-track the voice. But it's not double-tracked, because in fact it's voice with leakage from a speaker, as we didn't use headphones."   *Musician* (July 1987)

## INSTRUMENTATION
McCARTNEY: acoustic guitar                Session musicians: string quartet
(Epiphone Texan), vocal
*Record* and *Road* and *ATN*; guitar from *Guitar* (November 1987).

This was the first time a Beatle recorded solo.   *Forever* and *Record*

MARTIN: "The turning point probably came with the song 'Yesterday'. . . That was when, as I can see in retrospect, I started to leave my hallmark on the music, when a style started to emerge which was partly of my making. It was on 'Yesterday' that I started to score their music. It was on 'Yesterday' that we first used instruments or musicians other than the Beatles and myself. [Actually, 'You've Got to Hide Your Love Away' was first, but the participation by outside musicians was much less on that.]

"On 'Yesterday' the added ingredient was no more nor less than a string quartet; and that, in the pop world of those days, was quite a step to take. It was with 'Yesterday' that we started breaking out of the phase of using just four instruments and went into something more experimental, though our initial experiments were severely limited by the fairly crude tools at our disposal, and had simply to be molded out of my recording experience." *Ears*

## MISCELLANEOUS
This was the first Beatles song to capture the attention of the mass adult market. *Love*

More cover versions of this song have been recorded than of any other Beatles song (Harrison's "Something" is second), and it possibly is the most covered rock 'n' roll song of all time. By 1980 more than 2,500 artists—including Frank Sinatra, Ray Charles, Marianne Faithfull, Lou Rawls, Tom Jones, Jan and Dean, Liberace, the Supremes, and Marvin Gaye—had covered it. *Road* and *Love*

This was also the first Beatles recording that could not be accurately re-created in concert without additional musicians. *Forever*

Nonetheless, this song was part of the Beatles' live repertoire in 1965 and 1966. *Live* It was performed on *The Ed Sullivan Show* September 12, 1965 and also on their world tour—their last—in the summer of 1966. *Forever, Compleat*(b) agrees with 1966 tour.

It was one of five Beatles songs performed on McCartney's Wings over America tour in 1976.

McCartney performed it in the film *Give My Regards to Broad Street.* *Broad* He had to ask permission to use it, since he didn't own the publishing rights. *Beatles* Michael Jackson now does, after outbidding McCartney for them in the mid-'80s.

## COMMENTS BY BEATLES
LENNON: "Wow, that was a good 'un." *Hit Parader* (April 1972)

McCARTNEY: "I get made fun of because of it a bit. I remember George saying, 'Blimey, he's always talking about "Yesterday," you'd think he was Beethoven or somebody.' But it is the one, I reckon, that is the most complete thing I've ever written. It's very catchy without being sickly, too. When you're trying to write a song, there are certain times when you get the essence, it's all there. It's like an egg being laid, it's so there, not a crack nor a flaw in it." *Salewicz*

Some sources say this is McCartney's personal favorite of all the Beatles' songs; others say it is "Here, There and Everywhere."

LENNON: "I have had *so* much accolade for 'Yesterday.' That's Paul's song and Paul's baby. Well done. Beautiful—and I never wished I'd written it." September 1980, *Playboy Interviews*

●

# "DIZZY MISS LIZZY"

**AUTHORSHIP** Larry Williams (1.00)

**RECORDED**
May 10, 1965, at Abbey Road   *Abbey; Day* and *Road* and *ATN* say May 10 to 11.

**INSTRUMENTATION**

McCARTNEY: bass                    HARRISON: lead guitar
LENNON: Hammond organ, vocal       STARR: drums

*Record; Road* and *ATN* agree on vocal.

**MISCELLANEOUS**
This recording appeared first on the U.S. album *Beatles VI,* released in June 1965, about two months before *Help!* appeared.

The original recording by Larry Williams was released February 24, 1958. It was not a Top 40 hit.   *Road*

The Beatles recorded an unreleased version in late 1962.   *Day*

This song was part of the Beatles' live repertoire from 1960 to 1962 and again in 1965.   *Live*   It was performed on their North American tour in summer 1965 and on their U.K. tour that December.   *Forever*

●

# "DAY TRIPPER"

**CHART ACTION**
UNITED KINGDOM: Released as a single December 3, 1965, backed with "We Can Work It Out." Both were hits, but "Day Tripper" was considered the stronger of the two. Five days after release, it entered the chart at No. 1, where it stayed for five weeks.  *Road*

UNITED STATES: Released as a single December 6, 1965, backed with "We Can Work It Out," which got more airplay. "Day Tripper" was in the Top 40 for eight weeks beginning on December 25, 1965, and peaked at No. 5. *Road* and *Billboard*
　　　The monthly *Beatles Book* revealed in its January 1966 issue that the Beatles preferred "We Can Work It Out" as the A side, but others preferred "Day Tripper."  *Day*

**AUTHORSHIP** Lennon (.8) and McCartney (.2)
Lennon and McCartney said in a 1966 interview that "Day Tripper" was a "forced" composition, needed quickly for a new single.  *Abbey*

LENNON: "Me [I wrote it], but I think Paul helped with the verse."
*Hit Parader* (April 1972); *Road* agrees on McCartney's contribution; *ATN* credits only Lennon.

LENNON: "That's mine, including the lick, the guitar break, and the whole bit. It's just a rock 'n' roll song. Day trippers are people who go on a day trip, right? Usually on a ferryboat or something. But it was kind of—you know, 'you're just a weekend hippie.' Get it?"  September 1980, *Playboy Interviews*

　　　Pete Shotton wrote that Lennon loved to make the Beatles' records into word games and slip in allusions to sex, drugs, and other naughty subjects. This song contained Lennon's first deliberate reference to LSD and the line "She's a prick teaser," which was recorded as "She's a big teaser." Shotton (except for last).

**RECORDED**
October 16, 1965, at Abbey Road   *Abbey; Day* and *Road* and *ATN* say early November.

**INSTRUMENTATION**
McCARTNEY: bass, lead vocal            HARRISON: lead guitar
LENNON: rhythm guitar,                      STARR: drums
tambourine, lead vocal

*Record; Road* and *ATN* and *Transcriptions* agree on double lead vocals and Lennon's tambourine, but say Harrison sang backing vocal; *Transcriptions* says guitars were overdubbed.

**MISCELLANEOUS**
A promotional film clip was made for this song.   *A-Z*
    This song was part of the Beatles' live repertoire in 1965 and 1966.
*Live*   It was performed on the December 1965 U.K. tour and the 1966 world
tour.   *Forever*

●

# "WE CAN WORK IT OUT"

**CHART ACTION**
UNITED KINGDOM: Released December 3, 1965, as a double A-sided single
with "Day Tripper".   *Road*

UNITED STATES: Released as a single December 6, 1965. It entered the
Top 40 December 18 and hit No. 1 on January 8. After two weeks, it
dropped to No. 2 for one week, and rose to No. 1 again on January 29 for
one more week. It was in the Top 40 for a total of eleven weeks.   *Road* and
*Billboard*

**AUTHORSHIP** McCartney (.7) and Lennon (.3)
LENNON: "Paul did the first half, I did the middle-eight. But you've got Paul
writing . . . real optimistic, y'know, and me, impatient."
September 1980, *Playboy Interviews*
    McCartney's inspiration for this song was girlfriend Jane Asher.   *A-Z*

**RECORDED**
October 20, 1965, at Abbey Road, with a vocal overdub on October 29.
*Abbey; Day* and *Road* and *ATN* say early November.

**INSTRUMENTATION**

McCARTNEY: bass, lead vocal          HARRISON: tambourine

LENNON: acoustic guitar,             STARR: drums

harmonium, harmony vocal

*Record; Road* agrees on Lennon's harmonium but says Harrison provided backing vocal; *ATN* omits Harrison's vocal.

**MISCELLANEOUS**

A promotional film clip was made for this single.  *A-Z*

This song was part of the Beatles' live repertoire in 1965.  *Live*  It was performed on the December 1965 U.K. tour (McCartney and Lennon shared lead vocals).  *Forever*

This song was later used for Hewlett-Packard ads in the United Kingdom.  *B-Lists*

# RUBBER SOUL
## *ALBUM*

○

This album, considered by many to be one of the Beatles' best, becomes an even more remarkable feat when one realizes that it was recorded under strict time pressure for release during the 1965 Christmas season. When the sessions began October 12, Lennon and McCartney had little new material to work with and were forced to write and record a dozen originals, all in four weeks.

The Beatles responded to this pressure by coming up with such innovative pop songs as "Norwegian Wood (This Bird Has Flown)," "Nowhere Man," and "In My Life," and by stretching the sounds of the studio even more, employing the sitar, fuzz bass, and harmonium.

## CHART ACTION
UNITED KINGDOM: Released December 3, 1965. It entered the album chart five days later at No. 1, where it stayed for twelve weeks. *Road*

UNITED STATES: Released December 6, 1965. After selling 1.2 million copies in the first nine days, it rose to No. 1 in early January and stayed in the top spot for six weeks. The U.S. version of the album contained ten tracks from the U.K. version and two tracks from the U.K. *Help!* LP. *Road*

## RECORDED
Between October 12 and November 11, 1965, at Abbey Road. The Beatles ended up one song short so they resurrected "Wait" from the *Help!* sessions to fill out *Rubber Soul.*

*Abbey; Day* says October 12 to early November; *Diary* agrees on October 12; *Road* says mid-October through early November.

NORMAN SMITH: "With *Rubber Soul,* the clash between John and Paul was becoming obvious. Also, George was having to put up with an awful lot from Paul. We now had the luxury of four-track recording, so George would put his solo on afterward. But as far as Paul was concerned, George could do no right—Paul was absolutely finicky.

"So what would happen was that on certain songs Paul himself played the solos. I would wonder what the hell was going on, because George would have done two or three takes, and to me they were really quite okay. But Paul would be saying, 'No, no, no!' And he'd start quoting American records, telling him to play exactly as he'd heard on such-and-such a song. So we'd go back from the top, and George would really get into it. Then would come Paul's comment, 'Okay, the first sixteen bars weren't bad, but that middle . . .' Then Paul would take over and do it himself—he always had a left-handed guitar with him.

"Subsequently, I discovered that George Harrison had been hating Paul's bloody guts for this, but it didn't show itself. . . .

"Mind you, there is no doubt at all that Paul was the main musical force. He was also that in terms of production as well. A lot of the time George Martin didn't really have to do the things he did because Paul McCartney was around and could have done them equally well. The only thing he couldn't do was to put symbols to chords; he couldn't write music. But he could most certainly tell an arranger how to do it, just by singing a part—however, he didn't know, of course, whether the strings or brass could play what he wanted.

"But most of the ideas came from Paul." Salewicz

Producer George Martin experimented with a stereo mix that could also reproduce well for mono. That led him to "put lead voices on the right, bass on the left and not much in the middle." Capitol promo

McCartney used his Rickenbacker bass for many of the album's sessions. *Guitar* (November 1987)

## ALBUM PACKAGE
Lennon gave credit to McCartney for the title, which he supposed was a pun on "English soul." December 1970, *Remembers*

Before deciding on *Rubber Soul* for the title, the Beatles considered calling it *The Magic Circle*. B-Lists

Photographer Robert Freeman shot the front cover. The artist's name did not appear on it, probably the first time for any rock album. Forever

## COMMENTS BY OTHERS
MARTIN: "I think *Rubber Soul,* really, was the first of the Beatles' albums which presented a new Beatles to the world. Up till then we had been making albums rather like a collection of singles. Now we were really beginning to think about albums as a bit of art on their own, as entities of their own. And *Rubber Soul* was the first to emerge that way." Compleat(b)

BRIAN WILSON, of the Beach Boys: "I was sitting around a table with friends, smoking a joint, when we heard *Rubber Soul* for the very first time; and I'm smoking and I'm getting high and the album blew my mind because it was a whole album with all good stuff! It flipped me out so much, I said, 'I'm gonna try that, where a whole album becomes a *gas.*'" Crawdaddy (June

1976)  He then wrote the songs for the Beach Boys' *Pet Sounds* LP, which in turn impressed McCartney and spurred him to help create *Sgt. Pepper's Lonely Hearts Club Band.*

•

# "DRIVE MY CAR"

**AUTHORSHIP** McCartney (.7) and Lennon (.3)
Lennon attributed authorship to both himself and McCartney.
*Hit Parader* (April 1972)

McCartney originally wrote the song with the lyric "You can give me golden rings." In the studio, Lennon said the line was "crap" and they both came up with "You can drive my car," which they agreed was better. McCARTNEY: "The idea of the girl being a bitch was the same but it made the key line better." *Newsweek* via *Compleat*(b)

**RECORDED**
October 13, 1965, at Abbey Road  *Abbey*

There are small differences in John and Paul's vocals during the last verse. MARTIN: "That was never intended, but they did it that way. It was live, and things such as that slipped my attention. Once it went through and I saw it was there, I didn't think it was worthwhile calling them in again to replace a line; life's too short!" *Musician* (July 1987)

HARRISON: ". . . If [Paul] had written a song, he'd learn all the parts for Paul and then come in the studio and say (sometimes he was very difficult): 'Do this.' He'd never give you the opportunity to come out with something. But on 'Drive My Car' I just played the line, which is really like a lick off 'Respect,' you know, the Otis Redding version—*duum-da-da-da-da-da-da-dum*—and I played that line on the guitar and Paul laid that with me on bass. We laid the track down like that. We played the lead part later on top of it." *Crawdaddy* (February 1977)

**INSTRUMENTATION**

McCARTNEY: bass, piano, lead vocal

HARRISON: lead guitar, backing vocal

LENNON: tambourine, lead vocal

STARR: drums

*Record; Road* and *ATN* agree on vocals; *Guitar* (November 1987) says McCartney played slide guitar; *Crawdaddy* (February 1977) says McCartney played guitar.

•

# "NORWEGIAN WOOD
(THIS BIRD HAS FLOWN)"

**AUTHORSHIP** Lennon (.8) and McCartney (.2)
LENNON: "Me [I wrote it], but Paul helped me on the lyric."
*Hit Parader* (April 1972); *Road* supports McCartney's contribution.

LENNON: " 'Norwegian Wood' is my song completely. It was about an affair
I was having. . . . But I can't remember any specific woman it had to do
with." September 1980, *Playboy Interviews*
Lennon biographer Ray Coleman wrote that the woman was a "prominent journalist." Coleman; Shotton says "sophisticated lady journalist."

PETE SHOTTON: "He also managed to allude to his habit, back in his
poverty-stricken Art School days, of burning furniture in the fireplace of his
and Stuart [Sutcliffe]'s flat." Shotton

McCARTNEY: ". . . It was me who decided in 'Norwegian Wood' that the
house should burn down, not that it's any big deal."
*Time Out* via *Musician* (February 1985)

The lyrics were considered so good that they were included in an
anthology of classic British poetry. *Forever*

**RECORDED**
October 12, 1965, at Abbey Road, but remade October 21 *Abbey*
Lennon wanted Harrison's sitar on "Norwegian Wood," though it took
some doing to work it in. The instrument was still unfamiliar to George,
and John had thought up an accompaniment that challenged his new skill.
Trying and failing repeatedly to get the version they wanted frustrated John,
but Harrison kept at it, mastered the part, and it was dubbed in later.
December 1970, *Remembers*

**INSTRUMENTATION**
McCARTNEY: bass, harmony vocal     HARRISON: sitar
LENNON: acoustic guitar (Gibson J-     STARR: tambourine
160E [capoed]), lead vocal
*Record; Road* and *ATN* agree on vocals, Harrison's sitar; guitar from *Guitar* (November 1987).
A sitar was used here for the first time on a Beatles song. *A-Z* and *Record*
and *Love* and Capitol promo It was also the first time on any recording of a pop
song. *Road* Harrison tuned it to Western notes. *Record* He had first heard

the sitar played on the set of *Help!* and fell in love with it. *Love* (A sitar had been used in the lead-in to the title song on the American *Help!* album.)

HARRISON: "I had bought earlier a crummy sitar in London and played the 'Norwegian Wood' bit." *I Me Mine*

David Crosby introduced Harrison to the music of Indian musician Ravi Shankar. *20 Years*

## MISCELLANEOUS
Bob Dylan recorded a parody of this song. He called it "4th Time Around" and included it on *Blonde on Blonde. Forever* That made Lennon suspicious, and he felt very uncomfortable while Dylan played it for him in London. But he later realized that Dylan didn't mean any harm.
*RS* (November 23, 1968)

Paul McCartney alluded to this song in a Greenpeace campaign against acid rain during 1988 with a letter to thousands of Britons saying: "Do you remember 'Norwegian Wood'? Who would have guessed that the title would call to mind an image of dying forests. If your family loves the countryside, I urge you to help." *Beatlefan* (August-September 1988)

●

# "YOU WON'T SEE ME"

**AUTHORSHIP** McCartney (1.00)

## RECORDED
November 11, 1965, at Abbey Road, during the last session for the album
*Abbey*

## INSTRUMENTATION
McCARTNEY: bass, piano, lead vocal

HARRISON: lead guitar, backing vocal

LENNON: tambourine, backing vocal

STARR: drums

Mal Evans: Hammond organ

*Record; Road* and *ATN* agree on vocals, McCartney's piano, and Evans's organ; Capitol promo supports Evans's organ.

●

# "NOWHERE MAN"

## CHART ACTION
UNITED STATES: Also released as a single February 21, 1966, it entered the Top 40 March 5, hit No. 3, and spent nine weeks in the Top 40. *Road* and *Billboard*

## AUTHORSHIP Lennon (1.00)
LENNON: "I'd spent *five* hours that morning trying to write a song that was meaningful and good, and I finally gave up and lay down. Then 'Nowhere Man' came, words and music, the *whole* damn thing, as I lay down."
September 1980, *Playboy Interviews*

The song was not changed during the recording process from the way Lennon wrote it, a rare occurrence for the Beatles. *Abbey*

## RECORDED
October 21 and 22, 1965, at Abbey Road *Abbey*

## INSTRUMENTATION
McCARTNEY: bass, harmony vocal
LENNON: acoustic guitar (Fender Stratocaster [Sonic Blue tremolo]), lead vocal
HARRISON: lead guitar (Fender Stratocaster [Sonic Blue tremolo]), harmony vocal
STARR: drums

*Record* (except said all three shared lead vocals); *Road* and *ATN* say Lennon sang lead vocal, McCartney and Harrison provided backing vocals; guitars from *Guitar* (November 1987).

## MISCELLANEOUS
This song was part of the Beatles' live repertoire in 1965 and 1966. *Live* It was performed on the December 1965 U.K. tour and 1966 world tour. *Forever*

## COMMENTS BY BEATLES
Lennon later said he was disappointed in the lyrics. He thought they were trite. *A-Z*

McCARTNEY: "That was John after a night out, with dawn coming up. I think at that point in his life, he was a bit...wondering where he was going." *Playboy* (December 1984)

●

# "THINK FOR YOURSELF"

**AUTHORSHIP** Harrison (1.00)

**RECORDED**
November 8, 1965, at Abbey Road   *Abbey*

**INSTRUMENTATION**

McCARTNEY: fuzz bass, backing vocal

LENNON: tambourine, backing vocal

HARRISON: lead guitar, lead vocal

STARR: drums, maracas

*Record; Road* and *ATN* say Harrison played tambourine; Capitol promo supports McCartney's fuzz bass; bass.

McCartney played his Rickenbacker bass through a distortion box to get the fuzz effect.   *Guitar* (November 1987)

**COMMENTS BY BEATLES**
HARRISON: " 'Think for Yourself' must be about 'somebody' from the sound of it—but all this time later I don't quite recall who inspired that tune! Probably the government."   *I Me Mine*

●

# "THE WORD"

**AUTHORSHIP** Lennon (.6) and McCartney (.4)
LENNON: " 'The Word' was written together, but it's mainly mine. You read the words, it's all about—gettin' smart. It's the marijuana period. It's love, it's the love-and-peace thing. The word is 'love,' right?"
September 1980, *Playboy Interviews*

**RECORDED**
November 10, 1965, at Abbey Road   *Abbey*

**INSTRUMENTATION**

McCARTNEY: bass, piano, lead vocal

LENNON: rhythm guitar, lead vocal

HARRISON: lead guitar, lead vocal

STARR: drums, maracas

George Martin: harmonium

*Record; ATN* agrees on triple lead vocals; *Road* says Lennon sang lead vocal, agrees on McCartney's piano and Martin's harmonium; Capitol promo supports Martin's harmonium.

**COMMENTS BY BEATLES**
McCARTNEY: ". . . To write a *good* song with just one note in it—like 'Long Tall Sally'—is really very hard. It's the kind of thing we've wanted to do for some time. We get near it in 'The Word.' " *Compleat*(b)

●

## "MICHELLE"

**AUTHORSHIP** McCartney (.7) and Lennon (.3)
LENNON: "Both of us [wrote it]. I wrote the middle with him."
*Hit Parader* (April 1972)

LENNON: "He and I were staying somewhere and he walked in and hummed the first few bars, with the words, you know, and he says, 'Where do I go from here?' I had been listening to Nina Simone—I think it was 'I Put a Spell on You.' There was a line in it that went: 'I love *you,* I love *you,* I love *you.*' That's what made me think of the middle-eight for 'Michelle': 'I *love* you, I *love* you, I *l-o-ove* you.'

"So . . . my contribution to Paul's songs was always to add a little bluesy edge to them. Otherwise, y'know, 'Michelle' is a straight ballad, right?"
September 1980, *Playboy Interviews*

McCARTNEY: "I just fancied writing some French words. . . . I had a friend whose wife taught French . . . and I just asked her, you know, what we could figure out that was French. We got words that go together well." Fulton
The French teacher was Mrs. Ivan Vaughan, wife of the former Quarryman and childhood pal of McCartney and Lennon. *A-Z;* Vaughan spelling from *Live*

**RECORDED**
November 3, 1965, at Abbey Road *Abbey*

**INSTRUMENTATION**
McCARTNEY: bass, lead vocal
LENNON: acoustic guitar, backing vocal
HARRISON: acoustic guitar, backing vocal
STARR: drums

*Record; Road* says backing vocals were harmony; *Transcriptions* says backing vocals were multi-tracked, the acoustic guitar was double-tracked, and electric guitar was overdubbed.

**COMMENTS BY BEATLES**
McCARTNEY: " 'Michelle' was like a joke French tune for when you go to a party or something. That's all that was, and then after a while you say, well, that's quite a good tune, let's put some real words to it."
Probably early 1978, *Innersleeve*

## COMMENTS BY OTHERS

BOB DYLAN, on performing songs written by others, mid-March 1966: "It's the thing to do, to tell all the teeny-boppers, 'I dig the Beatles,' and you sing a song like 'Yesterday' or 'Michelle.' Hey, God knows, it's such a cop-out, man, both of those songs. If you go into the Library of Congress, you can find a lot better than that. There are millions of songs like 'Michelle' and 'Yesterday' written in Tin Pan Alley." *No Direction*

Composer Irving Berlin liked this song, according to historian Edward Jablonski. *New York Times* (May 1987)

ALLEN TOUSSAINT, recording artist, producer: "For melody and lyrics, the Beatles were unsurpassed, and I always loved Paul McCartney's bass lines. Songs like 'Michelle,' 'Norwegian Wood,' and 'Yesterday' are so indisputably excellent. In my mind, I always thought they stretched on forever in both directions." *Crawdaddy* (May 1975)

●

# "WHAT GOES ON"

## CHART ACTION

UNITED STATES: As one of the four songs left off the U.S. version of *Rubber Soul,* this was released as a single February 21, 1966, as the B side of "Nowhere Man." It was not a Top 40 hit. *Billboard*

## AUTHORSHIP Lennon (.6), McCartney (.2), and Starr (.2)

LENNON: "Me [I wrote it]. A very early song of mine. Ringo and Paul wrote a new middle-eight together when we recorded it." *Hit Parader* (April 1972)

This was the first song for which Starr got a composing credit.
STARR: "I used to wish that I could write songs like the others—and I've tried, but I just can't. I can get the words alright, but whenever I think of a tune and sing it to the others they always say, 'Yeah, it sounds like such-a-thing,' and when they point it out I see what they mean." *Own Words*

Starr later got complete composing credits on two songs for the Beatles: "Don't Pass Me By" on the White Album and "Octopus's Garden" on *Abbey Road.*

## RECORDED

November 4, 1965, at Abbey Road *Abbey*

McCartney tried to help Starr learn how to sing the song by providing him with a finished recording he had done alone. *A-Z*

**INSTRUMENTATION**

McCARTNEY: bass, harmony vocal
LENNON: rhythm guitar, harmony vocal

HARRISON: lead guitar
STARR: drums, lead vocal

*Record* (but says backing vocals); *Road* agrees on harmony vocals.

**MISCELLANEOUS**

During the song, Lennon is faintly heard answering Starr's "Tell me why" with "We already told you why," a reference to the previously released song, "Tell Me Why." Lennon says it at the end of the verse before the guitar break.

●

## "GIRL"

**AUTHORSHIP** Lennon (1.00)

LENNON: "This was about a dream girl. When Paul and I wrote lyrics in the old days we used to laugh about it, like the Tin Pan Alley people would. And it was only later on that we tried to match the lyrics to the tune. I like this one. It was one of my best."

*Own Words*

Lennon's lyrics also dealt with Christianity, and Catholicism in particular. He rejected the belief that suffering must precede happiness.

December 1970, *Remembers*

**RECORDED**

November 11, 1965, at Abbey Road, during the last session for the album

*Abbey*

McCARTNEY: "Listen to John's breath on 'Girl.' We asked the engineer to put it on treble, so you get this huge intake of breath and it sounds just like a percussion instrument." *Compleat*(b)

Lennon said that, as a joke, the backing singers repeat the syllable "tit."

*List*; Lennon quote in *Remembers* agrees.

**INSTRUMENTATION**

McCARTNEY: bass, backing vocal
LENNON: acoustic guitar, lead vocal

HARRISON: sitar, backing vocal
STARR: drums

*Record; Road* says McCartney and Harrison sang harmony vocals, doesn't mention sitar.

●

# "I'M LOOKING THROUGH YOU"

**AUTHORSHIP** McCartney (1.00)
McCartney wrote this song while he was separated from Jane Asher. She had left to go to Bristol on a theater tour. *A-Z* and *Road* (provides location).

**RECORDED**
October 24, 1965, but remade November 6 and again November 10, with vocals overdubbed November 11 at Abbey Road *Abbey*

**INSTRUMENTATION**

McCARTNEY: bass, lead vocal (double-tracked)
LENNON: acoustic guitar, harmony vocal

HARRISON: lead guitar, tambourine
STARR: drums, Hammond organ

*Record; Road* provides double-tracking; *Road* and *ATN* and Capitol and *Compleat*(b) support Starr's Hammond organ.

**MISCELLANEOUS**
An unreleased version has different instrumental breaks.
The U.S. stereo version contains two false guitar intros. *A-Z*

●

# "IN MY LIFE"

**AUTHORSHIP** Lennon (.65) and McCartney (.35)
This is one of two songs on which Lennon and McCartney significantly disputed authorship. ("Eleanor Rigby" is the other.) Lennon claimed he wrote the song with some help from McCartney. Paul said he wrote the music for the song.

LENNON: "Me [I wrote this]. I think I was trying to write about Penny Lane when I wrote it. It was about places I remembered. A nice song."
*Hit Parader* (April 1972)

McCARTNEY: "I think I wrote the tune to that; that's the one we slightly dispute. John either forgot or didn't think I wrote the tune. I remember he had the words, like a poem—sort of about faces he remembered. . . . I recall going off for half an hour and sitting with a Mellotron he had, writing the tune, which was Miracles inspired, as I remember. In fact, a lot of stuff was then."   *Playboy* (December 1984); *Musician* (February 1985) supports Miracles' inspiration.

LENNON: "Paul helped me write the middle-eight melody. The whole lyrics were already written before Paul had even heard it. In 'In My Life,' his contribution melodically was the harmony and the middle-eight itself."
September 1980, *Playboy Interviews*

LENNON: "I think 'In My Life' was the first song that I wrote that was really, consciously about my life. . . .

" 'In My Life' started out as a bus journey from my house on 250 Menlove Avenue to town, mentioning every place that I could remember. And it was ridiculous. This is before even 'Penny Lane' was written and I had Penny Lane, Strawberry Fields, Tram Sheds—Tram Sheds are the depot just outside of Penny Lane—and it was the most boring sort of 'What I Did on My Holiday's Bus Trip' song and it wasn't working at all. . . .

"But then I laid back and these lyrics started coming to me about the places I remember. . . . I'd struggled for days and hours trying to write clever lyrics. Then I *gave* up and 'In My Life' came to me."
September 1980, *Playboy Interviews*

The lines about living and dead friends were written primarily for Stu Sutcliffe, a dear friend of Lennon's and former Beatles bass player who died April 10, 1962, and Lennon's other longtime friend Pete Shotton.   Shotton

**RECORDED**
October 18, 1965, at Abbey Road, with the instrumental break overdubbed October 22   *Abbey*
A gap was left in the original recording for an unspecified solo. While the Beatles were out of the studio, George Martin decided to experiment with filling it with an Elizabethan-style keyboard sound. He wasn't able to play the solo fast enough, but played it at half-speed and then speeded up the tape to achieve the same result.   *Abbey* and *Musician* (July 1987)

**INSTRUMENTATION**

McCARTNEY: bass, harmony vocal   HARRISON: lead guitar
LENNON: lead vocal (double-   STARR: drums
tracked)   George Martin: piano

*Record; Road* and *ATN* agree on McCartney's vocal and Martin's piano; Capitol supports Martin's piano.

**MISCELLANEOUS**
This was one of Harrison's favorite Lennon-McCartney compositions, but he caused a furor by rearranging the music and some of the lyrics when he

performed this in concert in late 1974. *A-Z* One source said he had changed the line "In my life I love you more" to "In my life I love *God* more." *RS* (December 19, 1974) Another source claims he sang "I love *Him* more." *Yesterday*

## COMMENTS BY BEATLES

LENNON: ". . . It was, I think, my first real major piece of work. Up till then it had all been sort of glib and throwaway. And that was the first time I consciously put [the] literary part of myself into the lyric."

September 1980, *Playboy Interviews*

●

# "WAIT"

**AUTHORSHIP** Lennon (.5) and McCartney (.5)

*Road* says they both wrote it; *ATN* says Lennon.

## RECORDED

June 17, 1965, at Abbey Road, during the last session for *Help!* At the final session for *Rubber Soul* on November 11 one more song was needed, so the Beatles overdubbed bits and pieces onto the original recording, which already included the bass, drums, guitars, and lead vocals. *Abbey*

## INSTRUMENTATION

McCARTNEY: bass, lead vocal     HARRISON: lead guitar
LENNON: tambourine, lead vocal     STARR: drums

*Record; ATN* agrees on vocals; *Road* says McCartney and Harrison provided backing vocals.

●

# "IF I NEEDED SOMEONE"

**AUTHORSHIP** Harrison (1.00)

HARRISON: "It was written in D nut position (capoed at the 5th fret)."

*Guitar* (November 1987)

## RECORDED

October 16, 1965, at Abbey Road, with overdubs added October 18 *Abbey*

## INSTRUMENTATION

McCARTNEY: bass, backing vocal
LENNON: tambourine, backing vocal

HARRISON: lead guitar (Rickenbacker Fireglo 360/12 [capoed]), lead vocal (double-tracked)
STARR: drums
George Martin: harmonium

*Record; Road* provides double-tracking; *Road* and *ATN* agree on backing vocals; *Guitar* (November 1987) provides guitar but says Lennon played a Fender Stratocaster guitar, Sonic Blue tremolo model.

## MISCELLANEOUS

This song was part of the Beatles' live repertoire in 1965 and 1966. *Live* It was performed during their December 1965 U.K. tour and 1966 world tour. *Forever*

## COMMENTS BY BEATLES

HARRISON: " 'If I Needed Someone' is like a million other songs written around the D chord. If you move your finger about you get various little melodies. That guitar line, or variations on it, is found in many a song, and it amazes me that people still find new permutations of the same notes." *I Me Mine*

•

# "RUN FOR YOUR LIFE"

**AUTHORSHIP** Lennon (1.00)
LENNON: "[This was] just a sort of throwaway song of mine that I never thought much of, but it was always a favorite of George's. . . . It has a line from an old Presley song: 'I'd rather see you dead, little girl, than to be with another man' is a line from an old blues song that Presley did once."
September 1980, *Playboy Interviews*

The song was "Baby, Let's Play House," written by Arthur Gunter.

That line opens "Run for Your Life." Lennon said he wrote the song from it. December 1970, *Remembers*

## RECORDED

October 12, 1965, at Abbey Road, during the first session for the album
*Abbey*

**INSTRUMENTATION**

McCARTNEY: bass, backing vocal
LENNON: acoustic guitar, lead
vocal
HARRISON: lead guitar, backing
vocal

STARR: drums
George Martin: tambourine

*Record; Road* and *ATN* agree on vocals.

**COMMENTS BY BEATLES**
Lennon never liked this song. He had written it not because he had something to say, but simply because another song was needed.   Several sources

•

# "PAPERBACK WRITER"

**CHART ACTION**

UNITED KINGDOM: Released as a single June 10, 1966. It entered the chart five days later at No. 2, the first time since "She Loves You" that a Beatles single failed to *enter* the chart at No. 1. (Seven singles from "I Want to Hold Your Hand" through "Day Tripper" did so.) However, "Paperback Writer" went to the top spot one week later and stayed there for two weeks. *Road*

UNITED STATES: Released as a single May 30, 1966. It was in the Top 40 for ten weeks, beginning June 11, and rose to No. 1 for two weeks. *Billboard* and *Road*

The single was also a No. 1 hit in Singapore, Malaysia, Australia, New Zealand, Holland, Hong Kong, Denmark, West Germany, Austria, and Ireland. *Road*

▶ ## THE "BUTCHER" COVER

*The U.K. ad for this single in* New Musical Express *(June 3, 1966) used the "butcher" photo that was the original cover for the U.S.* Yesterday and Today *LP.* Day

LENNON: *"The original cover was the Beatles in white coats with figs 'n' dead bits o' meat and dolls cut up. It was inspired by our boredom and resentment at having to do another photo session and another photo thing. We were sick to death of it. Also, the photographer was into Dali and making surreal pictures. That combination produced that cover."* September 1980, *Playboy Interviews*

**AUTHORSHIP** McCartney (.8) and Lennon (.2)
LENNON: "Paul [wrote this]. I think I might have helped with some of the lyrics. Yes, I did. But it was mainly Paul's tune."

*Hit Parader* (April 1972); *Road* supports Lennon's contribution of lyrics; *ATN* credits McCartney.

McCartney had spent the first few days of 1966 helping set up the Indica Bookshop, owned by friends. The next single he wrote was "Paperback Writer."  Salewicz

## RECORDED
April 13, 1966, at Abbey Road, with an overdub on April 14

*Abbey; Beatles Monthly* agrees on dates; *ATN* and *Day* and *Diary* say April 13; *Road* says the basic track was recorded April 16 and that special effects were added a few days later.

Recording the song in its entirety took only ten hours.  Road

GEOFF EMERICK, recording engineer: " 'Paperback Writer' was the first time the bass sound had been heard in all its excitement. For a start, Paul played a different bass, a Rickenbacker. Then we boosted it further by using a loudspeaker as a microphone. We positioned it directly in front of the bass speaker and the moving diaphragm of the second speaker made the electric current." Despite the improvement, the inventor of the method, Ken Townsend, was reprimanded by Abbey Road management for incorrectly matching impedances.  Abbey

## INSTRUMENTATION
McCARTNEY: Rickenbacker bass, lead vocal
LENNON: rhythm guitar (Gretsch Nashville [model PX6120]), backing vocal

HARRISON: lead guitar (Gibson SG Standard), backing vocal
STARR: drums

*Record* (except guitar names); *Road* and *Transcriptions* agree on vocals but say McCartney also played Vox organ; *Guitar* (November 1987) provides guitar names and supports McCartney's Rickenbacker bass; *Abbey* says backing vocalists sang the French nursery rhyme "Frère Jacques"; *Lists* and *A-Z* say Frère Jacques was a singing group that provided falsetto vocals on this song; *Transcriptions* says backing vocals were looped to create a delay in the sound.

## MISCELLANEOUS
A film was shot May 20, 1966, at Chiswick House in London to promote the single on BBC-TV's *Top of the Pops.* Michael Lindsay-Hogg directed. The film was shown June 9, one day before the U.K. release of the single.

*Diary; Day* says film shot May 1966.

This song was performed during the 1966 world tour.  Forever

## COMMENTS BY BEATLES
LENNON: " 'Paperback Writer' is son of 'Day Tripper' . . . meaning a rock 'n' roll song with a guitar lick on a fuzzy, loud guitar."

September 1980, *Playboy Interviews*

•

# "RAIN"

**CHART ACTION**
UNITED KINGDOM: Released as a single June 10, 1966, the B side to "Paperback Writer." *Road*

UNITED STATES: Released as a single May 30, 1966. It entered the Top 40 on June 25, climbed to No. 23, and was Top 40 for five weeks. *Billboard* and *Road*

**AUTHORSHIP** Lennon (1.00)

**RECORDED**
April 14, 1966, at Abbey Road, with overdubs added April 16
*Abbey; Diary* says it was recorded April 25; *Road* and *Day* and *ATN* say late April.

This recording shows the first evidence of the Beatles' fascination with backward tape loops. *Lists* John was tripping at his little studio at the top of Kenwood when he put a rough version of "Rain" on the recorder backward. *Love*

LENNON: "I got home from the studio and I was stoned out of my mind on marijuana and, as I usually do, I listened to what I'd recorded that day. Somehow I got it on backwards and I sat there, transfixed, with the earphones on, with a big hash joint. I ran in the next day and said, 'I know what to do with it, I know . . . Listen to this!' So I made them all play it backwards. The fade is me actually singing backwards—'Sharethsmnowthsmeaness.' " *September 1980, Playboy Interviews*

The singing of the line "Rain, when the rain comes they run and hide their heads" is heard backward. *Road* and *Record*

MARTIN: "Once you started something, for a while it almost became the fashion. For example, once I'd turned John's voice around on 'Rain,' played his voice backward to him and put it on the track, it was 'Great! Let's try everything backward!' So George started doing backward guitar solos, there was backward cymbal on 'Strawberry Fields,' until that was exhausted and it was on to the next gimmick. It was a healthy curiosity to find new sounds and new ways of expressing themselves." *Musician* (July 1987)

GEOFF EMERICK: "One of the things we discovered when playing around with [tape] loops on 'Tomorrow Never Knows' [recorded a week before] was that the texture and depth of certain instruments sounded really good when slowed down. With 'Rain' the Beatles played the rhythm track really fast so that when the tape was played back at normal speed everything would be so much slower, changing the texture." *Abbey*

## INSTRUMENTATION

McCARTNEY: bass, backing vocal
LENNON: rhythm guitar, lead vocal

HARRISON: lead guitar, backing vocal
STARR: drums, tambourine

*Record; Road* and *ATN* agree on vocals.

## MISCELLANEOUS

A promotional film for this song was made in May 1966.

*Day; A-Z* agrees that a film was made.

This song was the first of many by Lennon (and Harrison) that emphasized that "reality" is just an illusion and a state of mind.

## COMMENTS BY BEATLES

STARR: "My favorite piece of me is what I did on 'Rain.' I think I just played amazing. I was into the snare and hi-hat. I think it was the first time I used this trick of starting a break by hitting the hi-hat first instead of going directly to a drum off the hi-hat. . . .

"I think it's the best out of all the records I've ever made. 'Rain' blows me away. It's out of left field. I know me and I know my playing, and then there's 'Rain.' " *Big Beat*

# REVOLVER
## *ALBUM*

○

The Beatles' songwriting and use of the studio reached a new peak with *Revolver*. Many consider it the best Beatles album in terms of the quality of the songs. The Beatles' consistent growth in the studio took a quantum leap during the recording of this album, which featured tabla and sitar, tape loops, instruments played backward, brass bands, and submarine sound effects. And overriding all of this were the most sophisticated—and some of the most obscure—lyrics the Beatles had yet written.

*Revolver,* a veritable pop extravaganza, set the stage for the breakthrough single, "Penny Lane" b/w "Strawberry Fields Forever," and, of course, its successor, *Sgt. Pepper's Lonely Hearts Club Band.*

### CHART ACTION
UNITED KINGDOM: Released August 5, 1966, the album entered the charts at No. 1, where it stayed for seven weeks.  *Road*

UNITED STATES: Released August 8, 1966. The United States version was much more McCartney-ish than the United Kingdom album—Lennon's "I'm Only Sleeping," "And Your Bird Can Sing," and "Doctor Robert" were missing. Those tracks had been used less than two months earlier on the U.S.-only *Yesterday and Today.* The shortage of songs didn't hurt *Revolver*'s sales. It was No. 1 by September 10 and stayed in the top position for six weeks.  *Road*  *Revolver* was the last album for which U.K. and U.S. versions differed, except for the special case of *Magical Mystery Tour.*

### RECORDED
From April 6 to June 21, 1966, at Abbey Road
*Abbey; Road* agrees on April 6; *ATN* says early April to mid-June; *Day* says late April to mid-June.

### ALBUM PACKAGE
PETE SHOTTON claims the sleeve design was created at Lennon's house, Kenwood: "John, Paul, and I devoted an evening to sifting through an enormous pile of newspapers and magazines for pictures of the Beatles, after which we cut out the faces and glued them all together. Our handiwork was later superimposed onto a line drawing by Klaus Voorman."
*Shotton; Road* said cover was "designed and drawn" by Voorman.

Voorman and the Beatles had been friends since the early days in Hamburg. Voorman later played bass on some of the Beatles' solo albums. *Road*

Among many poses, Lennon is shown on the cover in a suit of armor, above the ear of his large drawn face. He had bought the armor, named it "Sidney," and placed it in the hall of his house.  Coleman

## MISCELLANEOUS
The album was originally to be called *Abracadabra,* but it had already been used as the title of an album.  *Road* and *B-Lists*  Other titles considered: *Beatles on Safari, Bubble and Squeak, Free Wheelin' Beatles,* and *Magic Circles.* *B-Lists*

     This album was released a few days before the Beatles began their last tour. No *Revolver* songs were performed on the tour.
*Live;* tour of North America began August 12.

## COMMENTS BY BEATLES
McCARTNEY: "Just to show you how wrong one can be: I was in Germany on tour just before *Revolver* came out. I started listening to the album and I got really down because I thought the whole thing was out of tune. Everyone had to reassure me that it was all okay."  *Musician* (August 1980)

## COMMENTS BY OTHERS
Author Tom Wolfe found the Beatles' music profoundly influenced by the American climate of social drug experimentation. Hallucinogens were figuring prominently in artistic, literary, and intellectual expression. *Revolver* was the first of the Beatles' albums to reflect that environment, which, Wolfe believed, was thereafter both a focal point and source for their musical inspiration.  *RS* (December 10, 1987)

●

# "TAXMAN"

**AUTHORSHIP** Harrison (.9) and Lennon (.1)
LENNON: "I remember the day he called to ask for help on 'Taxman,' one of his first songs. I threw in a few one-liners to help the song along, because that's what he asked for."  September 1980, *Playboy Interviews*

## RECORDED
April 20, 1966, at Abbey Road, but remade April 21 with overdubbing on April 22 and May 16  *Abbey*

## INSTRUMENTATION

McCARTNEY: bass, backing vocal

LENNON: tambourine, backing vocal

HARRISON: lead guitar, lead vocal (double-tracked)

STARR: drums

*Record; Road* provides double-tracking, says Lennon and McCartney provided harmony vocals; *ATN* omits backing vocals; *A-Z* and Harrison quote in *Crawdaddy* (February 1977) say McCartney played lead guitar.

HARRISON: ". . . I was pleased to have [Paul] play that bit on 'Taxman.' If you notice, he did like a little Indian bit on it for me." *Guitar* (November 1987)

## MISCELLANEOUS

British prime ministers Edward Heath and Harold Wilson are mentioned in these bitter lyrics about taxation.

## COMMENTS BY BEATLES

HARRISON: " 'Taxman' was when I first realized that even though we had started earning money, we were actually giving most of it away in taxes; it was and still is typical. Why should this be so? Are we being punished for something we have forgotten to do?" *I Me Mine*

●

# "ELEANOR RIGBY"

## CHART ACTION

UNITED KINGDOM: Also released as a single August 5, 1966 (the same day as the album). On August 10 it entered the chart at No. 2; a week later it was No. 1, where it stayed for four weeks. *Road*

UNITED STATES: Also released as a single August 8, 1966 (the same day as the album). It entered the Top 40 September 10, climbed to No. 11, and spent six weeks in the Top 40. *Road* and *Billboard*

## AUTHORSHIP McCartney (.8) and Lennon (.2)

McCARTNEY: "That started off with sitting down at the piano and getting the first line of the melody, and playing around with words. I think it was 'Miss Daisy Hawkins' originally, then it was her picking up the rice in a church after a wedding. That's how nearly all our songs start, with the first line just suggesting itself from books or newspapers.

"At first I thought it was a young Miss Daisy Hawkins, a bit like 'Annabel Lee,' but not so sexy, but then I saw I'd said she was picking up the rice in church, so she had to be a cleaner; she had missed the wedding, and she was suddenly lonely. In fact, she had missed it all—she was the spinster type.

"Jane [Asher] was in a play in Bristol then, and I was walking 'round the streets waiting for her to finish. I didn't really like 'Daisy Hawkins'—I wanted a name that was more real." *Own Words*

McCARTNEY: "I got the name Rigby from . . . a shop called Rigby. And I think Eleanor was from Eleanor Bron, the actress we worked with in the film [*Help!*]. But I just liked the name. I was looking for a name that sounded natural. Eleanor Rigby sounded natural."

*Playboy* (December 1984); *A-Z* and *Road* say McCartney saw the name Daisy Hawkins above a Bristol shop, conflicting with the "Rigby" story.

McCARTNEY: "Then I took it down to John's house in Weybridge. We sat around, laughing, got stoned, and finished it off." September 1966, *Beatles*

McCARTNEY: "The next thing was Father MacKenzie. It was going to be Father McCartney, but then I thought that was a bit of a hang-up for my dad, being in this lonely song. So we looked through the phone book. That's the beauty of working at random—it does come up perfectly, much better than if you try to think it with your intellect."

*Own Words; Celebration* says "Father MacKenzie" may have been named after Tom McKenzie, the Beatles' compere, or emcee, from February 1962 to July 1963.

LENNON: "So we made it into MacKenzie, even though McCartney sounded better . . ." September 1980, *Playboy Interviews*

McCARTNEY: "Anyway, there was Father MacKenzie, and he was just as I had imagined him—lonely, darning his socks. We weren't sure if the song was going to go on. In the next verse we thought of a bin man, an old feller going through dustbins, but it got too involved—embarrassing. John and I wondered whether to have Eleanor Rigby and him have a thing going, but we couldn't really see how. When I played it to John we decided to finish it.

"That was the point anyway. She didn't make it, she never made it with anyone, she didn't even look as if she was going to." *Own Words*

The last verse was made up in the studio. *Road*

LENNON: "I wrote a good lot of the lyrics, about 70 percent."
*Hit Parader* (April 1972)

"The first verse was his and the rest are basically mine. . . .

"He had the whole start . . . he had the story and knew where it was going. . . . I do know that George Harrison was there when we came up with 'Ah, look at all the lonely people.' He and George were settling on that as I left the studio to go to the toilet, and I heard the lyric and turned around and said, 'That's *it!* '"   September 1980, *Playboy Interviews*

McCARTNEY: "I saw somewhere that [John] says he helped on 'Eleanor Rigby.' Yeah. About half a line."   May 3, 1981, *Beatles*

Pete Shotton claimed he witnessed the song's creation. He said it took place after dinner at Lennon's with the other Beatles and friends. The group watched TV for a while, until Lennon grew bored and suggested they play some music, so the Beatles retired to another room. McCartney, who had brought his guitar, played and sang the beginning of the song. The others all made suggestions except Lennon. McCartney had the cleric's name as "Father McCartney." Ringo came up with the line about Father McCartney "darning his socks in the night," which everybody liked. Shotton noted that people would think Father McCartney was Paul's dad, and, after looking through a phone book, suggested "Father MacKenzie." After a few more suggestions, McCartney said the problem was that he didn't know how to end the song. Shotton suggested that Father MacKenzie do the burial service for Eleanor Rigby—"the two lonely people coming together in the end"—but Lennon shot the idea down "with his first comment of the entire session." That prompted a profane retort from Shotton and ended the song-writing session.   Shotton

PETE SHOTTON: "Though John was to take credit, in one of his last interviews, for most of the lyrics, my own recollection is that 'Eleanor Rigby' was one 'Lennon-McCartney' classic in which John's contribution was virtually nil."   Shotton

## RECORDED
Instrumental backing was recorded April 28, 1966, at Abbey Road. Vocals were overdubbed April 29, and another McCartney vocal was added June 6.

*Abbey; Day* and *Diary* say vocal recorded April 20 and string backing April 27; *Road* says April 20 and 28.

McCARTNEY: "I thought of the backing, but it was George Martin who finished it off. I just go bash, bash on the piano. He knows what I mean." September 1966, *Beatles*

## INSTRUMENTATION
McCARTNEY: lead vocal (occasionally double-tracked) LENNON: harmony vocal

HARRISON: harmony vocal Session musicians: four violins, two violas, two cellos

*Abbey; Record* and *Road* and *ATN* agree on McCartney's vocal and session musicians; *A-Z* agrees on lack of Beatles instrumentation.

LENNON: "The violins backing was Paul's idea. Jane Asher had turned him on to Vivaldi, and it was very good."  September 1980, *Playboy Interviews*

## MISCELLANEOUS
A few days after the string track was recorded, on May 1, the Beatles performed their last concert before a paying audience in Britain. It was at the annual *New Musical Express* poll winners' concert at the Empire Pool in Wembley.  *Diary*

LENNON: "Ray Charles did a great version of this. Fantastic."
*Hit Parader* (April 1972)

## COMMENTS BY BEATLES
McCartney thought his singing on this song was not as good as on "Yesterday."  *A-Z*

## COMMENTS BY OTHERS
STUDS TERKEL, author: " 'Eleanor Rigby' I found a fantastic study of loneliness."  *Crawdaddy* (November 1974)

●

# "I'M ONLY SLEEPING"

**AUTHORSHIP** Lennon (1.00)

## RECORDED
April 27, 1966, at Abbey Road, with the lead vocal overdubbed April 29, backward guitar May 5, and backing vocals May 6
*Abbey; Day* says between late April and early May.

The hypnotic, yawning effect is a guitar recorded backward.  *Forever*
MARTIN: "In order to record the backward guitar on a track like 'I'm Only Sleeping,' you work out what your chord sequence is and write down the reverse order of the chords—as they are going to come up—so you can recognize them. You then learn to boogie around on that chord sequence, but you don't really know what it's going to sound like until it comes out again. It's hit or miss, no doubt about it, but you do it a few times, and when you like what you hear you keep it."

*Musician* (July 1987); *Lists,* supported by *Playboy Interviews,* says this solo was recorded straight, then overdubbed onto the tape backward.

**INSTRUMENTATION**

McCARTNEY: bass, backing vocal
LENNON: acoustic guitar, lead vocal

HARRISON: lead guitar, backing vocal
STARR: drums

*Record; Road* and *ATN* agree on vocals, except *Road* says McCartney and Harrison provided harmony vocals.

**COMMENTS BY OTHERS**

PETE SHOTTON: " 'I'm Only Sleeping' brilliantly evokes the state of chemically induced lethargy into which John had . . . drifted." Shotton

●

# "LOVE YOU TO"

**AUTHORSHIP** Harrison (1.00)

**RECORDED**

April 11, 1966, at Abbey Road, with overdubs added April 13   *Abbey*

**INSTRUMENTATION**

HARRISON: vocal (double-tracked)
Anil Bhagwat: tabla

Session musicians: other instruments
No other Beatles perform.

*Record; Road* provides double-tracking, agrees on tabla player, but says Harrison played sitar; *ATN* and Capitol agree on tabla player; note mention of guitars in next item.

HARRISON: " 'Love You To' was one of the first tunes I wrote for sitar. 'Norwegian Wood' was an accident as far as the sitar part was concerned, but this was the first song where I consciously tried to use the sitar and tabla on the basic track. I overdubbed the guitars and vocal later." *I Me Mine*

●

# "HERE, THERE AND EVERYWHERE"

**AUTHORSHIP** McCartney (1.00)

McCARTNEY: "I wrote that by John's pool one day."

*Playboy* (December 1984); Lennon quote in *Playboy Interviews* supports.

This love song was inspired by the Beach Boys' "God Only Knows."

*A-Z*

**RECORDED**
June 14, 1966, at Abbey Road, with overdubs added June 16 and 17  *Abbey*

**INSTRUMENTATION**

McCARTNEY: acoustic guitar, lead vocal (double-tracked)
LENNON: backing vocal

HARRISON: lead guitar, backing vocal
STARR: drums

*Record* (implies double-tracking); *Road* provides double-tracking and agrees on vocals; *ATN* omits backing vocals.

**MISCELLANEOUS**
Performed by McCartney in *Give My Regards to Broad Street.*  *Broad*

**COMMENTS BY BEATLES**
LENNON: "This was a great one of his."  *Hit Parader* (April 1972)

LENNON: "One of my favorite songs of the Beatles."
September 1980, *Playboy Interviews*

●

## "YELLOW SUBMARINE"

**CHART ACTION**
UNITED KINGDOM: Also released as a single August 5, 1966, as the B side to "Eleanor Rigby."  *Road*

UNITED STATES: Also released as a single August 8, 1966. It entered the Top 40 August 27, climbed to No. 2, and stayed in the Top 40 for eight weeks.  *Road* and *Billboard*

**AUTHORSHIP** McCartney (.8) and Lennon (.2)
McCARTNEY: "I wrote that in bed one night. As a kid's story. And then we thought it would be good for Ringo to do."  *Playboy* (December 1984)

LENNON: "Paul wrote the catchy chorus. I helped with the blunderbuss bit."  *Hit Parader* (April 1972)

LENNON: " 'Yellow Submarine' is Paul's baby. Donovan [Leitch] helped with the lyrics. I helped with the lyrics, too. We virtually made the track come alive in the studio, but based on Paul's inspiration. Paul's idea, Paul's title."  September 1980, *Playboy Interviews*

## RECORDED
May 26, 1966, at Abbey Road, with special effects overdubbed June 1

*Abbey; Road* says backing track was recorded in June and special effects were added two weeks later; *Day* says three versions were recorded June 7 to 10.

MARTIN: "... We used to try different things. That was always fun, and it made life a little bit more interesting. The most notable case was 'Yellow Submarine,' of course, where you can hear the noise of bubbles being blown into tanks, chains rattling, and that kind of thing. We actually did that in the studio. John got one of those little hand mikes, which he put into his Vox amp and was able to talk through. So all of that 'Full steam ahead' you hear was done live while the main vocal was going on, and we all had a giggle." *Musician* (July 1987)

GEOFF EMERICK, recording engineer: "For certain things, such as the background vocals on 'Yellow Submarine,' we always used to use live chambers. EMI did have echo plates then, but we never used them." *Musician* (July 1987)

## INSTRUMENTATION

McCARTNEY: acoustic guitar, backing vocal
LENNON: acoustic guitar, backing vocal
HARRISON: tambourine, backing vocal

STARR: drums, lead vocal
Session musicians: brass band
Chorus on fadeout: Mal Evans, Neil Aspinall, George Martin, Alf, Geoff Emerick, Patti Harrison, and studio staff

*Record; Road* and *B-Lists* and *ATN* agree on chorus members.

LENNON: blowing bubbles through a straw

HARRISON: swirling water in a bucket

*Road* and *ATN;* supported by Capitol promo; *Forever* adds that Starr was the one pushing rags in a bucket of water and says Harrison blew bubbles through a straw.

## MISCELLANEOUS
The "submarine crew" speaking in the middle of the song are Lennon and McCartney. *Road*

## COMMENTS BY BEATLES
McCARTNEY: "I knew it would get [drug] connotations, but it really was a children's song. I just loved the idea of kids singing it. With 'Yellow Submarine,' the whole idea was 'If someday I came across some kids singing it, that will be it,' so it's got to be very easy—there isn't a single big word. Kids will understand it easier than adults..." *Own Words*

STARR: "... It's simply a children's song with no hidden meanings. Many people have interpreted it to be a war song, that eventually all the world would be living in yellow submarines. That's not the case." *Own Words*

●

# "SHE SAID SHE SAID"

**AUTHORSHIP** Lennon (1.00)
LENNON: "That was written after an acid trip in L.A. during a break in the Beatles' tour [August 1965—his second acid trip] where we were having fun with the Byrds and lots of girls.... Peter Fonda came in when we were on acid and he kept coming up to me and sitting next to me and whispering, 'I know what it's like to be dead.' He was describing an acid trip he'd been on."

September 1980, *Playboy Interviews; Lennon supports in *Hit Parader* (April 1972); *Love* supports but adds Fonda was describing an operation during which he nearly died.

The song "She Said She Said" came out of that encounter with Fonda. For effect, Lennon turned "he" into "she." After the first verse ran through his head for a few days, he decided to create the middle-eight by writing whatever came to him. What came was a beat change in the new section— but it worked.   *RS* (November 23, 1968)

**RECORDED**
June 21, 1966, at Abbey Road, during the final session for the album. The Beatles took nine hours to rehearse and record the song, complete with overdubs.   *Abbey*

**INSTRUMENTATION**
McCARTNEY: bass                    HARRISON: lead guitar
LENNON: acoustic guitar, vocal     STARR: drums
*Record; Road* says McCartney and Harrison provided backing vocals; *ATN* omits backing vocals.

**COMMENTS BY BEATLES**
LENNON: "I like this one.... It's a nice song, too."   *Own Words*

LENNON: "It's an interesting track. The guitars are great on it."
September 1980, *Playboy Interviews*

●

# "GOOD DAY SUNSHINE"

**AUTHORSHIP** McCartney (1.00)
LENNON: "Paul [wrote this]. But I think maybe I helped him with some of the lyric."   *Hit Parader* (April 1972)

McCARTNEY: "Wrote that out at John's one day—the sun was shining. Influenced by the Lovin' Spoonful."   *Playboy* (December 1984)

## RECORDED
June 8, 1966, at Abbey Road, with overdubs added June 9   *Abbey*

## INSTRUMENTATION

McCARTNEY: bass, lead vocal          HARRISON: harmony vocal
LENNON: harmony vocal                STARR: drums
                                     George Martin: piano

*Record* (except bass); *Road* and *Transcriptions* agree on vocals but say McCartney played piano; *ATN* omits Lennon's and Harrison's harmony vocals; *ATN* and Capitol support Martin piano; *Transcriptions* says harmony vocals were multi-tracked and looped to create a "delay" effect.

## COMMENTS BY OTHERS
This song was praised, particularly for its construction, by Leonard Bernstein in a 1967 CBS news documentary.   *20 Years*

●

# "AND YOUR BIRD CAN SING"

**AUTHORSHIP** Lennon (1.00)

## RECORDED
April 20, 1966, at Abbey Road, but remade April 26
*Abbey; Road* says began in April; *Day* says between late April and early May.

## INSTRUMENTATION

McCARTNEY: bass, harmony vocal          HARRISON: lead guitar, harmony
LENNON: rhythm guitar, lead vocal       vocal
                                        STARR: drums, tambourine

*Record; Road* and *ATN* agree on vocals.

## MISCELLANEOUS
The working title was "You Don't Get Me."   *B-Lists*

## COMMENTS BY BEATLES
LENNON: "Another horror."   *Hit Parader* (April 1972)


LENNON: "Another of my throwaways."   September 1980, *Playboy Interviews*

HARRISON: "Listening to the [compact discs], there are some really good things [that can be heard], like 'And Your Bird Can Sing,' where I think it was Paul and me, or maybe John and me, playing in harmony—quite a complicated little line that goes right through the middle-eight." *Guitar* (November 1987)

●

## "FOR NO ONE"

**AUTHORSHIP** McCartney (1.00)
McCARTNEY: "I wrote that on a skiing holiday in Switzerland. In a hired chalet amongst the snow." *Playboy* (December 1984)

**RECORDED**
May 9, 1966, at Abbey Road, with the vocal overdubbed May 16, and French horn solo overdubbed May 19  *Abbey*

**INSTRUMENTATION**
McCARTNEY: bass, piano, vocal        Alan Civil: horn
STARR: drums, tambourine
*Record; Road* and *ATN* agree on McCartney's piano and Civil's horn; Capitol agrees on Civil as horn player.

**MISCELLANEOUS**
The working title was "Why Did It Die." *B-Lists*

**COMMENTS BY BEATLES**
McCARTNEY, on why he redid Beatle songs for the film *Give My Regards to Broad Street*: " 'For No One' I'd never done anywhere, ever. I'd written the song, took it to the studio, one day recorded it, end of story. It's just a record, a museum piece. And I hated the idea of them staying as museum pieces." Washington *Post* via *Musician* (February 1985)

LENNON: "Another of his I really liked." *Hit Parader* (April 1972)

●

## "DOCTOR ROBERT"

**AUTHORSHIP** Lennon (.75) and McCartney (.25)
LENNON: "Me [I wrote it]. I think Paul helped with the middle."
*Hit Parader* (April 1972); *Road* supports McCartney's contribution in middle.

LENNON: "It was about myself. I was the one that carried all the pills on tour and always [dispensed] them . . . in the early days. Later on, the roadies did it." September 1980, *Playboy Interviews*

PETE SHOTTON: "With 'Doctor Robert,' John paid sardonic tribute to an actual New York doctor—his real name was Charles Roberts, with an 's'— whose unorthodox prescriptions had made him a great favorite of Andy Warhol's entourage, and, indeed, of the Beatles themselves, whenever they passed through town. When John first played me the acetate of 'Doctor Robert,' he seemed beside himself with glee over the prospect of millions of record buyers innocently singing along." Shotton

Dr. Roberts was one of a number of doctors in New York City known as "speed doctors" or "acid doctors." Dr. Roberts would shoot up his star patients with various chemicals, including vitamins and LSD, but mainly speed. *Edie*

McCARTNEY: "Well, he's like a joke . . . about this fellow who cured everyone of everything with all these pills and tranquilizers, injections for this and that; he just kept New York high. That's what 'Doctor Robert' is all about: just a pill doctor who sees you all right. It was a joke between ourselves, but they go in in-jokes and come out out-jokes because everyone listens and puts their own thing on it, which is great. . . . You put your own meaning at your own level to our songs and that's what's great about them." *Own Words*

## RECORDED
April 17, 1966, at Abbey Road, with vocals overdubbed April 19
*Abbey; Day* says between late April and early May.

## INSTRUMENTATION
McCARTNEY: bass, harmony vocal        HARRISON: lead guitar
LENNON: harmonium, maracas,          STARR: drums
lead vocal (double-tracked)

*Record; Road* provides double-tracking information and agrees on McCartney's vocal; *ATN* says both share lead vocals.

●

# "I WANT TO TELL YOU"

**AUTHORSHIP** Harrison (1.00)

## RECORDED
June 2, 1966, at Abbey Road, with bass overdubbed June 3. This was the first bass overdub on a Beatles recording. They later became common

because recording the bass on a separate track allowed greater flexibility in tailoring the sound during the mixing process.   *Abbey*

## INSTRUMENTATION

McCARTNEY: bass, piano, harmony vocal
LENNON: tambourine, harmony vocal

HARRISON: lead guitar, lead vocal (double-tracked)
STARR: drums

*Record; Road* provides double-tracking information and agrees on vocals and McCartney's piano; *ATN* omits harmony vocals.

## COMMENTS BY BEATLES

HARRISON: "[This song] is about the avalanche of thoughts that are so hard to write down or say or transmit."   *I Me Mine*

●

# "GOT TO GET YOU INTO MY LIFE"

**AUTHORSHIP** McCartney (1.00)
LENNON: "I think George and I helped with some of the lyrics, I'm not sure."   *Hit Parader* (April 1972)
Lennon said this song was influenced by Motown music.   *RS* (November 23, 1968)

## RECORDED

April 7 and 8, 1966, at Abbey Road, with overdubs on April 11, May 18, and June 17   *Abbey*

## INSTRUMENTATION

McCARTNEY: bass, vocal (double-tracked)
LENNON: tambourine
HARRISON: lead guitar
STARR: drums
George Martin: organ

Eddy Thornton: trumpet
Ian Hamer: trumpet
Les Conlon: trumpet
Alan Branscombe: tenor sax
Peter Coe: tenor sax

*Record; Road* provides double-tracking information; *Road* and *ATN* agree on session musicians (except Conlon is Con*d*on and Eddy is Edd*ie*)

McCARTNEY: "It was the first one we used brass on, I think. One of the first times we used soul trumpets."   *Playboy* (December 1984)

## MISCELLANEOUS

McCartney performed this song at the Concert for the People of Kampuchea, December 29, 1979, with Wings.   *Kampuchea*

## COMMENTS BY BEATLES

LENNON: "I think that was one of his best songs, too, because the lyrics are good and I didn't write them."   September 1980, *Playboy Interviews*

●

# "TOMORROW NEVER KNOWS"

**AUTHORSHIP** Lennon (1.00)
LENNON: "This was my first psychedelic song."   *Hit Parader* (April 1972)

LENNON: "That's me in my Tibetan Book of the Dead period. I took one of Ringo's malapropisms as the title, to sort of take the edge off the heavy philosophical lyrics."

September 1980, *Playboy Interviews*; McCartney in 1984 *Playboy* interview agrees on Ringo malapropism; *A-Z* and *Day* also support it.

The song's concepts were inspired by Timothy Leary and Richard Alpert's *The Psychedelic Experience*, which was their interpretation of the Tibetan Book of the Dead.   *Lists, 20 Years, Forever* and McCartney 1984 *Playboy* interview; *A-Z* and Shotton say it was based directly on the Tibetan Book of the Dead   Lennon would read it while tripping on acid.   *Love*

**RECORDED**
April 6, 1966, at Abbey Road, during the first session for the album. Overdubs were added April 7 and 22.   *Abbey; Day* and *Road* and *Diary* agree on April 6.

MARTIN: "On 'Tomorrow Never Knows,' [John] wanted to sound like a Dalai Lama singing on a hilltop. He actually said to me: 'That's the kind of sound I need.' So I put his voice through a loudspeaker and rotated it. It actually did come out as that strangled sort of cry from the hillside."

Coleman; *Musician* (July 1987) says Lennon's voice was put through the Leslie rotating speaker of the Hammond organ; *Road* says Leslie speaker was used; *Record* says Lennon's vocal was partly sung through a megaphone.

Each Beatle worked at home on creating strange sounds to add to the mix. The various sounds were added at different speeds and often backward.   *Forever*

Lennon made eight tape loops, which were put through eight tape machines, then faded in and out as desired.   *Road; A-Z* says sixteen tape machines.

McCartney's tape loop of himself laughing is heard as the birdlike noises.   *A-Z*

McCartney got credit for "arranging" the sound effects.   *ATN* and *Record*

## INSTRUMENTATION

McCARTNEY: bass

LENNON: tambourine, vocal

HARRISON: lead guitar, sitar

STARR: drums

George Martin: piano

*Record*

## MISCELLANEOUS

This song's working title was "Mark I."

*Abbey; A-Z* and *Love* and *Road* say working title was "The Void."

## COMMENTS BY BEATLES

LENNON: "Often the backing I think of early on never comes off. With 'Tomorrow Never Knows' I'd imagined in my head that in the background you would hear thousands of monks chanting. That was impractical, of course, and we did something different. It was a bit of a drag, and I didn't really like it. I should have tried to get near my original idea, the monks singing; I realize now that was what it wanted."   Circa 1968, *Beatles*

McCARTNEY: "That *was* an LSD song. Probably the only one."

*Playboy* (December 1984)

●

# "PENNY LANE"

**CHART ACTION**
Capitol Records forced the release of this and "Strawberry Fields Forever" when it demanded a new Beatles single. The songs were originally meant to be part of an album about the Beatles' childhood. Instead, the Beatles recorded *Sgt. Pepper.* *Compleat*

UNITED KINGDOM: Released as a single February 17, 1967. It held the No. 2 position on the chart for two weeks without going to No. 1. *Road*

DEREK TAYLOR, one-time Beatles press agent and insider: "What a fuss there was in the British music press and in the Schadenfreudian columns of some of the regular press: 'Beatles Fail to Reach the Top,' 'First Time in Four Years,' 'Has the Bubble Burst?' " *20 Years*

The song that kept the Beatles out of the top spot in the United Kingdom was Engelbert Humperdinck's "Release Me." *Road*

DEREK TAYLOR: "The Beatles were so serene that they didn't even mind that Humperdinck had kept them off the top of the British charts." *20 Years*

UNITED STATES: Released as a single February 13, 1967. It entered the Top 40 March 4, hit No. 1, and remained in the Top 40 for nine weeks.
*Billboard* and *Road*

**AUTHORSHIP** McCartney (.8) and Lennon (.2)
Lennon helped write some of the lyrics.
*Road* and Lennon quote in *Hit Parader* (April 1972)

McCARTNEY: " 'Penny Lane' is a bus roundabout in Liverpool and there is a barber's shop.... There's a bank on the corner so we made up the bit about the banker in his motor car. It's part fact, part nostalgia for a place which is a great place—blue suburban skies as we remember it, and it's still there." *Own Words*

The song might have been inspired by "Fern Hill," a poem by Dylan Thomas that McCartney said he had been reading. In it, the poet reminisces nostalgically about childhood. *Forever*

## RECORDED

December 29, 1966, at Abbey Road, with overdubs December 30, and in seven sessions during January 1967

*Abbey; ATN* says December; *Day* says three versions were recorded; *Diary* says three versions were recorded on December 16; *Ears* implies recording took place before Christmas; *Forever* implies in December; *Road* says in the first two weeks of January.

## INSTRUMENTATION

McCARTNEY: bass, Arco string bass, flute, lead vocal
LENNON: piano, harmony vocal
HARRISON: conga drum, firebell

STARR: drums
George Martin: piano
David Mason: piccolo trumpet
Philip Jones: trumpet

*Record* (but Phillip); *Road* agrees on Lennon's vocal and piano, Martin's piano, Mason's piccolo trumpet (sped-up piccolo B-flat trumpet) and Jones's trumpet, but it says Lennon played conga drum, Frank Clarke played string bass, and adds flutes, piccolos, flugelhorn; *ATN* says it was McCartney, not Lennon, on piano, omits Lennon's vocal; Salewicz agrees on Mason; *Transcriptions* says McCartney and Martin played piano, Lennon played congas, and Frank Clarke played string bass, but agrees on Mason and Jones.

George Martin said it was McCartney's idea to use a "fantastic high trumpet" he had heard at a concert of Bach's *Brandenburg Concerti.* Salewicz  The piccolo trumpet plays an octave above a traditional trumpet. *Compleat*(b)

MARTIN: "We had no music prepared [for the trumpet]. We just knew that we wanted little piping interjections. . . . As we came to each little section where we wanted the sound, Paul would think up the notes he wanted, and I would write them down for David [Mason]." *Ears*

## MISCELLANEOUS

The song deliberately contained at least two slang obscenities. One was "finger pie," which was an old Liverpool obscenity about females. The other was the phallic inference of the fireman who "keeps his fire engine clean." *Beatles*

McCARTNEY: ". . . We put in a joke or two: 'Four of fish and finger pie.' The women would never dare say that, except to themselves. Most people wouldn't hear it, but 'finger pie' is just a nice little joke for the Liverpool lads who like a bit of smut." *Own Words*

A promotional film was made for this song. *Compleat*

The photograph for the cover of the single, showing the Beatles under bright lights, was shot during a photo session while the group was in the studio recording *Sgt. Pepper* in January 1967. Photos from the same session were printed in many magazines and newspapers because the Beatles having facial hair was considered big news and "proof" that the group was about to break up or had gone crazy. *Diary*

The recording originally had a trumpet solo at the end and that version was distributed for promotional purposes. But the trumpet ending was deleted when it was released commercially. The version on the U.S. *Rarities* LP is not the true original; the promotional single was in mono, so for *Rarities* Capitol Records simply dubbed the solo onto the stereo version of the song. *Road*

●

# "STRAWBERRY FIELDS FOREVER"

**CHART ACTION**
UNITED KINGDOM: Released as a single February 17, 1967, as the B side to "Penny Lane." *Road*

UNITED STATES: Released as a single February 13, 1967. It was in the Top 40 for seven weeks, entering on March 11, 1967, and peaking at No. 8. *Road* and *Billboard*

**AUTHORSHIP** Lennon (1.00)
Lennon wrote the song in Almeria, Spain, during autumn 1966 while he was filming *How I Won the War.*

Despite idyllic surroundings on the southern coast of Spain, writing "Strawberry Fields" was a struggle. Lennon was trying for a natural, spoken quality with the lyrics. The song was about Liverpool, but Lennon used real place names only for the images they evoked. The lyrical Strawberry Fields was, in fact, a Salvation Army home in the neighborhood where he grew up. As a child he had attended parties there and enjoyed himself. The name brought back happy memories. *RS* (November 23, 1968) and *Playboy Interviews*

**RECORDED**
Began November 24, 1966, at Abbey Road, with additional work on November 28 and 29 and December 8, 9, 15, and 21

*Abbey; Road* says December; *Day* says one version was recorded December 10; *Diary* says a version was recorded December 16.

MARTIN: "That November John came into the studio, and we went into our regular routine. I sat on my high stool with Paul standing beside me, and John stood in front of us with his acoustic guitar and sang the song. It was absolutely lovely. Then we tried it with Ringo on drums, and Paul and George on their bass and electric guitars. It started to get heavy—it wasn't the gentle song that I had first heard. We ended up with a record which was very good heavy rock." *Ears*

A week later Lennon wanted to try recording it again with more orchestration. He and Martin decided on cellos and trumpets. After Martin wrote a score for the instruments, the Beatles recorded the song again. Martin was pleased with this version, but Lennon liked the beginning of the first version and the end of the second and asked Martin to join them together. Martin pointed out that the two versions were in different tempos and different keys.

As the producer listened to the two versions again, he suddenly realized that if he slowed down one of them and speeded up the other, the slower version was only a semi-tone flat compared with the faster. He combined the two versions together with a variable-control tape machine. *Compleat*(b) and other sources

## INSTRUMENTATION

McCARTNEY: bass, piano, bongos, flute

LENNON: lead guitar, harpsichord, vocal

HARRISON: lead guitar, tympani

STARR: drums

Mal Evans: tambourine

Philip Jones: alto trumpet

Session musicians: two cellos, two horns

*Record; Road* and *ATN* say McCartney played tympani, bongos and Mellotron (at the beginning, using the flute stop), Harrison played tympani, bongos and tabla harp, and Starr played electric drum track, but both agree on Evans's tambourine, say recording also included flutes, cellos, harpischord and brass; *Musician* (July 1987) says a cymbal was used.

Backward tape loops were used. *A-Z* A cymbal was recorded backward on this, according to Martin. *Musician* (July 1987)

## MISCELLANEOUS

A promotional video was made for this song. The bizarre, psychedelic film shows the Beatles frolicking in a park, overturning a dinner table, and destroying a piano.

"PAUL IS DEAD" HYSTERIA: At the end of the song, Lennon can be heard saying what sounds very much like "I buried Paul." Lennon said he said "cranberry sauce." *Lists* and Forever

McCARTNEY: "That wasn't 'I buried Paul' at all, that was John saying 'cranberry sauce.' . . . That's John's humor. John would say something totally out of sync, like 'cranberry sauce.' If you don't realize that John's apt to say 'cranberry sauce' when he feels like it, then you start to hear a funny little word there, and you think, aha!' " *Own Words*

The Central Park memorial to Lennon is called "Strawberry Fields."

## COMMENTS BY BEATLES

In 1970, Lennon claimed that of all his compositions, only two qualified as *honest* songs: "Help!" and "Strawberry Fields Forever." December 1970, *Remembers*

LENNON: "The awareness apparently trying to be expressed is—let's say in one way I was always hip. I was hip in kindergarten. I was different from the others. I was different all my life. The second verse goes, 'No one I think is in my tree.' Well, I was too shy and self-doubting. Nobody seems to be as hip as me is what I was saying. Therefore, I must be crazy or a genius —'I mean it must be high or low,' the next line. There was something wrong with me, I thought, because I seemed to see things other people didn't see. I thought I was crazy or an egomaniac for claiming to see things other people didn't see." *Playboy* (January 1981)

## COMMENTS BY OTHERS
ADRIAN BELEW, musician: ". . . When 'Strawberry Fields Forever' was being broadcast and thousands of housewives were listening to this bizarre piece of music—I'd like to see that happen again." ENS (October 25, 1987)

# SGT. PEPPER'S
# LONELY HEARTS CLUB BAND
### ALBUM

○

*Sgt. Pepper* not only changed pop music, but transformed how we perceived that music and, in a very literal sense, how we perceived ourselves. A product largely of the mid-sixties Swinging London scene, the album became the soundtrack for the flowering of the hippie movement in the United States during its "Summer of Love."

*Sgt. Pepper* broke the rules of what went before and by so doing gave support to new ways of thinking and alternative life styles. The front cover, showing the mustachioed Beatles in brightly colored uniforms next to drab waxen figures of themselves as they used to look, plainly showed the metamorphosis that had occurred. They had been reborn, and it was a new age.

Before this album, pop music had limits. The common unit was the single, about two or three minutes in length. In the United States Top 40 radio was king. Albums, especially in the United States, had been mainly a way to get more sales from a hit song. Generally, if a pop artist had one or two chart hits (or even almost-hits), the record companies would slap together another ten arbitrarily chosen songs and issue them as an album. The songs would not be thematically related, and their collection on the same slice of vinyl was determined mainly by chance.

Things were a little different in Britain. The Beatles had been releasing hit singles without pressing them on albums. With *Sgt. Pepper,* they went a step further.

The music never stops for long on *Sgt. Pepper*—songs simply segue into other songs or there's only a split-second of silence, far shorter than the normal gaps on pop albums. This reflects the album's concertlike format, perhaps spurred by the Beatles' tradition-shattering 1966 decision to play no more concerts.

The album begins with concert noises: an orchestra tuning up and an audience full of anticipation. Then come the first hard-rock notes and the first lyric—an introduction to Sgt. Pepper's Lonely Hearts Club Band—followed by the lines "We hope you will enjoy the show . . ." and the bulk of the album-*cum*-concert. There is even a reprise at the end of the album that signals that the concert is over. Finally, to round out the concert allegory, there is the encore—"A Day in the Life."

Judged as a group, the songs are generally not up to the standard of those contained in *Revolver* and *Rubber Soul,* but they have more layers. Heavy overdubbing, despite the use of what now seems like crude recording equipment, was an innovation touched upon by *Revolver* and the single "Penny Lane" b/w "Strawberry Fields Forever" the previous winter. "Strawberry Fields" had seemed strange—almost like an LSD dream. On *Sgt. Pepper,* the Beatles were speaking with a far different vocabulary from the one they had used on "I Want to Hold Your Hand." They wanted to "turn you on" and sang, "with our love we could save the world." Despite the inclination of some to read *too* much into it all, the spirit of the album was certainly drug-induced—liberated by the power of LSD, a drug all four Beatles had taken by then.

Several localized events penetrated their altered sensibilities and spurred the creation of songs. The first part of "A Day in the Life" came from items John read in a newspaper. A news report on the generation gap and teenage runaways inspired McCartney to write "She's Leaving Home." And a TV commercial for cornflakes provided the title and spirit of "Good Morning, Good Morning."

Spawned from pop culture, the *Sgt. Pepper* album helped to elevate pop art even higher. It was quite the rage for a while; covered heavily in the magazines of the day, it influenced TV and films, interior decorating and fashion.

The art on the front cover of *Sgt. Pepper* celebrates pop culture. Behind the Beatles stand pop icons and friends, including Bob Dylan (who turned them on to marijuana in 1964), Marilyn Monroe and her English clone Diana Dors, Marlon Brando, Lenny Bruce, and many others. Beatles manager Brian Epstein fought against the cover design. But this was a new age, and the new Beatles were doing things their way.

The Beatles' headstrong demand for creative control would lead to artistic disaster with the *Magical Mystery Tour* film later in the year, but as of the release of *Sgt. Pepper,* they had never lost. Like others of their generation, they felt that they had the power to change the world for the better.


**CHART ACTION**
UNITED KINGDOM: Released June 1, 1967. It sold 250,000 copies within the first week and entered the album charts at No. 1. Sales mounted to 500,000 within the first month and 1 million by April 1973. *Road*

UNITED STATES: Released June 2, 1967. Advance sales were 1 million, and within the first three months more than 2.5 million copies were sold. It occupied the top spot on the *Billboard* album chart for fifteen weeks, stayed in the Top 100 for 85 weeks, and, partly due to a resurgence in 1969–70, was in the Top 200 for a total of 113 weeks.

*Road;* AP agrees on the 113 figure.

Sales in other parts of the world were also outstanding, including 100,000 copies in its first week of release in West Germany. It was the biggest-selling British album of all time until *Abbey Road* in January 1971. By 1981 more than 10 million copies of *Sgt. Pepper* had been sold world-wide. *Road*  By mid-1987 15 million copies had been sold.  Capitol via AP

## RECORDED
Between December 6 and April 3, 1967, at Abbey Road and Regent Sound Studio. A small snatch of gibberish for the end of the album was recorded April 21.

*Abbey; Road* says recording occurred between December 10 and April 2.

*Sgt. Pepper* took more than seven hundred hours to record and cost about $75,000.  A-Z; CD agrees with length of recording time.

Wanting *Sgt. Pepper* to have a radically new feel, the Beatles recorded every instrument and voice with some kind of studio manipulation. They distorted, compressed, echoed, and equalized, turning the studio into a laboratory for experiments in sound.

GEOFF EMERICK, recording engineer: "We were driving the equipment to its limit. . . .

"Technically, *Pepper* still stands up as the best album, knowing what we were going through. I mean, although it was a bit laborious and it can't be done today, every time we either changed tape or we copied something, everything was meticulously lined up and re-biased. . . .

"On *Pepper* we were using the luxury of utilizing one track for bass overdub on some of the things. . . . We used to stay behind after the sessions, and Paul would dub all the bass on. I used to use a valve C12 microphone on Paul's amp, sometimes on figure-eight, and sometimes positioned up to eight feet away, believe it or not. Direct injection wasn't used on the guitars until *Abbey Road.*" *Musician* (July 1987)

PETER VINCE, engineer for "Getting Better," described the *Sgt. Pepper* recording sessions: "Lots of their friends would come in, dressed in the beads and bells of the time, and would just be sitting around playing sitars, tablas, you name it! They would all be playing together, there would be no screening between the individual instruments, and everything would be drowning everything else out!" *Musician* (July 1987)

SIR JOSEPH LOCKWOOD, EMI Records managing director: "I knew there was some possible connection with cannabis in the studios—'smells' were noted—but I never pursued it. I had a pretty close relationship with the Beatles, largely because they were so successful." *20 Years*

McCARTNEY: ". . . I was into [cocaine] just before the entire record industry got into it. I was into it at the time of *Sgt. Pepper,* actually. And the guys
in the group were a bit, kind of, 'Hey, wait a minute, that's a little heavier
than we've been getting into.' And I was doing the traditional coke thing—
'No problem, man, it's just a little toot, no problem.' It was all very lightweight, really. But I remember one evening I went to a club, and somebody
was passin' coke around, and I was feelin' so great, and I came back from
the toilet—and suddenly I just got *the plunge,* you know? The *drop.* . . .
Anyway, I could never stand that feelin' at the back of the throat—it was
like you were chokin', you know? So I knocked that on the head. I just
thought, 'This is not fun.' " *RS* (September 11, 1986)

MARTIN: ". . . Of course I knew they were smoking [marijuana]. They tried
to hide it from me; they'd go out into the canteen one at a time. Neil
[Aspinall] and Mal [Evans] would have the joints already rolled out there.
They'd come back and it would be obvious, but it seemed to help and they
had an enormous enthusiasm for recording in those days. They worked
very hard." *20 years*

NEIL ASPINALL: "They were workaholics. . . . They took a lot longer than
before because they weren't on the road—they took three months and
instead of working from 2 in the afternoon till 3 in the morning, it was from
6 p.m. to 1 a.m. with weekends off." *20 Years*

HARRISON: "Most of the songs we did we had to do as if we were recording
live, like mono. We spent hours getting drum, bass, and guitar sounds, then
balancing them and then doing the take. That was in effect a backing track
and then we later added overdubs. Nowadays you can overdub individually
with each person having his own channel to record on. Then we'd have to
think of all the instrumental overdubs, say a guitar coming in on the second
verse and a piano in the middle and then a tambourine. And we'd routine
all of that, get the sound and the balance and the mix and do it as one
performance. And if one person got it wrong we'd have to back up and do
the entire overdub of all the parts again." *20 Years*

Jane Asher departed Britain January 16, 1967, for a three-month tour
of the United States with the Old Vic troupe of actors. McCartney concentrated on *Sgt. Pepper* and made a deadline that all work be completed in
time for him to see Jane in Denver, Colorado, on her twenty-first birthday,
April 5. Work on *Sgt. Pepper* ended April 2, and Paul flew to the United
States April 3. *Love*

Lennon told Derek Taylor later that he was the happiest he had ever
been in the studio during the *Sgt. Pepper* sessions. (This probably only
includes Beatles sessions.) *20 Years*

David Crosby, of the Byrds, sang harmony on one track, according to Derek Taylor. *20 Years* Crosby reportedly has denied that, saying he only visited the studio during sessions for "A Day in the Life." *Beatlefan,* January 1989

The Byrds were old friends of the Beatles. Some of them were at the party during which Lennon and Harrison took LSD for the second time. The experience prompted the creation of "She Said She Said." *Love* and others

## INSTRUMENTATION

According to *The Beatles Book,* a monthly fan publication, in a report from the session: "The Beatles play far more instruments [now]. The total count at the moment is fourteen guitars, a tamboura, one sitar, a two-manual [double keyboard] Vox organ, and Ringo's Ludwig kit. Plus various pianos and organs supplied by EMI." *Guitar* (November 1987)

McCARTNEY: "On the *Pepper* stuff, I got into the more melodic bass lines. In fact, some of the best-paced bass playing I ever did was at that time." *Musician* (February 1988)

## ALBUM PACKAGE

McCartney became convinced during the recording sessions that *Sgt. Pepper* was a great artistic work and insisted the album have a cover to match. *Core*

PETER BLAKE, who staged the album cover photo: "Paul explained that [the concept] was like a band you might see in a park. So the cover shot could be a photograph of them as though they were a town band finishing a concert in a park, playing on a bandstand with a municipal flowerbed next to it, with a crowd of people around them. I think my main contribution was to decide that if we made the crowd a certain way the people in it could be anybody." *20 Years*

When Blake asked band members to pick onlookers for the park scene on the cover, George wanted gurus. Ringo, not especially interested in the fanciful audience, left it up to his mates. John wanted Jesus, Gandhi, and Hitler. Because his comment that the Beatles were more popular than Jesus had recently sparked demonstrations and album burnings in the States, John's choice of Jesus was vetoed. CD

McCARTNEY: "The rest of us said names we liked the sound of, like Aldous Huxley, H. G. Wells, Johnny Weissmuller.... These were all just cult heroes." Washington *Post,* by English designer Alan Aldridge, via *20 Years.*

EMI nixed one face from the crowd scene—Mahatma Gandhi, which was to be above and to the left of Diana Dors on the cover—because it feared offending India. EMI also insisted that every person be approached (or their executors if dead) for permission and that the Beatles indemnify EMI for several million pounds in case of lawsuits.  *20 Years*

WENDY MOGER, Epstein's former personal assistant: "He [Brian Epstein] asked me to try and get legal clearance from everybody within a week. EMI wasn't very keen on the cover, but Paul wanted to do it. It was an incredible job. I spent many hours and pounds on the telephone to the States. Some people agreed to it, others wouldn't. Fred Astaire was very sweet about it, but Shirley Temple wanted to hear the record first. I got on famously with Marlon Brando."  *Core*

Mae West refused to be pictured, asking, "What would I be doing in a lonely hearts club band?" She agreed only after all four Beatles wrote her saying how much they wanted her on the cover. Leo Gorcey, of the Bowery Boys, was the only one to decline being pictured and asked for a fee, which EMI refused. He was deleted. About half the famous faces couldn't be found to gain their permission, but the album cover was printed as planned. *20 Years*

Brian Epstein didn't like the idea for the cover and feared lawsuits. While the negotiations were going on, he had to fly back to London from New York. Afraid the plane would crash, he scribbled a note to his New York attorney, Nat Weiss, which instructed that brown paper jackets should be used for the album.  *Road*

PETER BLAKE: "All the figures which you see behind the Beatles only filled a space about two feet deep, and then there was a line of figures in front of them which were the waxworks. The actual Beatles stood on a platform about four feet deep in all with the drum in front of them, and in front of that there was a flowerbed which was pitched at an angle, maybe ten feet deep. So that from front to back the whole thing was only about fifteen feet deep."  *20 Years*

It took Blake two weeks to construct the collage.  CD

Mal Evans spent more than four hours polishing the instruments held by the Beatles on the cover.  *Celebration*

The three-hour session took place in photographer Michael Cooper's studio in Chelsea on March 30. Later that night the Beatles recorded over-dubs for "With a Little Help from My Friends."  *Diary* and *Abbey* and CD

Contrary to rumor, the plants on the edge of the cover photo were not marijuana plants, according to Peter Blake.  *20 Years*

A *photograph* of a garden gnome that appears on the album cover sold for $9,740 at a London auction on August 26, 1987.  AP

"PAUL IS DEAD" HYSTERIA: The album cover allegedly provided many "clues" to prove that McCartney had met his end. The hand above Mc-

Cartney's head supposedly was a sign of death. The Beatles were standing around his freshly dug grave. The yellow hyacinth bass guitar in the foreground marked Paul's grave, but according to Peter Blake, the flower arrangement was only a guitar, suggested and made by a young boy helping set up the shot.  *20 Years*

The Beatles hold golden instruments, except for Paul, whose clarinet is black, supposedly signifying death. On the back cover Harrison's finger is pointing to the first line of "She's Leaving Home," which says "Wednesday morning at 5 o'clock as the day begins," the time of the "fatal" accident.

In fact, McCartney did have a car crash on a Wednesday at 5 a.m. It happened on November 9, 1966, after an all-night recording session, and was coincidentally the morning after John met Yoko.

*Diary; Macs* alludes to a crash on a motorbike that caused "severe facial injuries to one half of his baby face"; *Abbey* disputes November 8 recording session.

The Paul on the cover photo was supposedly an actor named William Campbell, who had plastic surgery and had taken Paul's place to keep the group functioning.  *Love*  The inside photo showed McCartney wearing an arm patch reading O.P.D., which many took to mean "Officially Pronounced Dead" instead of "Ontario Police Department." The photo on the back also gave support to the hysteria—McCartney has his back turned.

*CD* says McCartney was there and shows pictures of him in poses similar to back cover; *Road* says the "Paul" in the back-cover photo is Mal Evans and that McCartney couldn't attend the photo session, having flown to America to be with girlfriend Jane Asher on her twenty-first birthday.

McCARTNEY: "We realized for the first time that someday someone would actually be holding a thing that they'd call the Beatles' new LP and that normally it would just be a collection of songs or a nice picture on the cover, nothing more. So the idea was to do a complete thing that you could make what you liked of—just a little magic presentation. We were going to have a little envelope in the center with the nutty things you can buy at Woolworth's—a surprise packet."

*Washington Post,* written by English designer Alan Aldridge, via *20 Years*

The album package included a set of cardboard cutouts: a moustache, sergeant stripes, two badges, a picture card, and a "stand-up" of the Beatles as Sgt. Pepper's band.  *Road*

For the original release, the inner record sleeve was decorated with a wash of reds and pinks in a design created by The Fool, a Dutch group of designers. It's believed that this was the first time a pop record had something other than the regular inner sleeve. The colorful sleeve was discontinued after the early pressings of the album.  *Road*

The center spread was also supposed to be done by The Fool but they hadn't found out what the physical size of the album was so the design was out of scale. Consequently the photo of the Beatles in their Victorian regalia was shot and printed there.  *20 Years*

NEIL ASPINALL: "The back [of the cover] took some time and had to be left till last because we were printing lyrics and they had to be designed and we had to have a running order and we couldn't have that until everyone had decided on it. I remember Paul and I walking along, I think Kingly Street in the West End, trying to work out some clever word using the initial letter of each song—the first would have to be *S* for 'Sgt. Pepper' and then we'd try and get a vowel, say—but we couldn't get it right, so the running order was decided in another way." *20 Years*

The original planned sequence of the first side of the album:
"Sgt. Pepper's Lonely Hearts Club Band"
"With a Little Help from My Friends"
"Being for the Benefit of Mr. Kite!"
"Fixing a Hole"
"Lucy in the Sky with Diamonds"
"Getting Better"
"She's Leaving Home" *Abbey*

*Sgt. Pepper* was the first time song lyrics were printed in full on an album cover, at least on a major pop release.
*Forever* and the London *Times* (May 30, 1987)

**MISCELLANEOUS**
McCartney and photographer Linda Eastman, who would later become his wife, got to know each other at the release party of *Sgt. Pepper,* May 19, 1967, at Brian Epstein's Mayfair house. They had met briefly during one of the Beatles' U.S. tours. *Core;* Salewicz provides date and location.

The album was originally titled *Dr. Pepper's . . .* until the Beatles realized an American soft-drink company had rights to that name. *A-Z*

PETE SHOTTON: "It was Mal [Evans] who not only coined the memorable name 'Sgt. Pepper's Lonely Hearts Club Band,' but also made the invaluable suggestion that this fictitious ensemble be presented as the Beatles' alter egos—the entire album as an uninterrupted performance by Sgt. Pepper's 'band.' " Shotton; Starr in *Big Beat* agrees title was Evans's idea.

McCARTNEY: "[*Sgt. Pepper*] was an idea I had, I think, when I was flying from L.A. to somewhere. I thought it would be nice to lose our identities, to submerge ourselves in the persona of a fake group. We would make up all the culture around it and collect all our heroes in one place. So I thought, a typical stupid-sounding name for a Dr. Hook's Medicine Show and Traveling Circus kind of thing would be Sgt. Pepper's Lonely Hearts Club Band. Just a word game, really." *Playboy* (December 1984)

McCARTNEY: "... After you have written that down you start to think: 'There's this Sgt. Pepper who has taught the band to play, and got them going so that at least they found one number. They're a bit of a brass band in a way, but also a rock band because they've got the San Francisco thing.' And I had the idea that instead of Hell's Angels, they put up pictures of Hitler and the latest Nazi signs and leather and that. We went into it just like that: just us doing a good show."  *Own Words*

A high-frequency note at about 18 kilocycles per second was originally added to the run-out groove on the second side of the album. It is inaudible to humans but dogs can hear it.  *Road; Love* says about 20 kilocycles; *Abbey* says 15 kilocycles.

A few seconds of gibberish was also included for the run-out groove. McCartney suggested it for the benefit of people who had a turntable that didn't shut off. The needle would go around and around in the groove without shutting off, and some gibberish in that groove was deemed better than hiss. Recording the two seconds of gibberish took a full night, from 7 p.m. to 3 a.m., more than half the time it took to record the Beatles' entire first album.

The London *Times* (May 30, 1987); *Abbey* says session ended at 1:30 and included the mixing of a song.

## COMMENTS BY BEATLES

McCARTNEY: 'I think the big influence [on *Sgt. Pepper*] was *Pet Sounds* by the Beach Boys. That album just flipped me out. Still is one of my favorite albums—the musical invention on that is just amazing. I play it for our kids now, and they love it. When I heard it I thought, 'Oh, dear, this is the album of all time. What the hell are we going to do?' My ideas took off from that standard."  *Musician* (August 1980)

Another influence, according to biographer Philip Norman, was Frank Zappa's acidy *Freak Out*, released in 1966. "Throughout the *Sgt. Pepper* sessions, Paul McCartney kept saying: 'This is our *Freak Out*.'"

The London *Times* (May 30, 1987)

STARR: "*Sgt. Pepper* was supposed to have been this complete musical montage with all the songs blending into each other. That idea went out the window two tracks in, after 'Sgt. Pepper' and 'Little Help from My Friends.'"  *Musician* (February 1982)

LENNON: "*Sgt. Pepper* is called the first concept album, but it doesn't go anywhere. All my contributions to the album have absolutely nothing to do with this idea of Sgt. Pepper and his band; but it works 'cause we *said* it worked."  September 1980, *Playboy Interviews*

While the idea behind *Sgt. Pepper* left Lennon cold (as did the production of the album), he knew it was a high point of achievement in his collaboration with Paul, and for the Beatles.  December 1970, *Remembers*

According to Lennon biographer Ray Coleman, Lennon initially worried that they had gone too far and that it wouldn't be accepted by the public.  *20 Years*

McCARTNEY: "We write songs; we know what we mean by them. But in a week someone else says something about it, says that it means that as well, and you can't deny it. Things take on millions of meanings. I don't understand it.

"A fantastic example is the [few seconds of gibberish] on the back of *Sgt. Pepper* that plays for hours if your automatic [turntable] doesn't cut off. It's like a mantra in Yoga and the meaning changes and it all becomes dissociated from what it is saying. You get a pure buzz after a while because it's so boring it ceases to mean anything."  *Own Words*

McCARTNEY: "Until this album we'd never thought of taking the freedom to do something like *Sgt. Pepper.* Marijuana started to find its way into everything we did. It colored our perception, and we started to realize there weren't as many barriers as we'd thought, we could break through with things like album covers, or invent another persona for the band."
*20 Years*

HARRISON, on the compact-disc version: "On *Sgt. Pepper,* I keep hearing this horrible-sounding tambourine that leaps out of the right speaker. It was obviously in the original mix, but it was never that loud."
Denver *Post* (October 18, 1987)

STARR: "With *Sgt. Pepper,* I felt more like a session man because we were interested in making an *album* with strings and brass and *parts.* Everyone says that record is a classic, but it's not my favorite album."  *Big Beat*

## COMMENTS BY OTHERS
Critical reaction was spectacular. Kenneth Tynan said *Sgt. Pepper* represented "a decisive moment in the history of Western civilization."
The London *Times* (May 30, 1977)

The *New York Review of Books* said it ushered in "a new and golden renaissance of song."  *Forever*

*Sgt. Pepper* was selected as the best rock album of all time by critics and broadcasters (mostly in Britain and the United States) in Paul Gambaccini's *The Top 100 Rock 'n' Roll Albums.* It won in both the 1977 and 1987 editions.  Los Angeles *Times* (mid-March 1987)

MARTIN: "[*Sgt. Pepper*] was the turning point, something that will stand the test of time as a valid art form: sculpture in music . . ."  *20 Years*

"That was an incredible thing because it took on its own character, it grew despite us. It was a complete change of life, a very long and arduous series of recordings, and I suppose that looking back on it, *Pepper* would never have been formed in exactly that way if the boys hadn't got into the drug scene, and if I hadn't been a normal person. I don't think it would have been as coherent. . . . I just had to be patient. You can't do much with a guy when he's giggling all the time. If they hadn't been on drugs, it's possible something like *Pepper* would have happened but not quite so flowery, maybe."  Coleman

PETER TOWNSHEND of the Who described *Sgt. Pepper* as "incredibly non-physical."  *RS* (September 14, 1968)

TIMOTHY LEARY: "The *Sgt. Pepper* album . . . compresses the evolutionary development of musicology and much of the history of Eastern and Western sound in a new tympanic complexity. . . . The Beatles are Divine Messiahs. . . . Prototypes of a new young race of laughing freemen."
1968 essay via *Beatles Book*

AL KOOPER, musician, producer: "*Sgt. Pepper,* for one thing, was the album that changed drumming more than anything else. Before that album, drum 'fills' in rock 'n' roll were pretty rudimentary, all much the same, and this record had what I call 'space fills' where they would leave a tremendous amount of air. It was most appealing to me musically. Also the sound of the drums got much better. . . . It will always be a great record. Timeless."
*20 Years*

JOHN SEBASTIAN, of the Lovin' Spoonful: "It was like throwing down a hat in the center of a ring, it was a tremendous challenge. . . . It seemed like an almost insurmountable task to come up with anything even in the same ballpark."  *20 Years*

MICHELLE PHILLIPS, of the Mamas and the Papas: "*Sgt. Pepper* was what we listened to for the next days and weeks: that record, played over and over again. It was the theme of the people working for the [Monterey Pop] Festival."  *20 Years*

ABBIE HOFFMAN, social critic: "Hearing *Sgt. Pepper,* smoking reefers, and planning the revolution in my friend's loft, we were just overwhelmed by their vision."  *20 Years*

DAVID CROSBY, musician: "Somehow *Sgt. Pepper* did not stop the Vietnam War. Somehow it didn't work. Somebody isn't listening. . . . I would've thought *Sgt. Pepper* could've stopped the war just by putting too many good vibes in the air for anybody to have a war around." *RS* (July 23, 1970)

STUDS TERKEL, author: "It's sort of a study . . . of working-class people, of life today." *Crawdaddy* (November 1974)

ROGER McGUINN, of the Byrds: "I was already involved in the psychedelic thing when *Sgt. Pepper* came out so it wasn't the big wonderful surprise for me I think it was for the rest of the audience, but it really had a strong impact on the world, and it did change a lot of things. But, listening to the album recently, it didn't have the continuity I at first thought it had." *20 Years*

Bob Dylan reportedly growled "turn that off" when someone played him *Sgt. Pepper* for the first time. *Forever*

●

# "SGT. PEPPER'S LONELY HEARTS CLUB BAND"

**AUTHORSHIP** McCartney (1.00) *Road* and *Hit Parader* (April 1972)
    Mal Evans received some of the songwriting royalties but no credit.
*A-Z*

**RECORDED**
February 1, 1967, at Abbey Road, with overdubbing February 2 and March 3 and 6

*Abbey; Day* and *Diary* say a version was recorded with horns but without Starr February 1; *Road* agrees recording began February 1; *Day* says a version with Starr was recorded March 29.

MARTIN: ". . . When we had finished [recording] it, Paul said, 'Why don't we make the album as though the Pepper band really existed, as though Sgt. Pepper was making the record?' I loved the idea, and from that moment it was as though *Pepper* had a life of its own. . . ." *Ears*

REPRISE: Recorded April 1, 1967, at Abbey Road, in a hurried session that was to bc McCartncy's last for the album

*Abbey; Road* says recording began March 17; *Diary* says reprise was recorded March 29.

GEOFF EMERICK: ". . . The way Ringo's bass and snare drums sort of thunder out on the *Sgt. Pepper* theme and the reprise—no one had heard that in those days. The bass drum was just padded with woolen articles; later on we would take the front skin of the bass drum off. Before that, people recorded bass drums purely for the note and the beat value. So it became quite exciting to actually have it right up front and sort of slapped in your face. I used to position the mike about six inches away from the front, angled toward the floor a little bit to stop the wind-blast bashing its diaphragm. Later, when we took the front skin off the bass drum, we would normally place the mike inside, of course. We wanted to get the snap of the hammer hitting the skin, and again we'd stuff the drums with cushions or rags to deaden it and make a solid note within there. That's now normal practice, but it wasn't then."   *Musician* (July 1987)

## INSTRUMENTATION
McCARTNEY: bass, lead vocal        STARR: drums
LENNON: lead guitar, backing vocal     George Martin: organ
HARRISON: lead guitar, backing       Session musicians: four horns
vocal

*Record; Road* agrees on four session horns, Martin's organ, omits backing vocals.

## REPRISE
McCARTNEY: bass, lead vocal        HARRISON: lead guitar, lead vocal
LENNON: lead guitar, maracas, lead     STARR: drums
vocal

*Record; Road* says Lennon and Harrison sang backing vocals.

Audience sounds were dubbed in to make the recording seem as if it were being performed live.   *Road*

## MISCELLANEOUS
McCartney, Harrison, and Starr performed this song together on May 19, 1979, at the wedding reception for Eric and Patti Boyd Harrison Clapton. *A-Z*

It was Neil Aspinall's idea that the song be reprised near the end of the album leading into the last song.   *20 Years*

## COMMENTS BY BEATLES
According to McCartney, the Beatles used "Billy Shears" for the name's poetic ring, for the rhyme, and as an introduction to Ringo's following song. The name itself had no particular relevance.   *RS* (January 31, 1974)

●

# "WITH A LITTLE HELP FROM MY FRIENDS"

**AUTHORSHIP** McCartney (.75) and Lennon (.25)
McCartney and Lennon finished writing this in mid-March 1967.  *Day*

**RECORDED**
March 29, 1967, at Abbey Road, with overdubs added March 30
*Abbey; Road* and *Day* say recording began March 30; *Diary* says it was recorded March 30.

**INSTRUMENTATION**
McCARTNEY: bass, piano, backing vocal
LENNON: backing vocal

HARRISON: tambourine
STARR: drums, lead vocal

*Record; Road* agrees on vocals and McCartney's piano.

**MISCELLANEOUS**
Joe Cocker had a big hit with his cover of this song. His version was No. 1 on the British chart in November 1968.  *Road*

The song was originally called "Badfinger Boogie." Later, the word Badfinger would be used as the name of an Apple band produced by McCartney.  *Road; Record* supports.

**COMMENTS BY BEATLES**
Against assumptions to the contrary, Lennon insisted that "With a Little Help from My Friends" was not endorsing drug use. He defended the explicit but deeper meaning of the lyrics.  December 1970, *Remembers*

**COMMENTS BY OTHERS**
RICHIE HAVENS, musician, introducing the song in concert on July 12, 1968: "I'd like to sing my favorite song in the whole universe."
On LP *Richard P. Havens, 1983*, released in 1968.

●

# "LUCY IN THE SKY WITH DIAMONDS"

**AUTHORSHIP** Lennon (.8) and McCartney (.2)
LENNON: "My son Julian came in one day with a picture he painted about

a school friend of his named Lucy. He had sketched in some stars in the sky and called it *Lucy in the Sky with Diamonds.* Simple."
September 1980, *Playboy Interviews*

For the rest of his life Lennon consistently maintained that his four-year-old son Julian's name for a painting inspired the title, which many thought was a reference to LSD.

PETE SHOTTON: "I also happened to be there the day Julian came home from school with a pastel drawing of his classmate Lucy's face against a backdrop of exploding, multicolored stars. Unusually impressed with his son's handiwork, John asked what the drawing was called. 'It's *Lucy in the Sky with Diamonds,* Daddy," Julian replied. . . . Though John was certainly ingesting inordinate amounts of acid around the time he wrote 'Lucy in the Sky with Diamonds,' the pun was indeed sheer coincidence." Shotton

LENNON: "The images were from *Alice in Wonderland.* It was Alice in the boat. She is buying an egg, and it turns into Humpty Dumpty. The woman serving in the shop turns into a sheep and the next minute they are rowing in a rowing boat somewhere, and I was visualizing that. There was also the image of the female who would someday come save me—a 'girl with kaleidoscope eyes'—who would come out of the sky. It turned out to be Yoko, though I hadn't met Yoko yet. So maybe it should be 'Yoko in the Sky with Diamonds.' " September 1980, *Playboy Interviews*

Actually, Lennon had probably met Yoko by then. He met her November 8, 1966, and presumably wrote the song later, during the recording sessions.

Lennon said the "newspaper taxis" line was McCartney's and that he might have helped with the last verse.
December 1970, *Remembers; Hit Parader* (April 1972)

Lennon worked deliberately on the poetic quality of the lyrics, but later said they were "self-conscious." December 1970, *Remembers*

## RECORDED
March 1, 1967, at Abbey Road, with overdubs added March 2
*Abbey; Day* and *Diary* say recording began March 2; *Road* says both March 2 and May 2 (latter must be a typographical error).

## INSTRUMENTATION
McCARTNEY: bass, Hammond organ, harmony vocal
LENNON: lead guitar, lead vocal
HARRISON: sitar, harmony vocal
STARR: drums

*Record; Road* says McCartney's and Harrison's vocals were backing, agrees on McCartney's Hammond organ; *Forever* agrees on Harrison's sitar.

The Hammond organ had a special organ stop that produced the bell-like sound resembling a celeste.  *Road*

## MISCELLANEOUS
Banned by the British Broadcasting Company because of the LSD acronym.

Elton John released a version of this song in 1974 with Lennon helping out on vocal and guitar. It was a big hit: No. 1 on the *Billboard* chart for two weeks.  *Billboard*

A three-million-year-old skeleton, discovered in 1974 and considered an archeological treasure, was named Lucy because this song had been played over and over during her discoverers' celebration party.  *Newsweek* (January 11, 1988)

## COMMENTS BY BEATLES
Lennon claimed that until it was pointed out to him, he was not aware of the LSD acronym in the song title.  December 1970, *Remembers*

McCARTNEY: "... People came up and said, very cunningly, 'Right, I get it. L-S-D,' and it was when all the papers were talking about LSD, but we never thought about it.... We did the whole thing like an *Alice in Wonderland* idea, being in a boat on the river, slowly drifting downstream, and great cellophane flowers towering over your head. Every so often it broke off and you saw 'Lucy in the Sky with Diamonds' all over the sky. This Lucy was God, the big figure, the white rabbit."  *Own Words*

LENNON: "...I heard 'Lucy in the Sky with Diamonds' on the radio last night. It's *abysmal*, you know. The track is just *terrible*. I mean, it's great, but it wasn't made right."  *Playboy* (January 1981)

●

# "GETTING BETTER"

AUTHORSHIP McCartney (.65) and Lennon (.35)
McCartney was walking his dog, Martha, during the early spring of 1967 when the sun came out and he thought, "It's getting better," which reminded him that Jimmy Nichols used to say that same phrase frequently. (Nichols had filled in for an ill Ringo Starr during part of an Australian tour years before.) When Lennon came over that day to continue writing material for *Sgt. Pepper*, McCartney suggested they write a song called "Getting Better." They worked on it for twelve hours, stopping once for a quick

meal. They introduced the song to George and Ringo and recorded some of the instrumentation the next night.    *Beatles*

McCARTNEY: "Wrote that at my house in St. John's Wood. All I remember is that I said, 'It's getting better all the time,' and John contributed the legendary line, 'It couldn't get much worse,' which I thought was very good. Against the spirit of that song, which was all super-optimistic—then there's that lovely little sardonic line. Typical John."    *Playboy* (December 1984)

Lennon said he wrote the lines about being cruel and beating the woman.

LENNON: "I used to be cruel to my woman, and physically—any woman. I was a hitter. I couldn't express myself, and I hit."
September 1980, *Playboy Interviews;* supported by *Road.*

**RECORDED**
March 9, 1967, at Abbey Road, with overdubbing March 10, 21, and 23
*Abbey; Road* and *Day* and *Diary* agree recording began on March 9.

▶    **TRIPPING IN THE STUDIO**

*While overdubbing vocals for this song on March 21, Lennon felt ill.* *Abbey*

*LENNON: "I suddenly got so scared on the mike. I thought I felt ill, and I thought I was going to crack. I said I must get some air."* *Own Words*

*MARTIN: "The problem was where to go; there were the usual five hundred or so kids waiting for us at the front, keeping vigil like guard-dogs, and if we had dared to appear at the entrance there would have been uproar and they would probably have broken the gates down. So I took him up to the roof, above No. 2 studio. I remember it was a lovely night, with very bright stars. Then I suddenly realized that the only protection around the edge of the roof was a parapet about six inches high, with a sheer drop of some ninety feet to the ground below, and I had to tell him, 'Don't go too near the edge, there's no rail there, John.' "* *Ears*

LENNON: *"They all took me upstairs on the roof, and George Martin was looking at me funny, and then it dawned on me I must have taken acid. I said, 'Well, I can't go on, you'll have to do it, and I'll just stay and watch.' You know I got very nervous just watching them all. I was saying, 'Is it all right?' And they were saying, 'Yeah.' They had all been very kind, and they carried on making the record."* Own Words

McCartney offered to take John home, and when they got there Paul took LSD, too, to keep him company. McCartney said that was his first LSD experience. *RS* (September 11, 1986) and *Ears*

## INSTRUMENTATION

McCARTNEY: bass, lead and backing vocal
LENNON: lead guitar, backing vocal
HARRISON: lead guitar, tamboura, backing vocal

STARR; drums, bongos
George Martin: piano (striking the strings instead of the keys)

*Record; Road* agrees on Martin's piano (and striking strings) and Harrison's tamboura but omits his vocal.

The tamboura is an unfretted lute, a huge Indian instrument with four strings that produce a droning resonant note. *Road*

•

# "FIXING A HOLE"

**AUTHORSHIP** McCartney (1.00)
McCARTNEY: "I wrote that." *Playboy* (December 1984)

Paul wrote this after repairing the roof on his Scottish farm, hence, perhaps, the title. *Salewicz*

Mal Evans, the Beatles' longtime assistant, claimed to have helped write this song. He was not credited but was paid for his help. *A-Z*

**RECORDED**
February 9, 1967, at Regent Sound Studio, with overdubbing February 21 at Abbey Road. The February 9 session was the first the Beatles had held outside an EMI studio since they had signed their recording contract.
*Abbey; Day* and *Road* and *Diary* say the song was recorded February 21 at Abbey Road.

McCARTNEY: "The night we went to record that, a guy turned up at my house who announced himself as Jesus. So I took him to the session. You know, couldn't harm, I thought. Introduced Jesus to the guys. Quite reasonable about it. But that was it. Last we ever saw of Jesus."
*Playboy* (December 1984)

## INSTRUMENTATION

McCARTNEY: bass, lead guitar, harpsichord, lead vocal
LENNON: maracas, backing vocal

HARRISON: lead guitar and solo (double-tracked) (Sonic Blue Fender Stratocaster, tremolo model), backing vocal
STARR: drums

*Record; Road* provides double-tracking information and agrees with McCartney's harpsichord and Harrison's solo; *ATN* omits instruments; guitar from *Guitar* (November 1987)

## MISCELLANEOUS

Some listeners interpreted the title to mean a junkie shooting up.

McCARTNEY: "This song is just about the hole in the road where the rain gets in; a good old analogy—the hole in your makeup which lets the rain in and stops your mind from going where it will. . . . It's about fans, too. . . . If you're a junkie sitting in a room fixing a hole, then that's what it will mean to you, but when I wrote it, I meant if there's a crack or if the room is uncolorful, then I'll paint it."   *Own Words*

## COMMENTS BY BEATLES

McCARTNEY: "I liked that one."   *Playboy* (December 1984)

LENNON: "That's Paul, *again* writing a good lyric."
September 1980, *Playboy Interviews*

●

# "SHE'S LEAVING HOME"

**AUTHORSHIP** McCartney (.65) and Lennon (.35)
McCartney wrote the theme, based on a story he read in a newspaper about a runaway girl. Lennon assisted on some lyrics.   *Road; A-Z* agrees it was a newspaper article.

McCARTNEY: "It's a much younger girl than Eleanor Rigby, but the same sort of loneliness. That was a *Daily Mirror* story again: this girl left home and her father said: 'We gave her everything, I don't know why she left home.' But he didn't give her that much, not what she wanted when she left home." *Own Words; Road* says newspaper was *Daily Mail.*

The lyrics about parental sacrifice in this song were taken from Lennon's own childhood. The phrases came naturally—John was quoting his Aunt Mimi. *Hit Parader* (April 1972)

## RECORDED
March 17, 1967, at Abbey Road, with vocals overdubbed March 20

*Abbey; Road* agrees on starting date but says strings and harp were added after April 3; *Day* and *Diary* say it was recorded March 17.

## INSTRUMENTATION
McCARTNEY: lead and backing vocal

LENNON: lead and backing vocal
Session musicians: strings, harp

*Record*

The Beatles did not play any instruments on the track. The vocals were doubled so they sounded like a quartet. *Road*

The strings and harp were arranged by Mike Leander.

*Road* and *ATN* and *Abbey*

According to George Martin, McCartney called him and asked him to write the arrangement for this song the following afternoon. Martin said he couldn't because he had a recording session scheduled. So McCartney contacted Leander. Martin has said he was very hurt that Paul couldn't wait for him. *Ears*

McCARTNEY: "He [Martin] was busy, and I was itching to get on with it; I was inspired. I think George had a lot of difficulty forgiving me for that. It hurt him; I didn't mean to." *Playboy* (December 1984)

## MISCELLANEOUS
The line about the man from the motor trade might have been inspired by the Beatles' friend Terry Doran. He had been a car salesman and ran Brian Epstein's Brydor Auto car dealership in Houndslow, Middlesex, where the Beatles bought their many cars. *A-Z* and *Love*

## COMMENTS BY BEATLES
McCARTNEY: "My kind of ballad from that period. My daughter likes that one. *One* of my daughters likes that. Still works." *Playboy* (December 1984)

●

# "BEING FOR THE BENEFIT OF MR. KITE!"

**AUTHORSHIP** Lennon (1.00)

LENNON: " 'Mr. Kite' was a straight lift. I had all the words staring me in the face one day when I was looking for a song. It was from this old poster I'd bought at an antique shop. We'd been down in Surrey or somewhere filming a piece.... There was a break, and I went into this shop and bought an old poster advertising a variety show which starred Mr. Kite. It said the Hendersons would also be there, late of Pablo Fanques Fair. There would be hoops and horses and someone going through a hogshead of real fire. Then there was Henry the Horse. The band would start at ten to six. All at Bishopsgate. Look, there's the bill, with Mr. Kite topping it. I hardly made up a word, just connecting the lists together. Word for word, really."  *Beatles*

PETE SHOTTON: "John composed 'Mr. Kite' squinting across the room at the framed poster, while his fingers found suitable melodic patterns."
Shotton

McCARTNEY: "... 'The Hendersons'—you couldn't make that up."
*Own Words*

The poster was bought during the filming of the "Penny Lane" and "Strawberry Fields Forever" film clips. The performance it advertised was for February 14, 1843.  *20 Years*

LENNON: "I wasn't very proud of that. There was no real work. I was just going through the motions because we needed a new song for *Sgt. Pepper* at that moment."  *Beatles*

**RECORDED**
February 17, 1967, at Abbey Road, with overdubbing February 20 and March 28, 29, and 31  *Abbey; Day* and *Road* and *Diary* agree recording began February 17.

MARTIN: "Paul would sit down and ask what I planned to do with his songs, every note virtually.... Lots of the arrangements to his songs were very much his ideas which I would have to implement. John would be more vague in what he wanted. He would talk in metaphors about his ideas. I'd have to get inside his brain to find out what he wanted. It would be more of a psychological approach.

"He'd say—for example, on 'Being for the Benefit of Mr. Kite!'—'This song's about a fairground. A little bit mystified. I want to get the feeling of

the sawdust and the feel of the ring. Can you do something about it?' I'd then have to think how that imagery could be transformed into sound."
Coleman

Lennon wanted the authentic sound of a steam organ, but Martin told him none that existed could be played by hand (they were all played by punched cards). *Road*

So Martin took tapes of old Victorian steam organs and asked the engineer to cut them into small sections, about a foot long. Then he told him to fling them up into the air and put them back together again at random. The result, of course, made no sense in strictly musical terms, but it did produce the kind of aural wash Martin was looking for.
*Forever* and *Compleat* and *Road* and *Record*

## INSTRUMENTATION
McCARTNEY: bass, lead guitar
LENNON: Hammond organ (main melody), lead vocal
HARRISON: harmonica
STARR: harmonica

George Martin: Wurlitzer organ (countermelody), piano
Mal Evans: harmonica
Neil Aspinall: harmonica

*Record* (except for melodies); *Road* agrees on McCartney's guitar solo and Lennon's Hammond organ and Martin's Wurlitzer organ but says Starr, Harrison, and Aspinall play harmoniums and Evans plays bass harmonium; *Compleat* provides melodies.

The last half of McCartney's guitar solo was on an acoustic with its tone altered.   *Road* with *Guitar* (November 1987)

## COMMENTS BY BEATLES
LENNON: "People want to know what the inner meaning of 'Mr. Kite' was. There wasn't any. I just did it. I shoved a lot of words together, then shoved some noise on. I just did it. I didn't dig that song when I wrote it. I didn't believe in it when I was doing it. But nobody will believe it. They don't want to. They want it to be important."   *Beatles*

LENNON: "The story that Henry the Horse meant heroin was rubbish."
*Hit Parader* (April 1972)

LENNON: "It's all just from that poster. The song is pure, like a painting, a pure watercolor."   September 1980, *Playboy Interviews*

•

# "WITHIN YOU WITHOUT YOU"

**AUTHORSHIP** Harrison (1.00)
Harrison wrote this after dinner one night at Klaus Voorman's house in Hampstead, London. *Road*

HARRISON: "Klaus Voorman had a harmonium in his house, which I hadn't played before. I was doodling on it, playing to amuse myself, when 'Within You Without You' started to come. The tune came initially, and then I got the first line ['We were talking']. It came out of what we'd been discussing that evening." *Celebration*

**RECORDED**
March 15, 1967, at Abbey Road, with overdubbing March 22 and April 3
*Abbey, Road* and *Day* and *Diary* agree that recording began March 15.
  The Indian musicians were concerned when they heard their instruments being amplified. The recording engineer had to use close miking, compression, and equalization. *Musician* (July 1987)

PETER BLAKE, who staged the album cover photo: "I remember one evening George was recording [this]. There was a carpet laid out, there was an Indian musician, and the whole atmosphere was different to other times."
*20 Years*

**INSTRUMENTATION**
HARRISON: tamboura, vocal
Neil Aspinall: tamboura

Indian session musicians: dilruba, tamboura, tabla, swordmandel
Session musicians: eight violins, three cellos

*Record; Road* agrees no other Beatles participated and on Harrison's tamboura, Indian musicians' instruments (except has Harrison also playing swordmandel), and number of violins and cellos; *Celebration* agrees with Aspinall's tamboura and number of violins and cellos but says sitar was also played by session musicians.
  A swordmandel is a zither-like Indian instrument. A dilruba is a bowed instrument. *Road*

  George Martin helped out as overall producer and arranger, as well as conductor for the violinists and cellists. *Celebration*

MARTIN: "I worked very closely with [George] on the scoring of it, using a string orchestra, and he brought in some friends from the Indian Music

Association to play special instruments. I was introduced to the dilruba, an Indian violin, in playing which a lot of sliding techniques are used. This meant that in scoring for that track I had to make the string players play very much like Indian musicians, bending the notes, and with slurs between one note and the next." *Ears*

## MISCELLANEOUS
The burst of laughter at the end was Harrison's idea to lighten the mood of the music. *Road* and *A-Z*

## COMMENTS BY BEATLES
HARRISON: "The best part of it for me is the instrumental solo in the middle which is in 5/4 time—the first of the strange [Indian] rhythm cycles that I caught onto—1-2, 1-2-3, 1-2-1-2-3." *I Me Mine*

LENNON: "One of George's best songs. One of my favorites of his, too. He's clear on that song. His mind and his music are clear. There is his innate talent; he brought that sound together." September 1980, *Playboy Interviews*

## COMMENTS BY OTHERS
Stephen Stills, songwriter and performer, was so impressed by the lyrics that he had them carved on a stone monument in his yard. *Forever*

●

# "WHEN I'M SIXTY-FOUR"

AUTHORSHIP McCartney (.85) and Lennon (.15)
McCARTNEY: "I wrote the tune when I was about fifteen [or sixteen], I think, on the piano at home, before I moved from Liverpool. It was kind of a cabaret tune."
*Playboy* (December 1984); *Day* says written in 1962 or 1963; *Innersleeve* quotes McCartney as saying he had the tune at age sixteen.

When he wrote this song, it was not yet clear to McCartney in what direction his career would develop. "When I'm Sixty-four" was conceived as a sort of show tune that he imagined might be useful at a later point.
*RS* (January 31, 1974)

He put lyrics to it years later in honor of his father's sixty-fourth birthday. *A-Z*

LENNON: "I think I helped Paul with some of the words."
*Hit Parader* (April 1972)

## RECORDED
December 6, 1966, at Abbey Road, during the first session for what turned out to be *Sgt. Pepper.* Overdubs were added December 8, 20, and 21.

*Abbey; Road* and *Celebration* and *Diary* say recording began December 10; *Day* says it was recorded in December.

George Martin wrote accompaniment for clarinets to give McCartney the "tooty sound" he was after.  *Ears*

## INSTRUMENTATION
McCARTNEY: bass, piano, lead and backing vocal
LENNON: lead guitar (Sunburst Epiphone Casino), backing vocal

HARRISON: backing vocal
STARR: drums
Session musicians: bass clarinet, two clarinets

*Record; Road* agrees with McCartney's piano and Lennon's lead guitar and vocals (wordless harmony on chorus) and session musicians' instruments; *ATN* says McCartney only sang lead vocal; guitar from *Guitar* (November 1987)

## MISCELLANEOUS
One source includes a song called "When I'm Sixty-four" in a list of songs performed by the Beatles during 1962. McCartney was credited with the composition and lead vocal. Was it the same song with different lyrics?  *Live*

## COMMENTS BY BEATLES
McCARTNEY: ". . . So many of my things, like 'When I'm Sixty-four' and those, they're tongue-in-cheek! But they get taken for real! [Sarcastic] 'Paul is saying, "Will you love me when I'm sixty-four?" ' But I say, 'Will you still *feed* me when I'm sixty-four?' That's the tongue-in-cheek bit. And similarly with 'Lovely Rita'—the idea of a parking-meter attendant's being sexy was tongue-in-cheek at the time."  *Playboy* (December 1984)

LENNON: "I would never even *dream* of writing a song like that."
September 1980, *Playboy Interviews*

●

# "LOVELY RITA"

**AUTHORSHIP** McCartney (1.00)
McCARTNEY: "I was bopping about on the piano in Liverpool when someone told me that in America, they call parking-meter women meter maids. I thought that was great, and it got to 'Rita Meter Maid' and then 'Lovely Rita Meter Maid' and I was thinking vaguely that it should be a hate song: 'You took my car away and I'm so blue today.' And you wouldn't be liking

her; but then I thought it would be better to love her and if she was very freaky too, like a military man, with a bag on her shoulder. A foot stomper, but nice.

"The song was imagining if somebody was there taking down my number and I suddenly fell for her, and the kind of person I'd be, to fall for a meter maid, would be a shy office clerk, and I'd say, 'May I inquire discreetly when you are free to take some tea with me.'

"Tea, not pot. It's like saying, 'Come and cut the grass' and then realizing that could be pot, or the old teapot could be something about pot. But I don't mind pot and I leave the words in. They're not consciously introduced just to say pot and be clever." *Own Words*

## RECORDED
February 23, 1967, at Abbey Road, with overdubbing February 24 and March 7 and 21. *Abbey; Road* and *Day* and *Diary* say recording began February 22.

TONY KING, an associate of George Martin and later general manager of the American Apple record label: "One night they were doing 'Lovely Rita.' You know those funny noises on the song? Well, they were done with combs and paper. George [Martin] said to me, 'Would you mind going into some of the other recording sessions to see if you can find anybody who's got a metal comb?' Then we were all in the bathroom, tearing up toilet tissue to make the right sound through the comb. The Beatles had the luxury of being able to spend an hour of their recording time getting the right combs and right strength of toilet tissue." *Ballad*

## INSTRUMENTATION
McCARTNEY: bass, piano, comb and paper, lead and backing vocal
LENNON: acoustic guitar, comb and paper, backing vocal

HARRISON: acoustic guitar, comb and paper, backing vocal
STARR: drums
George Martin: honky-tonk piano

*Record; Road* agrees but omits acoustic guitars, drums, and bass.

## COMMENTS BY BEATLES
LENNON: "That's Paul writing a pop song. . . . He makes 'em up like a novelist." September 1980, *Playboy Interviews*

•

# "GOOD MORNING, GOOD MORNING"

**AUTHORSHIP** Lennon (1.00)
LENNON: "I often sit at the piano, working at songs, with the telly on low in the background. If I'm a bit low and not getting much done then the words on the telly come through. That's when I heard 'Good Morning, Good Morning' . . . it was a cornflakes advertisement." *Own Words*

**RECORDED**
February 8, 1967, at Abbey Road, with overdubbing February 16 and March 13, 28, and 29
*Abbey; Road* and *Diary* say recording began February 16; *Day* says recorded on February 8.

MARTIN: "We weren't averse to putting recorded effects in, too. There were all sorts of sound effects that you could get on record, so in the case of 'Good Morning, Good Morning,' for instance, there was a whole farmyard of animals dubbed in from a [sound-effects] disc." *Musician* (July 1987)

GEOFF EMERICK: "John said to me during one of the breaks that he wanted to have the sound of animals escaping and that each successive animal should be capable of frightening or devouring its predecessor. So those are not just random effects, there was actually a lot of thought put into all that." *Abbey*

MARTIN: "Imagine my delight when I discovered that the sound of a chicken clucking at the end of 'Good Morning' was remarkably like the guitar sound at the beginning of 'Sgt. Pepper' [reprise]. I was able to cut and mix the two tracks in such a way that the one actually turned into the other. That was one of the luckiest edits one could ever get." *Ears*

**INSTRUMENTATION**
McCARTNEY: bass, lead guitar and solo (right-handed Fender Esquire), backing vocal
LENNON: lead and backing vocal
HARRISON: lead guitar
STARR: drums
Sounds Incorporated: three saxophones, two trombones, French horn

*Record; Road* agrees on McCartney's vocal and guitar solo and number of instruments by Sounds Incorporated; guitar from *Guitar* (November 1987); *ATN* gives only Lennon vocal and Sounds Incorporated participation.

Sounds Incorporated was a British band that appeared on the same bill as the Beatles on the '64 British fall tour, '64 Christmas shows, and '65 North American summer tour.  A-Z

**COMMENTS BY BEATLES**
LENNON: "A bit of a gobble-de-gook one, but nice words."
*Hit Parader* (April 1972)

LENNON: "It's a throwaway, a piece of garbage."
September 1980, *Playboy Interviews*

McCARTNEY: "That was our first major use of sound effects, I think. We had horses and chickens and dogs and all sorts running through it."
*Playboy* (December 1984)

●

# "SGT. PEPPER'S LONELY HEARTS CLUB BAND (REPRISE)"

(*See:* "Sgt. Pepper's Lonely Hearts Club Band" song entry.)

●

# "A DAY IN THE LIFE"

**AUTHORSHIP** Lennon (.6) and McCartney (.4)
LENNON: "I was reading the paper one day and noticed two stories. One was about the Guinness heir who killed himself in a car. That was the main headline story. He died in London in a car crash. On the next page was a story about four thousand potholes in the streets of Blackburn, Lancashire, that needed to be filled. Paul's contribution was the beautiful little lick in the song, 'I'd love to turn you on,' that he'd had floating around in his head and couldn't use. I thought it was a damn good piece of work."
September 1980, *Playboy Interviews*

McCartney also contributed the middle section of the song that refers to waking up and catching a bus.

The Guinness heir was Tara Browne, a friend of the Beatles and other rock groups. On December 18, 1966, Browne went through red lights at

110 mph in his Lotus Elan and smashed into the back of a parked van in South Kensington. He was dead at age twenty-one.

*Macs;* Salewicz agrees on date, spelling of name, car, parked van, location.

LENNON: ". . . There was a paragraph about four thousand holes in Blackburn, Lancashire, being discovered, and there was still one word missing in that particular verse when we began to record. I knew the line should go: 'Now they know how many holes it takes to (blank) the Albert Hall.' It was a nonsense verse really, but for some reason I just couldn't think of the bloody verb! What did the holes do to the Albert Hall? It was actually Terry Doran who finally said: 'Fill the Albert Hall, John.' "    *Celebration* and *Own Words*

## RECORDED

In sessions between January 19 (basic track) and February 10, 1967 (orchestral track), at Abbey Road, with an overdub February 22 (the one-chord ending)    *Abbey;* widespread agreement on two main sessions

Lennon's part of the song was recorded first, with him on guitar and McCartney on piano.    *Road*

GEOFF EMERICK: "Lennon's voice on 'A Day in the Life'—that was achieved with tape echo. We used to send the feed from the vocal mike into a mono tape machine. They had separate record and replay heads, so we'd be recording the vocal on the tape, taking the replay and feeding it back through the machine itself. There was a big pot on the front of the machines, and we used to turn up the record level until it started to slightly feed back on itself, and gave this sort of twittery vocal sound. Of course John was hearing echo in his [headphones] as he was singing—it wasn't put on after—and he used that as a rhythmic feel for singing. That tape echo on the vocal always suited John's voice, because he had a cutting voice that used to trigger it so well."    *Musician* (July 1987)

The need for a middle section became apparent. McCartney offered some lyrics that he was intending for another song. After discussion, they were accepted, as long as the connecting part was very rhythmic. George Martin suggested the connecting passages have a definite length.    *Road*

MARTIN: "In order to keep time, we got Mal Evans to count each bar, and on the record you can still hear his voice as he stood by the piano counting: 'one, two, three, four . . .' For a joke, Mal set an alarm clock to go off at the end of twenty-four bars, and you can hear that too. We left it in because we couldn't get it off!"    *Ears*

Martin then asked what should be used in those long connecting passages. McCartney answered that he wanted a symphony orchestra to "freak out" during them. Martin disagreed, but McCartney persisted. They compromised on a smaller, forty-one-piece orchestra.

*Road; Ears* indicates Lennon came up with the idea of using an orchestra.

Lennon's only instruction to George Martin was that the sound must rise up to "a sound like the end of the world."

The London *Times* (May 30, 1987); *Ears* says Lennon was more explicit. "I'd like it to be from extreme quietness to extreme loudness, not only in volume, but also for the sound to expand as well" and more.

MARTIN: "[John] did explain what he wanted sufficiently for me to be able to write a score. For the 'I'd like [sic] to turn you *onnnnn*' bit, I used cellos and violas. I had them playing those two notes that echo John's voice. However, instead of fingering their instruments, which would produce crisp notes, I got them to slide their fingers up and down the frets, building in intensity until the start of the orchestral climax.

"That climax was something else again. What I did there was to write, at the beginning of the twenty-four bars, the lowest possible note for each of the instruments in the orchestra. At the end of the twenty-four bars, I wrote the highest note each instrument could reach that was near a chord of E major. Then I put a squiggly line right through the twenty-four bars, with reference points to tell them roughly what note they should have reached during each bar. The musicians also had instructions to slide as gracefully as possible between one note and the next. In the case of the stringed instruments, that was a matter of sliding their fingers up the strings. With keyed instruments, like clarinet and oboe, they obviously had to move their fingers from key to key as they went up, but they were asked to 'lip' the changes as much as possible too." *Ears*

McCartney suggested that Martin and the orchestra come to the session in evening dress. *Ears*

PETE SHOTTON: "The predominantly middle-aged [orchestra members] were each handed a paper mask or some other such party novelty. The orchestra leader, for instance, was given a bright red false nose, while the main violinist was obliged to clutch his bow in a giant gorilla's paw." Shotton

PETE SHOTTON: "[The musicians] were even more bemused, if not downright aghast, by Paul McCartney's instructions that they all play as out of tune and out of time as possible.... Only after repeated tries did the musicians finally deliver a performance sufficiently chaotic to suit the Beatles' requirements." Shotton

ERICH GRUENBERG, orchestra leader: "... They wanted certain effects from the string players which were very difficult to convey in writing, but they explained what they wanted. It was an intensification of sound or a rise in pitch—if you remember there's a sort of spiraling chord that starts on a semitone 'swirrel' and then rises up. The particular effect was created by everyone doing his own thing, in a sense, because it's the mixture of all these different ingredients that gives this special effect."

20 Years; Ears says orchestra leader was David McCallum and spells Erich as "Eric."

McCARTNEY: ". . . I suggested that what we should do was write all but fifteen bars properly so that the orchestra could read it, but where the fifteen bars began we would give the musicians a simple direction: 'Start on your lowest note and eventually, at the end of the fifteen bars, be at your highest note.' How they got there was up to them, but it all resulted in a crazy crescendo. It was interesting because the trumpet players, always famous for their fondness for lubricating substances, didn't care, so they'd be there at the note ahead of everyone. The strings all watched each other like little sheep: 'Are you going up?' Yes. 'So am I.' And they'd go up. 'A little more?' Yes. And they'd go up a little more, all very delicate and cozy, all going up together. You listen to those trumpets. They're just freaking out."

20 Years

McCARTNEY: "The orchestra crescendo and that was based on some of the ideas I'd been getting from Stockhausen and people like that, which is more abstract." Playboy (December 1984)

GEOFF EMERICK: "On the orchestral rush at the end of the track, by careful fader manipulation I was gradually building the crescendo to a peak. My technique then was a little bit psychological, because I would bring it up to a point and then slightly fade it back in level, as I had a long time to do so. It was just a case of really feeling the music, more than the technical side." Musician (July 1987)

MARTIN: "I wanted that [final piano] chord to last as long as possible, and I told Geoff Emerick it would be up to him, not the boys, to achieve that." Ears

About twenty-four seconds into the sound of the final chord, Emerick turned the sound level so high that the studio's air-conditioners became audible. Lists; Love supports.

DEREK TAYLOR: "The final bunched chords came from all four Beatles and George Martin in the studio, playing three pianos. All of them hit the chords simultaneously, as hard as possible, with the engineer pushing the volume-input faders way down on the moment of impact. Then, as the noise gradually diminished, the faders were pushed slowly up to the top. It took forty-five seconds, and it was done three or four times, piling on a huge sound—one piano after another, all doing the same thing." *20 Years*

## INSTRUMENTATION

LENNON: lead vocals on the first, second, and last verses

McCARTNEY: lead vocals on the section that begins "Woke up, fell out of bed"

## BASIC TRACK

LENNON: Gibson J-160E acoustic guitar

McCARTNEY: piano
Mal Evans: alarm clock

## ORCHESTRAL TRACK

LENNON: lead guitar (at beginning)
LENNON, McCARTNEY, STARR, and Mal Evans: three pianos (at end)

George Martin: harmonium
McCARTNEY: conducts forty-one-piece orchestra

*Road* and *ATN; Ears* and *A-Z* and *Love* say forty-two-piece; *20 Years* and *Ears* say all Beatles and Martin played final chord on three pianos; *Record* and *Celebration* agree with forty-one-piece; *Record* omits lead guitar (but does agree with acoustic) and adds Harrison playing bongos, Starr playing drums and maracas, and McCartney playing bass; guitar from *Guitar* (November 1987).

The Mellotron, a keyboard that electronically produces programmed taped sounds, was used for the first time. It would later become standard equipment for rock bands. *A-Z*

Martin harbored reservations about the orchestral sequences: "One part of me said, 'We're being a bit self-indulgent, we're going a little bit over the top,' and the other part of me said, 'It's bloody marvelous! I think it's fantastic!' I was then thoroughly reassured before I put the thing together, when I actually let an American visitor hear a bit of 'A Day in the Life.' When that happened he did a handstand, and I then knew my worries were over." *Musician* (July 1987)

MARTIN: "[Ringo's] use of toms was also very inventive. The 'A Day in the Life' tympani sound on the toms was very characteristic." *Musician* (July 1987)

## MISCELLANEOUS

The final piano note lasts either 42, 43½, or 45 seconds, depending upon your source or your sense of hearing.

The film referred to is *How I Won the War,* in which Lennon appeared.

"PAUL IS DEAD" Hysteria: The line "He blew his mind out in a car" supposedly told how McCartney died.

The working title was "In the Life of . . ."   *Abbey*

The song was banned by the BBC because of Paul's lyric about having a smoke and going into a dream, construed as being about marijuana. The four thousand holes in Blackburn, Lancashire, were thought by some to be about the tracks in a junkie's arm.   *Love*

## COMMENTS BY BEATLES

McCARTNEY: "There'd been a story about a lucky man who'd made the grade, and there was a photograph of him sitting in his big car, and when John saw it he just had to laugh! That's all just a little black comedy, you know. The next bit was another song altogether, but it happened to fit well with the first section. It was really only me remembering what it was like to run up the road to catch the school bus, having a smoke, and then going into class. We decided: 'Bugger this, we're going to write a real turn-on song!' It was a reflection of my school days—I would have a Woodbine then, and somebody would speak and I would go into a dream. This was the only one in the album written as a deliberate provocation to people. But what we really wanted was to turn you on to the truth rather than just bloody pot!"   *Celebration* and *Own Words*

McCARTNEY: "I remember being very conscious of the words, 'I'd love to turn you on,' and thinking, 'Well, that's about as risqué as we dare get at this point.' Well, the BBC banned it. . . ."   *Playboy* (December 1984)

## COMMENTS BY OTHERS

LEONARD BERNSTEIN, composer, conductor: ". . . Three bars of 'A Day in the Life' still sustain me, rejuvenate me, inflame my senses and sensibilities."
*The Beatles* by Geoffrey Stokes (1979), via *Companion*

This song is one of Julian Lennon's favorites. Circa 1984, Coleman

●

# "ALL YOU NEED IS LOVE"

**CHART ACTION**
UNITED KINGDOM: Released as a single July 7, 1967. In five days it was
No. 1, where it remained for four weeks.  *Road*

UNITED STATES: Released as a single July 17, 1967. It entered the Top 40
chart July 29, hit No. 1 for one week, and spent nine weeks in the Top 40.
*Billboard* and *Road*

**AUTHORSHIP** Lennon (1.00)
McCartney said on July 22, 1967, that the song was written in two weeks
as a message to the world.  *Day*
　　　The song was written in late May 1967  *Road*  for live performance via
satellite on the *Our World* TV spectacular on June 25. *Our World* was the
first live worldwide TV program, six hours long, and seen in twenty-four
countries by an estimated 400 million people.
*A-Z* and *Day* and *Road; Love* says 200+ million; *Diary* says twenty-six countries.
　　　It featured live performances from the various participating countries;
the Beatles represented Britain and were shown recording this song.
*Diary* says show's title changed to *Across the World* when five Communist countries dropped out at the
last minute.
　　　Other nations' contributions included a Van Cliburn piano recital from
the United States and segments on lady streetcar conductors in Australia,
and eccentric painters in France.  *Diary*

**RECORDED**
Recording began June 14, 1967, at Olympic Studios, where a backing track
—ten minutes long—was done. The song was added to at a session at
Abbey Road and shortened to six minutes. During the *Our World* performance, the backing track was used to which the Beatles sang and played
live.  *Road; Abbey* agrees on date.

MARTIN: "[The song] had to be kept terribly secret, because the general
idea was that the television viewers would actually see the Beatles at work
recording their new single—although, modern recording being what it is,
we obviously couldn't do that for real; so we laid down a basic rhythm
track first of all. I remember that one of the minor problems was that

George had got hold of a violin which he wanted to try to play, even though he couldn't!

"I did a score for the song, a fairly arbitrary sort of arrangement since it was at such short notice. . . . The mixture I came up with was culled from the 'Marseillaise' [the French national anthem], a Bach two-part invention, 'Greensleeves,' and a little lick from 'In the Mood.' I wove them all together, at slightly different tempos so that they all still worked as separate entities."
*Ears*

McCARTNEY: "George Martin always has something to do with it, but sometimes more than others. For instance, he wrote the end of 'All You Need Is Love' and got into trouble because the 'In the Mood' bit was copyrighted. We thought of all the great clichés because they're a great bit of random. It was a hurried session, and we didn't mind giving him that to do—saying, 'There's the end, we want it to go on and on.' Actually, what he wrote was much more disjointed, so when we put all the bits together we said, 'Could we have "Greensleeves" right on top of that little Bach thing?' And on top of that we had the 'In the Mood' bit.

"George is quite a sage. Sometimes he works with us, sometimes against us; he's always looked after us. I don't think he does as much as some people think. He sometimes does all the arrangements and we just change them."    *Own Words*

Lennon's lead vocal was re-recorded before this song was released as a single.    *Diary* and *Ears*

## INSTRUMENTATION
### BACKING TRACK
McCARTNEY: string bass played with a bow

LENNON: harpsichord

HARRISON: violin (first time he ever played it)

STARR: drums

*Road; Diary* says Lennon played clavichord, McCartney ran violin bow across Arco bass guitar.

### ABBEY ROAD TRACK
McCARTNEY: electric bass

LENNON: vocal

HARRISON: guitar

STARR: drums

George Martin: piano

Session musicians: two trumpets, two trombones, two saxophones, one accordion, four violins, and two cellos

*Road; Diary* omits vocal.

LIVE *OUR WORLD* PERFORMANCE

| | |
|---|---|
| McCARTNEY: backing vocal | A studio orchestra |
| LENNON: lead vocal | Chorus included: Mick Jagger, Gary |
| HARRISON: backing vocal | Leeds, Keith Richards, Marianne |
| | Faithfull, Jane Asher, Patti Harrison, |
| | Keith Moon, and Graham Nash |

*Road* and *Record; Diary* adds Eric Clapton, Brian Epstein, Mike McGear (Mike McCartney) to chorus; *Record* adds Gary Brooker to chorus.

McCartney sang a chorus of "She Loves You" as the song faded.   *Road*; Coleman says Lennon sang it.

## MISCELLANEOUS

Acceptance of the offer to appear on *Our World* forced the Beatles to delay work on a *Sgt. Pepper* TV special and the *Magical Mystery Tour* project. *Diary*

The group produced this single faster than any other: written in late May, recorded by June 25, and released on July 7 (in the United Kingdom). *Road* "A Hard Day's Night" was written and recorded in less time but not released as quickly. *Compleat*(b)

At the Abbey Road session, McCartney wore a shirt he painted himself. McCARTNEY: "I stayed up all night the night before. I didn't mean to but I was drawing on a shirt. I had these pen things that you used to draw with and the ink didn't wash out. I stayed up all night doing it, and the shirt was nicked the next day. Who has it, I don't know. One of these days Sotheby's [an auction house] will tell." *20 Years*

## COMMENTS BY BEATLES

HARRISON: "John has an amazing thing with his timing—he always comes across with very different time signatures, you know. For example, on 'All You Need Is Love' it just sort of skips a beat here and there and changes time. But when you question him as to what it is he's actually doing, he really doesn't know. He just does it naturally...." *Celebration*

McCARTNEY, 1967: "We had been told we'd be seen recording it by the whole world at the same time. So we had one message for the world—love. We need more love in the world." July 1967, Salewicz

McCARTNEY, 1987: "I don't know what you need." The London *Times* (May 30, 1987)

## COMMENTS BY OTHERS

ALBERT GORE, politician, and wife TIPPER, crusader against "obscene" rock lyrics, played this song as their wedding recessional.
*Newsweek* (December 21, 1987)

BRIAN EPSTEIN: "It is a wonderful, beautiful, spine-chilling record. It cannot be misinterpreted. It is a clear message saying that love is everything."
July 1967, *Melody Maker* via *20 Years*

KEITH RICHARDS, Rolling Stones: "Try *livin'* off of it."   *RS* (December 10, 1987)

●

# "BABY YOU'RE A RICH MAN"

## CHART ACTION

UNITED KINGDOM: Released as a single July 7, 1967, as the B side to "All You Need Is Love."   *Road*

UNITED STATES: Released as a single July 17, 1967. It entered the Top 40 August 12, climbed to No. 34, and stayed in the Top 40 for two weeks.
*Billboard* and *Road*

## AUTHORSHIP Lennon (.5) and McCartney (.5)

Working independently, Lennon and McCartney were each responsible for writing half this song. John said he wrote the bit about "the beautiful people" and that the title refrain section was Paul's.
September 1980, *Playboy Interviews;* Lennon quote in *Hit Parader* (April 1972) supports.

HARRISON, on the songwriters' aim: "For a while we thought we were having some influence, and the idea was to show that we, by being rich and famous and having all these experiences, had realized that there was a greater thing to be got out of life—and what's the point of having that on your own? You want all your friends and everybody else to do it, too."
20 Years

## RECORDED

May 11, 1967, at Olympic Sound Studios

*Abbey; Road* agrees on date and studio; *Day* says it was recorded at Abbey Road; *Diary* says recording began May 3 and concluded May 11 at Olympic with Rolling Stone Mick Jagger present; *ATN* says May.

## INSTRUMENTATION

McCARTNEY: bass, piano, harmony vocal

LENNON: clavioline, piano, lead vocal

HARRISON: tambourine, harmony vocal

STARR: drums, maracas

Session musician: vibes

*Record* (except "studio engineers" for "session musician"); *Road* agrees on Lennon's and McCartney's piano, Harrison's vocal, and vibes by an unknown player, but says Rolling Stone Brian Jones played oboe; *ATN* credits both Lennon and McCartney with lead vocals, omits instruments.

The clavioline is an amplified keyboard that plays one note at a time. It's heard at the beginning of the song.   *Road* with *Record*

## MISCELLANEOUS

The two songs that make up "Baby You're a Rich Man" are believed to have been recorded separately but never released, not even as bootlegs.   *Record*

The song was originally intended for the *Yellow Submarine* sound-track.   *Road*

Some listeners believe that at the end of this song, the Beatles sing "Baby, you're a rich fag Jew," which they interpret as a slur on Brian Epstein.   *Lists*   One source says Lennon originally dedicated this song to Epstein as "Baby You're a Rich Fag Jew."   Coleman

This song was sung by Harrison as he walked through Golden Gate Park and Haight-Ashbury in San Francisco when he and wife Patti visited the famous hippie center August 8, 1967.   *Diary; Day* and *A-Z* support.

•

# ''HELLO GOODBYE''

## CHART ACTION

UNITED KINGDOM: Released as a single November 24, 1967. It entered the chart November 29 at No. 3 and was No. 1 by December 6. It stayed in the top spot for six weeks.   *Road*

UNITED STATES: Released as a single November 27, 1967. It entered the Top 40 December 9, climbed to No. 1 for three weeks, and remained in the Top 40 for ten weeks.   *Billboard* and *Road*

**AUTHORSHIP** McCartney ( 1.00 )

## RECORDED

October 2, 1967, at Abbey Road, with overdubs October 19, 20, and 25 and November 2

*Abbey; Road* agrees work began October 2 and spread over weeks; *Day* and *Diary* and *ATN* say November 4 and 5.

## INSTRUMENTATION

McCARTNEY: bass, piano, bongos, conga drum, lead and backing vocal
LENNON: lead guitar, organ, backing vocal

HARRISON: lead guitar, tambourine, backing vocal
STARR: drums, maracas
Session musicians: two violas

*Record; Road* agrees on McCartney's piano, two lead guitars and Starr's maracas, but says two violins were used; *ATN* omits backing vocals, lead guitars, violas.

## MISCELLANEOUS

A promotional film was shot for this song. The BBC banned it when McCartney showed he was lip-syncing the vocal, which went against rules of the British musicians' union. *A-Z* The film was shot November 10 at the Saville Theater, London, with McCartney directing. *Diary; Day* omits direction credit.

The instrumentation shown in the film was probably used to record the song—Lennon: Martin D-28 guitar. McCartney: Rickenbacker bass. Harrison: Epiphone Casino guitar. *Guitar* (November 1987)

## COMMENTS BY BEATLES

Lennon always hated this song and felt insulted because this was the A side of the single, relegating his own "I Am the Walrus" to the B side.

December 1970, *Remembers*

LENNON: "It wasn't a great piece; the best bit was the end, which we all adlibbed in the studio."

September 1980, *Playboy Interviews*

# MAGICAL MYSTERY TOUR
## ALBUM

○

*Magical Mystery Tour* became a full album only as an afterthought. The project was conceived shortly after *Sgt. Pepper* was recorded, primarily as an avant-garde film Paul McCartney wanted to make. The project was delayed by the group's decision to tape "All You Need Is Love" for a live, worldwide television show.

The summer of 1967 reached its end with the Beatles simultaneously enraptured by the presence of the Maharishi Mahesh Yogi and somewhat blown away by the death of their manager, Brian Epstein. The Beatles decided to manage themselves, and *Magical Mystery Tour* became their first self-managed project. The film was their first project that received widespread critical scorn.

## CHART ACTION
UNITED KINGDOM: The six soundtrack songs were released December 8, 1967, on two extended-play discs with a twenty-four-page booklet. It only got as high as No. 2 on the singles chart because the Beatles' own single, "Hello Goodbye," occupied the top spot. *Road; Diary* says thirty-two-page booklet.

UNITED STATES: The Beatles' 1967 singles were combined with the soundtrack songs to make up *Magical Mystery Tour,* released November 27, 1967. The album brought in more than $8 million within three weeks of its release. It was No. 1 by January 8, and stayed there for eight weeks. By mid-January, the album had sold 1.75 million copies.

The U.S. version of the album was EMI's biggest-selling import in the United Kingdom, with sales of more than 50,000. EMI released the U.S. version in the United Kingdom November 19, 1976, and again on compact disc in early October 1987. *Road* The U.S. version is now accepted as the definitive version.

## RECORDED
April 25 through November 7, 1967, at the Abbey Road, De Lane Lea, and Chappell recording studios, London.

*Abbey; Road* says late April through late September; *ATN* says September and October.

## ALBUM PACKAGE
The original U.S. album contained several photos from the film of the same name and lyrics for the songs used in the film.

"PAUL IS DEAD" HYSTERIA: This album has many "clues" used by sleuths to "prove" that McCartney was dead. The album cover shows a black walrus, which is considered a symbol of death in some parts of Scandinavia, and Lennon sang a year later in "Glass Onion": "The walrus was Paul." The booklet shows McCartney with a hand above his head in several photos, supposedly another sign of death. In one photo from the film, McCartney is seen wearing a black carnation while the other Beatles are wearing red carnations. Another photo shows McCartney seated behind a desk with a sign on it that says, "I WaS."

## FILM

McCartney came up with the idea for the film while flying from Los Angeles to London on April 11, 1967. He also wrote the tune and one line, apparently, for the title song on that flight. *Diary; Beatles* agrees McCartney thought of it in April. He was influenced by reports of Ken Kesey's Merry Pranksters, who had toured the United States in a psychedelically painted bus and filmed whatever happened.

The Beatles discussed the project September 1 (four days after Epstein's death) at Paul's house in St. John's Wood.

*Abbey; Love* says September 2 and that the title song was partially written at this time; *Diary* says September 1 and that plans for filming and recording sessions were scheduled then.

Participants gathered at 10:45 a.m., September 11, at Allsop Place in London, but the bus was late (the MMT logo had to be painted at the last minute). McCartney boarded in London, while the other Beatles joined up at Virginia Water. Filming began on the way to Teignmouth. The bus left Teignmouth September 12, and scenes with "tour hostess Wendy Winters" were filmed; later, scenes with "courier Jolly Jimmy Johnson" were filmed. On September 13 Lennon and Harrison directed a scene with "Happy Nat the Rubber Man" around a hotel pool, while McCartney directed Starr with "Auntie Jessie" and "Alf the chauffeur." On September 14 scenes around a tent in a field were shot and the lunch was filmed. On September 15 filming was held at a snack bar in Taunton, and later the participants headed for London to accordion accompaniment. This was followed between September 19 and 24 by filming in unused hangars at the Royal Air Force base in West Malling, Kent, for scenes including the grand finale.

*Diary; Love* agrees on beginning date and tour description; *Live* says Alf Bicknell was the group's chauffeur.

The film was the group's first venture after Brian Epstein's death. McCartney and Starr were the main directors, but each Beatle supervised in all production matters. *A-Z*

Lennon disliked the film project. He was upset at the expense—£75,000—for "the most expensive home movie ever," and by McCartney assuming effective control of the band after Epstein's death. But Lennon was also a man of contradictions: On the entry form for a British newspaper's Valentine Awards in 1969, he handwrote *Magical Mystery Tour* as the "top TV show." Coleman And he later said he enjoyed the "fish and chips" atmosphere of the film.

Two tunes heard in the film were not included on the U.S. album or the British EPs—"Shirley's Wild Accordion" and "Jessie's Dream." Diary

The film was a critical disaster—the Beatles' first failure. But actually, *Magical Mystery Tour* was way ahead of its time. It is one long music video.

## COMMENTS BY BEATLES
McCARTNEY: "John said, '*Magical Mystery Tour* was just a big ego trip for Paul.' God. It was for their sake, to keep us together, keep us going, give us something new to do . . ." May 1981, *Beatles*

●

# "MAGICAL MYSTERY TOUR"

**AUTHORSHIP** McCartney (.9) and Lennon (.1)
LENNON: "Paul [wrote it]. I helped with some of the lyric."
*Hit Parader* (April 1972)

The song was conceived by McCartney while he was returning from the United States, immediately after *Sgt. Pepper* was completed. A-Z

## RECORDED
When the Beatles began recording this song on April 25, 1967, only the title, one line of the lyrics and a tiny snatch of the music had been determined.

The first part of the session was primarily a rehearsal, with McCartney explaining to the other Beatles what ideas he had for the song. At the piano, he played the opening bars and said loudly, "flash, flash," indicating that the song should sound like a television commercial. As Mal Evans took notes, McCartney said he wanted trumpets to provide a fanfare for the opening "Roll up, roll up" lyric, the only line written by then. McCartney told Evans to write down the first chords of the music, D-A-E.

The Beatles then turned their attention to recording a basic backing track, using the piano, two guitars and drums. In a couple of hours they had finished it.

McCartney left the playing area and went up to the control room. As he instructed the recording engineers on the sound he wanted, the other Beatles amused themselves; Lennon played the piano, alternating between quiet and wild tunes, Harrison drew a picture with crayons he took from his jacket, and Starr smoked cigarets. After McCartney was finally satisfied with the backing track, he rejoined his bandmates and said he wanted to add to the song. In an attempt to write more of the lyrics, the Beatles shouted out ideas as Evans took notes—"trip of a lifetime," "satisfaction guaranteed"—but they soon grew bored and decided to sing whatever words came to them later.

At that point, McCartney said he wanted to add more instruments to the song and recorded a bass track. Then, at his suggestion, all of the Beatles, plus Evans and Neil Aspinall, picked up any instruments in the studio, such as maracas and tambourines, and played along to the backing track they heard on their headphones.  *Beatles* and *Abbey; Road* supports; *Day* and *Road* and *Diary* agree with April 25.

Overdubs were recorded April 26, 27 (vocals), May 3 (brass), and November 7.

*Abbey; Road* agrees on April 27 vocal and May 3 brass overdubs; *Diary* agrees on April 27 date.


### INSTRUMENTATION
McCARTNEY: bass, piano (with echo effects), lead vocal
LENNON: acoustic guitar, backing vocal

HARRISON: lead guitar, backing vocal
STARR: drums, tambourine
Session musicians: three trumpets

*Record; Road* provides piano effects, agrees with McCartney's piano, Lennon's and Harrison's backing vocals, and three trumpets, and says assorted other instruments; *ATN* omits Harrison's vocals, trumpets, and piano.


### MISCELLANEOUS
The film of the same name went into production almost five months after the song was recorded.


●

# "THE FOOL ON THE HILL"


### AUTHORSHIP McCartney (1.00)
McCartney first played the song to Lennon in mid-March 1967 while they were trying to write lyrics for "With a Little Help from My Friends" at McCartney's house in St. John's Wood. Lennon suggested that McCartney write the words down so he wouldn't forget them; there was no further discussion.  *Beatles*


### RECORDED
September 25 at Abbey Road with overdubbing September 26 and October 20 (flutes)  *Abbey; Road* and *Day* and *Diary* agree recording began September 25.

## INSTRUMENTATION

McCARTNEY: piano, recorder (double-tracked), flute, vocal
LENNON: harmonica, maracas

HARRISON: lead guitar, harmonica
STARR: finger cymbals

*Record; Road* provides double-tracking information and agrees with McCartney's instruments, both harmonicas, Starr's finger cymbals, and Harrison's lone guitar; *ATN* omits guitar, finger cymbals.

## MISCELLANEOUS

This segment in the film *Magical Mystery Tour* was shot November 1 and 2, 1967, in Nice, France, with only Paul. He had lots of problems: He forgot his passport and had to have it sent via air freight while he was detained at French customs, his credit was not accepted because he had left his wallet at home, and he had to wire for money before he could continue work on the film. *A-Z; Diary* supports Paul's troubles and provides dates.

McCartney also didn't have the right lenses for the camera and had to have them sent. It cost £4,000 to film the scene of McCartney on the hill in Nice. *Love*

The title of this song was used for the name of a fifty-year retrospective on the BBC in December 1986, *Fools on the Hill.*

## COMMENTS BY BEATLES

LENNON: "Another good lyric. Shows he's capable of writing complete songs." September 1980, *Playboy Interviews*

●

# "FLYING"

**AUTHORSHIP** Lennon (.25), McCartney (.25), Harrison (.25), and Starr (.25)
This was the first composition to be written by all members of the group and the only instrumental the Beatles recorded for Parlophone.

## RECORDED

September 8, 1967, at Abbey Road, with overdubbing September 28
*Abbey; Road* and *Day* and *Diary* agree recording began September 8.

## INSTRUMENTATION

McCARTNEY: guitars, chanting
LENNON: Mellotron, chanting

HARRISON: guitars, chanting
STARR: drums, maracas, chanting

*Record; Road* agrees on Lennon's Mellotron and McCartney's and Harrison's guitars, plus chanting by all.

The electronic sounds at the end were put together by Lennon and Starr using tape loops.  *Road*

**MISCELLANEOUS**
This was heard in the film *Magical Mystery Tour.*

●

# "BLUE JAY WAY"

**AUTHORSHIP** Harrison ( 1.00 )
Harrison wrote the song August 1, 1967.
*Day; Diary* agrees on that date for his arrival; *Road* says early summer.

He was visiting Los Angeles and had just arrived at the Hollywood Hills house on Blue Jay Way he and Patti had rented. He was waiting for his friend Derek Taylor to come and see them.  *Beatles*

HARRISON: "Derek got held up. He rang to say he'd be late. I told him on the phone that the house was on Blue Jay Way. He said he could find it okay, he could always ask a cop. I waited and waited. I felt really nackered with the flight, but I didn't want to go to sleep till he came. There was a fog and it got later and later. To keep myself awake, just as a joke to fill in time, I wrote a song about waiting for him in Blue Jay Way. There was a little Hammond organ in the corner of this rented house, which I hadn't noticed. I messed around on this and the song came."  *Beatles*
       The lyrics were written on stationery of Robert Fitzpatrick Associates, a Los Angeles firm. Harrison later got the original back from Beatles biographer Hunter Davies.  *Beatles*

**RECORDED**
September 6, 1967, at Abbey Road, with overdubbing September 7 and October 6  *Abbey; Day* and *Road* and *Diary* say recorded on September 6.

**INSTRUMENTATION**
McCARTNEY: bass, backing vocal      STARR: drums
LENNON: tambourine      Session musician: cello
HARRISON: Hammond organ, lead
(double-tracked) and backing vocal
*Record; Road* agrees on double-tracking, Harrison's Hammond organ, single cello, and backing vocals.
       The vocal, organ, and drums were all "phased." The original sounds were recorded on two tape machines and played back slightly out of syn-

chronization to create a swirling effect. Electronic sounds and other studio effects were also used.   *Record; Road* supports phasing of vocal and organ and "studio effects."

**MISCELLANEOUS**
Performed in the film *Magical Mystery Tour.*
    The phrase "Don't be long" is sung twenty-nine times.   *Forever*

●

# "YOUR MOTHER SHOULD KNOW"

**AUTHORSHIP** McCartney (1.00)

**RECORDED**
August 22, 1967, at Chappell Recording Studios, London, with overdubbing August 23, remade September 16 (but not used) and overdubbing September 29

*Abbey; Road* says recording began August 22 at Chappell and re-recorded in September; *Day* says August 22 but that recording ended September 25; *Diary* says August 22 but that it was re-recorded the first week of September.

**INSTRUMENTATION**

McCARTNEY: bass, piano, lead and backing vocal
LENNON: organ, backing vocal

HARRISON: tambourine, tabla, backing vocal
STARR: drums

*Record; Road* agrees with McCartney's piano and Lennon's organ.

**MISCELLANEOUS**
Performed in the film *Magical Mystery Tour.* It was used during the grand finale, when the Beatles, wearing tuxedos, descend a long spiral staircase.

"PAUL IS DEAD" HYSTERIA: In the filmed performance of this song, McCartney wears a black carnation; the others wear white. (McCartney later said that they had run out of white carnations.)   *Lists*

●

# "I AM THE WALRUS"

**CHART ACTION**
UNITED KINGDOM: Also released as a single November 24, 1967, as the B side to "Hello Goodbye."   *Road*

UNITED STATES: Also released as a single November 27, 1967. It did not crack the Top 40, reaching only No. 56; it was in the Top 100 for four weeks.   *Road*

**AUTHORSHIP** Lennon ( 1.00 )
The rhythm came from a shrieking police-car siren Lennon heard in the distance while he was at home. It consisted of two repeating notes, up and down.   *Beatles; Road* generally supports.

LENNON: "The first line was written on one acid trip one weekend. The second line was written on the next acid trip the next weekend, and it was filled in after I met Yoko. . . .

   "[The walrus] came from 'The Walrus and the Carpenter.' *Alice in Wonderland.* To me, it was a beautiful poem. . . . [Later I] realized that the walrus was the bad guy in the story, and the carpenter was the good guy. I thought, 'Oh, shit, I picked the wrong guy. I should have said, "I am the carpenter." ' But that wouldn't have been the same, would it?"
September 1980, *Playboy Interviews*

   According to Pete Shotton, the song's genesis came when he and Lennon read a fan letter from a student at Quarry Bank, their old school. The fan wrote, much to their amusement, that the school's literature class was analyzing the Beatles' songs. This prompted them to remember a song they used to sing while attending the school: "Yellow matter custard, green slop pie / All mixed together with a dead dog's eye . . ."

   According to Shotton, Lennon then scribbled the line "Yellow matter custard dripping from a dead dog's eye." Lennon then came up with the most ludicrous images he could—"semolina" (an insipid pudding) and "pilchard" (a sardine usually fed to cats)—resulting in "Semolina Pilchard climbing up the Eiffel Tower. . . ." It was an effort to confuse the masters at his old school.   Shotton; *A-Z* supports intent.

**RECORDED**
September 5, 1967, at Abbey Road, with overdubbing September 6 and 27.

*Abbey; Diary* says two versions were recorded September 7 and recording was completed September 27 to 29; *Day* gives September 7 date but excludes other Beatles; *Road* says work continued throughout September.

**INSTRUMENTATION**
McCARTNEY: bass, backing vocal
LENNON: Mellotron (at beginning), lead vocal
HARRISON: tambourine, backing vocal
STARR: drums

Session musicians: eight violins, four cellos, three horns
Choir: six boys singing "Oompah, oompah, stick it up your jumper," six girls singing "Everybody's got one"

*Record; Road* agrees on Mellotron opening, session instruments, number in choir, provides lyrics for choir; *Diary* adds three cor anglais and says six Mike Sammes singers.

LENNON, on what it is everybody has one of: "You name it. One penis, one vagina, one asshole—you name it."  September 1980, *Playboy Interviews*

## MISCELLANEOUS

A surrealistic performance was included in the *Magical Mystery Tour* film.

The U.S. and U.K. versions of this song differ. Capitol made the U.S. *Rarities* version by editing the few extra beats in the middle of the U.S. single version with the U.K. version, which has the introductory riff repeated six times instead of four.  *Road*

At the end there are voices speaking. Lennon taped the voices from a BBC radio program and years later finally found out which play it was— Shakespeare's *King Lear* (act IV, scene 6).

*A-Z* provides taping and *King Lear,* and *Forever* provides complete play information.

"PAUL IS DEAD" HYSTERIA: The Shakespearean actors say these ominous lines near the end of the song: "What, is he dead?" "Bury my body," and "O, untimely death."  *B-Lists*

## COMMENTS BY BEATLES

LENNON: "I like that one. That was the time when I was putting Hare Krishna and all that down. I hadn't taken it up then."  *Hit Parader* (April 1972)

## COMMENTS BY OTHERS

The Electric Light Orchestra was formed years later to continue from where "I Am the Walrus" left off, artistically.  Promo material with first ELO LP    ELO went on to have many successful albums.

•

# "LADY MADONNA"

## CHART ACTION

UNITED KINGDOM: Released as a single March 15, 1968. In five weeks the single was No. 6 on the chart and, a week later, was at No. 1, where it stayed for two weeks. *Road*

UNITED STATES: Released as a single March 18, 1968. It entered the Top 40 March 23 and stayed for ten weeks, climbing to No. 4. *Billboard* and *Road*

This was the first Beatles A side single not to be No. 1 on at least two of the three main U.S. record charts *(Billboard, Cashbox, Record World)* since the February 1966 release of "Nowhere Man"/"What Goes On." There were five No. 1s in between. *Record2*

At the last minute this song replaced the original version of "Across the Universe" as the single's A side. *Record2*

This was the last Beatles single to be released on Parlophone (in the United Kingdom) and Capitol (in the United States). Henceforth, releases were on the group's Apple label.

## AUTHORSHIP McCartney (1.00)

The Beatles admitted that the melody and arrangement were based on "Bad Penny Blues," an old recording. *Forever*

## RECORDED

February 3, 1968, at Abbey Road, with overdubbing February 6.

*Abbey; Road* and *ATN* say it was recorded February 3 and 4; *Day* and *Diary* say McCartney and session musicians recorded this February 3.

GEOFF EMERICK: "We spent a lot of time getting the right piano sound for 'Lady Madonna.' We ended up using a cheaper type of microphone and heavy compression and limiting." *Abbey*

## INSTRUMENTATION

McCARTNEY: Rickenbacker bass, piano, lead vocal
LENNON: backing vocal
HARRISON: lead guitar, backing vocal

STARR: drums
Ronnie Scott: saxophone
Harry Klein: saxophone
Bill Povey: saxophone
Bill Jackman: saxophone

*Record; Road* agrees on McCartney's contributions and sax players (but Jack*son* instead of Jack*man*), but says Lennon and McCartney play guitars through the same amp; *ATN* agrees on Jackman and backing vocals; Rickenbacker from *Guitar* (November 1987); *Transcriptions* says Jack*son* and that Lennon and Harrison played guitar through same amp, piano was double-tracked, and two drum tracks were used (brushes and sticks).

The backing vocalists sang with hands cupped around mouths.  *Road* and *A-Z* and *Transcriptions*

## MISCELLANEOUS

A promotional film was shot for this song on February 11, 1968, at Abbey Road.  *Abbey; Diary* says February 8; *Day* says two films were shot in February 1968.  The Beatles recorded "Hey Bulldog" while the film crew worked around them.  *Road* and *Compleat*(b) and *Abbey*

McCartney designed the ads for the single release.  *A-Z*

This was one of five Beatle songs performed on McCartney's Wings over America tour in 1976.

## COMMENTS BY BEATLES

McCARTNEY: "Lady Madonna's all women. How do they do it?—bless 'em —it's that one, you know. Baby at your breast, how do they get the time to feed them? Where do you get the money? How do you do this thing that women do?"  *Musician* (October 1986)

STARR: "It sounds like Elvis, doesn't it? No—no, it doesn't sound like Elvis. It is Elvis—even those bits where he goes very high."  *Own Words*

LENNON: "Good piano lick, but the song never really went anywhere." September 1980, *Playboy Interviews*

## COMMENTS BY OTHERS

ELVIS COSTELLO, musician, upon finding "Lady Madonna" on the radio: "It's a bit sad when you have to wait for a ten-year-old record to come on the radio to turn it up."  *Crawdaddy* (March 1978)

•

# "THE INNER LIGHT"

## CHART ACTION

UNITED KINGDOM: Released as a single March 15, 1968, as the B side to "Lady Madonna."  *Road*

UNITED STATES: Released as a single March 18, 1968. It failed to make the Top 40, but was in the Top 100 for one week, at No. 96, on March 30.  *Road*

This was Harrison's first song to appear on a single.
*Road* and *Diary* and *Abbey*

**AUTHORSHIP** Harrison (1.00)

Harrison said he wrote the lyrics from a translation of the "Tao Te Ching [XLVII]," in a book named *Lamps of Fire* sent to him by Juan Mascaro, the Sanskrit teacher at Cambridge University. Harrison used the first verse from it verbatim and altered the rest slightly. "It was nice, the words said everything."

*I Me Mine; A-Z* and *Record* and *Forever* say lyrics were from the translation of a Japanese poem by Roshi.

**RECORDED**

All of the music was recorded by Indian musicians under Harrison's direction at EMI Studios in Bombay, India, January 12, 1968.

*Road; Abbey* supplies date; *Day* and *Diary* say January 11.

Harrison overdubbed his lead vocal February 6 at Abbey Road, and Lennon and McCartney added their background vocals February 8.

*Abbey; Road* and *Diary* agree Harrison's vocal was recorded February 6 in England.

JERRY BOYS, tape operator: "George had this big thing about not wanting to sing it because he didn't feel confident that he could do the song justice. I remember Paul saying, 'You must have a go, don't worry about it, it's *good.*' " *Abbey*

**INSTRUMENTATION**

McCARTNEY: backing vocal
LENNON: backing vocal

HARRISON: lead vocal
Session musicians: all instruments

*Abbey* and *Road* and *ATN; Record* omits Lennon and McCartney vocals; *A-Z* says no Beatles other than Harrison are on the recording.

**COMMENTS BY BEATLES**

McCARTNEY: "Forget the Indian music and listen to the melody. Don't you think it's a beautiful melody? It's really lovely." *Own Words* and *Forever*

●

# "HEY JUDE"

**CHART ACTION**

UNITED KINGDOM: Released as a single August 26, 1968. It hit No. 1 within two weeks and held that position for three weeks. *Road*

UNITED STATES: Released as a single August 26, 1968. It entered the Top 40 September 14, held the No. 1 position for nine weeks, and remained on the chart for nineteen weeks. *Road* and *Billboard*

This was the Beatles' most successful single. It was a No. 1 hit in Holland, Ireland, Belgium, West Germany, Denmark, Singapore, Malaysia, New Zealand, Norway, and Sweden, with world sales totaling more than 5 million by the end of 1968 and 7.5 million by October 1972.  *Road* and *Forever*

*Billboard* published a special chart in 1976 which listed the biggest hits of the past two decades. "Hey Jude" placed second, behind Chubby Checker's "The Twist."  *Forever*

McCartney said he was "worried stiff" while this song was being released because he wasn't sure whether it was any good. He said he isn't able to make that kind of critical distinction.  *RS* (April 30, 1970)

"Revolution" was originally going to be the A side (it was recorded earlier) and "Hey Jude" was going to be the B side. But those plans were reversed.  *Diary*  Lennon reluctantly agreed to relegate his song to the B side.  Coleman

**AUTHORSHIP** McCartney (1.00)
PETER BROWN, Beatles associate: "[During the breakup of John and Cynthia Lennon] Paul drove out to Weybridge in his Aston Martin to visit her and Julian. On the way he made a song to cheer the little boy."  *Love*

McCARTNEY said he was idly singing "Hey Jules" while he was driving: "And then I just thought a better name was Jude. A bit more country and western for me."  *Own Words*

An influence on McCartney when he began writing this was the Drifters' "Save the Last Dance For Me."  *A-Z*

McCartney and Lennon finished writing the song at Paul's house, on July 26, 1968.  *Road* and *Diary*

▶    **PAUL AS LYRICIST**

*Lennon helped McCartney decide on some of the lyrics.*

*McCARTNEY, describing a demo tape he made of the song: "I remember I played it to John and Yoko, and I was saying, 'These words won't be on the finished version.' Some of the words were, 'The movement you need is on your shoulder,' and John was saying, 'It's great!' I'm saying, 'It's crazy, it doesn't make any sense at all.' He's saying, 'Sure, it does, it's great.' I'm always saying that, by the way, that's me, I'm always never sure if it's good enough. That's me, you know."  RS (January 31, 1974)*

LENNON: ". . . Paul is quite a capable lyricist who doesn't think he is. . . . 'Hey Jude' is a damn good set of lyrics, and I made no contribution to that. A couple of lines he's come up with show indications he's a good lyricist, but he just never took it anywhere."
September 1980, *Playboy Interviews*

## RECORDED

Rehearsed by all four Beatles on Monday, July 29, 1968, at Abbey Road. The next night they recorded it while being filmed for a feature about the music of Britain. On Wednesday they discarded that version and recorded the song again, at Trident Studios. On Thursday a forty-piece orchestra was used to hold single notes for long periods and to clap and sing the "la-la-la" chorus. (McCartney wanted a full symphony orchestra, but George Martin said booking one so quickly was impossible.) The final remix was done early Friday, and by the afternoon acetates were made.

*Road; Abbey* agrees on dates; *Day* differs; *Diary* says in different places that filming was on July 29 and 30, that equipment was moved to Trident for the Wednesday session, and that Lennon, McCartney, Martin, and technicians worked through from Thursday session to get a rough proof-pressing by late afternoon Friday.

McCARTNEY: "I remember on 'Hey Jude' telling George not to play guitar. He wanted to echo riffs after the vocal phrases, which I didn't think was appropriate. He didn't see it like that, and it was a bit of a number for me to have to *dare* to tell George Harrison—who's one of the greats—not to play. It was like an insult. But that's how we did a lot of our stuff." *Musician* (February 1985)

"The rule was whosoever's song it was got to say how we did the arrangement for it. That pissed him off . . ." *Musician* (October 1986)

McCARTNEY: " 'Hey Jude' was a very special take when we did it. In actual fact, Ringo was in the toilet. I started the song without drums, I thought he was in his drum booth. He heard me starting—'Hey Jude, don't make it . . .' Hey, he does up his fly, leaps back into the studio, and he's creeping past me, I'm doing this take realizing the drummer is trying to make his way back to the booth. He makes his way very quietly, just got there in time for his entry, so it was kind of a magic take." Washington *Post* via *Musician* (February 1985)

## INSTRUMENTATION

McCARTNEY: bass, piano, lead vocal

LENNON: acoustic guitar (Gibson J-160E), backing vocal

HARRISON: lead guitar, backing vocal

STARR: drums, tambourine

Forty-piece orchestra

*Record; Road* agrees on McCartney's piano, Harrison's electric guitar, Starr's tambourine, and forty-piece orchestra, but says Starr also sang backing vocal; guitar from *Guitar* (November 1987)

The song begins with McCartney's piano and vocal and, after instruments are added one by one, concludes with about fifty instruments playing and a large number of voices. *Forever*

## MISCELLANEOUS

"Hey Jude" is the Beatles' longest single—7:11 long—four minutes of which is the fadeout.

*Record; Forever* and *ATN* and *B-Lists* support time; *Road* says 7:15; CD says 7:09.

This single was the Beatles' first release on Apple. *Forever*

During the week the Beatles were working on the song, they closed their Apple Boutique clothing store, one of the first indications of their disillusionment with running their own company. *Day*

PETER BROWN, Beatles associate: "To help publicize the release of 'Hey Jude,' Paul decided to put the closed boutique at Baker and Paddington streets to some good use. Late one night he snuck into the store and whitewashed the windows. Then he wrote HEY JUDE across it in block letters. The following morning, when the neighborhood shopkeepers arrived to open their stores, they were incensed; never having heard of the song 'Hey Jude*n*' before, they took it as an anti-Semitic slur. A brick was thrown through the store window before the words could be cleaned off and the misunderstanding straightened out." *Love*

A promotional video was made at Twickenham Studios. The group was filmed for five hours, and about fifty to sixty invited fans participated in singing the long fadeout. The Beatles warmed up for their performance by playing versions of "Hang Down Your Head, Tom Dooley" and other songs. *Day* In the promo Lennon and Harrison are both playing instruments different from the ones they used during the recording session.

*Guitar* (November 1987)

The song was performed live on David Frost's British TV show in September 1968. *A-Z*

## COMMENTS BY BEATLES

LENNON: "That's his best song." *Hit Parader* (April 1972)

LENNON: "... I always heard it as a song to me. If you think about it ... Yoko's just come into the picture. He's saying, 'Hey Jude'—"Hey John.' I know I'm sounding like one of those fans who reads things into it, but you *can* hear it as a song to me. The words 'go out and get her'—subconsciously he was saying, 'Go ahead, leave me.' On a conscious level, he didn't want me to go ahead. The angel in him was saying, 'Bless you.' The devil in him didn't like it at all, because he didn't want to lose his partner."

September 1980, *Playboy Interviews*

●

# "REVOLUTION"

## CHART ACTION
UNITED KINGDOM: Released as a single August 26, 1968, the B side to "Hey Jude." *Road*

UNITED STATES: Released as a single August 26, 1968. It entered the Top 40 September 14, rose to No. 12, and stayed in the Top 40 for eleven weeks. *Billboard* and *Road*

## AUTHORSHIP Lennon ( 1.00 )
Lennon wrote it while in India early in 1968. *Road*

## RECORDED
ALBUM: This was the first of the two versions to be recorded. Work began May 30, 1968, at Abbey Road, with overdubbing May 31 and June 4 and 21. One performance was at least ten minutes long.

*Abbey; Diary* agrees on May 30; *Day* says both May 30 and early June; *Road* corroborates June period and ten-minute length; *Crawdaddy* (August 1975) says twenty-two minutes.

LENNON: "The Beatles were getting real tense with each other. I did the slow version and I wanted it out as a single, as a statement of the Beatles' position on Vietnam and the Beatles' position on revolution. . . . George and Paul were resentful and said it wasn't fast enough."

September 1980, *Playboy Interviews*

SINGLE: Lennon decided to record a fast, loud version. The remake was rehearsed with the tapes running July 9 and recording began July 10, at Abbey Road. Overdubs were added July 11 and 12.

*Abbey; Road* says late July; *Diary* agrees on the version for single; *Day* says only Lennon and McCartney recorded this version on July 31.

Lennon's vocal for the single version was recorded many times. *Record and Abbey* Finally he lay down on his back on the studio floor because he was so stoned and sang it again.

*Love* says he was stoned; *A-Z* says he recorded it on his back; *Forever* and *Record* say he lay down for the single version to get the right feel for his vocal; *Abbey* says vocal for the album version was recorded this way.

MARTIN: "[The guitar distortion] was done deliberately because John wanted a very dirty sound on guitar, and he couldn't get it through his amps. What we did . . . was just overload one of the preamps." *Forever*

## INSTRUMENTATION
SINGLE VERSION
McCARTNEY: bass, organ                 STARR: drums
LENNON: lead guitar, vocal             Nicky Hopkins: piano
HARRISON: lead guitar

*Record* (except Hopkins credit); *Record* and *Road* say McCartney also plays piano and omit Hopkins; *Ballad* and *RS* (May 17, 1969) and *Abbey* say Hopkins played on a version; *RS* and *Abbey* say he played on the single version; *Ballad* and *Abbey* say he played piano.

ALBUM VERSION
McCARTNEY: bass, piano, harmony        HARRISON: guitar, harmony vocal
vocal                                  STARR: drums
LENNON: guitar, lead and harmony       Session musicians: brass backing
vocal

*Road* provides vocals and piano, and *Abbey* provides bass and drums.

## MISCELLANEOUS
A promotional film was made of the single version.

PETE SHOTTON: ". . . Paul made little effort to mask his distaste for a few of John's more 'way out' compositions, specifically 'Revolution' and 'Revolution 9.' 'Revolution,' however, meant more to John at the time than any song he'd written in years, and he was determined that it should appear as the A side of the Beatles' debut release on their soon-to-be-launched Apple Records. Apart from marking a return to the high adrenalin, no-frills rock 'n' roll that had always remained his first musical love, 'Revolution' was the first Beatles song to constitute an explicitly political statement. Which in turn is precisely why Paul felt so wary about it; nonpolitical to the core, he would have much preferred the Beatles to steer clear of such 'heavy' topics." *Shotton*

In the lyrics, Lennon comes out against violence on the single version but is equivocal on the White Album's slower version, following "count me out" with "in." *Author*

LENNON: "It's a yin-yang thing. We all have a streak of violence underneath." *Forever*

## SELLING SHOES

*The single version of "Revolution" was used many years later, in 1987, as part of a $7 million campaign to sell Nike shoes.* ENS (May 14, 1987) *Nike reportedly paid $250,000 to Capitol Records, which holds the North American licensing rights to the recording, for use of the Beatles' original version. Through Apple Records, the three surviving Beatles and Yoko Ono sued Nike, its ad agency, Capitol, and EMI Records, which holds licensing rights outside North America. The suit claimed that Nike was using the Beatles' "persona and goodwill" in its ads without permission. Nike contended it had a valid contract and was innocently entangled in the Beatles' dispute with Capitol and EMI.* AP (February 24, 1988)

*Capitol later claimed that Yoko Ono insisted that Nike use the Beatles' version.* RS (October 22, 1987) *Asked what she thought of the deal, Yoko Ono was quoted as saying, "John's songs should not be part of a cult of glorified martyrdom. They should be enjoyed by kids today."* ENS (May 14, 1987)

*Capitol supplied Jim Bredouw, co-owner of Admusic in Hollywood, with a first-generation tape of the master, which is in stereo, while the single was released in mono. Bredouw listened to both sides of the stereo version and heard mistakes muffled in mono. Bredouw said, "There were a couple of terrible drum mistakes that sounded like Ringo dropped a drum stick...."*
Los Angeles *Times* news service (May 9, 1987)

*McCARTNEY: "... What has happened is some people have used it [the Beatles catalog] without the right to use it. People who haven't got the right have been giving away the right.... But the most difficult question is whether you should use songs for commercials. I haven't made up my mind.... Generally, I don't like it, particularly with the Beatles stuff. When twenty more years have passed, maybe we'll move into the realm where it's okay to do it."*
*Musician* (February 1988)

*HARRISON: "If it's allowed to happen, every Beatles song ever recorded is going to be advertising women's underwear and sau-*

*sages. We've got to put a stop to it in order to set a precedent. Otherwise, it's going to be a free-for-all. . . . It's one thing if you're dead, but we're still around! They don't have any respect for the fact that we wrote and recorded those songs, and it was our lives. . . ."* Musician (November 1987)

*Nike allowed its option to use the recording to lapse March 22, 1988. The company said it was satisfied with the yearlong ad campaign and that sales rose substantially.* AP (February 24, 1988)

## COMMENTS BY BEATLES
LENNON: "I should never have put that in about Chairman Mao. I was just finishing off in the studio when I did that." Hit Parader (April 1972)

LENNON: ". . . The underground left only picked up on the [version] that said 'count me out.' The original version which ends up on the LP said 'count me in' too; I put in both because I wasn't sure. . . . On the version released as a single I said, 'When you talk about destruction you can count me out.' I didn't want to get killed." Red Mole (March 8-22, 1971) via Companion

## COMMENTS BY OTHERS
JAMES TAYLOR, singer, songwriter: "For me and my generation that song I watched John Lennon creating at the Abbey Road studios was an honest statement about social change, really coming out and revealing how *he* felt. . . . It was the truth—but now it refers to a *running shoe.*"
Musician (April 1988)

JOHN FOGERTY, singer, songwriter: "I was one of the people who reacted violently the first time I saw the Nike commercial. I think I was in a hotel room somewhere, and I was *jumping up and down!* I was real pissed off. Goddamnit, I was mad, you know, because when John Lennon wrote that song, he wasn't doing it for the money. And to be using it for any corporate thing . . . it made me angry." RS (December 10, 1987)

●

# YELLOW SUBMARINE
## *ALBUM*

○

This album is undoubtedly the weakest of all officially released Beatles albums. Issued shortly after *The Beatles* (the White Album), almost half of the forty-minute album consists of George Martin orchestrations used in the animated film of the same name, plus two other tracks—the title song and "All You Need Is Love"—that were not only previously released but relatively ancient by then. That left only four "new" Beatles songs, although they were hardly new, having been recorded months before the White Album.

In addition to offering so few new songs, the group didn't even put much effort into them. The Beatles were unhappy about the idea of being portrayed in a cartoon, the result of one of Brian Epstein's last deals. (The movie's critical and popular success changed their minds.) So now they offered the dregs: "All Together Now," a pleasing but lightweight McCartney sing-along; "Only a Northern Song," one of the worst songs Harrison ever wrote; Lennon's "Hey Bulldog," a good rocker that was recorded during filming of a promotional film for another song; and "It's All Too Much," a fleshed-out Harrison psychedelic extravaganza that is probably the album's standout, if only by default.

**CHART ACTION**
UNITED KINGDOM: Released January 17, 1969. It entered the album chart five days later at No. 9. It climbed to No. 3, where it stayed for two weeks. Meanwhile, the White Album was in the No. 1 spot. *Road*

UNITED STATES: Released January 13, 1969. On February 8 it finally entered the Top 100 at No. 86 and then climbed to No. 2 for one week. *Road*

**RECORDED**
The new material was recorded sporadically between February 13, 1967, and February 11, 1968, at the Abbey Road and De Lane Lea Music Recording Studios, London. *Abbey;* other sources disagree.

MARTIN: "As we recorded songs for future albums, they would try out some little bit of nonsense at the end of the session, and, as long as it worked moderately well, they would say: 'Right, that's good enough for the film. Let them have that.' So the film scraped the bottom of the Beatle barrel as far as new material was concerned." *Ears*

**MISCELLANEOUS**
These are the titles of the George Martin orchestrations that make up half the album: "Pepperland," "Sea of Time," "Sea of Holes," "Sea of Monsters," "March of the Meanies," "Pepperland Laid Waste," and "Yellow Submarine in Pepperland." The last is an orchestration of the original "Yellow Submarine" song. *Road*

Because of the speed at which the film was made, Martin's scoring and the film's animation work were done simultaneously.

**COMMENTS BY BEATLES**
HARRISON: "There were albums which weren't any good as far as I was concerned, like *Yellow Submarine.*" *Crawdaddy* (February 1977)

●

# "YELLOW SUBMARINE"

(*See:* the song's entry as part of the *Revolver* LP.)

●

# "ONLY A NORTHERN SONG"

**AUTHORSHIP** Harrison (1.00)
Sources differ on how this song was written. The most common belief is that Harrison wrote it in about one hour while an orchestra was waiting. The producer of the *Yellow Submarine* film insisted at 2 a.m. one morning that he needed one more song for the film. Harrison volunteered to write one and went off to do so, returning in about one hour. The lyrics indicate he wasn't thrilled about it. *Road; Forever* says it was written and recorded within an hour.

A conflicting source says this was recorded during the *Sgt. Pepper* sessions nearly two years before it was released to the public. *Abbey*

**RECORDED**
February 13, 1967, at Abbey Road, during the early work on *Sgt. Pepper.* Lead vocals were overdubbed February 14 and more overdubs were added April 20. *Abbey; Day* and *Diary* say February 11, 1968; *Road* says mid-February 1968.

## INSTRUMENTATION

McCARTNEY: bass, discordant
instruments
LENNON: piano, discordant
instruments

HARRISON: organ, discordant
instruments, vocal (occasionally
double-tracked)
STARR: drums, discordant
instruments
Session musicians: brass

*Record* (except session musicians credit); *Road* provides double-tracking and brass backing information, agrees there is organ, says there was various percussion.

## COMMENTS BY BEATLES

HARRISON: " 'Northern Song' was a joke relating to Liverpool, the Holy City in the North of England. In addition, the song was copyrighted Northern Songs Ltd., which I don't own."   *I Me Mine*

●

# "ALL TOGETHER NOW"

**AUTHORSHIP** McCartney (1.00)

## RECORDED

May 12, 1967, at Abbey Road   *Abbey; Day* and *Road* say mid-June; *Diary* says June 22.

## INSTRUMENTATION

McCARTNEY: bass, acoustic guitar,
lead vocal
LENNON: banjo, backing vocal

HARRISON: harmonica, backing
vocal
STARR: drums, finger cymbals

*Record; Road* agrees on McCartney's guitar, but says Lennon sang vocal on "bom bom—look at me" part and probably played harmonica, and all Beatles sang vocals on the chorus; *ATN* only credits McCartney with vocals.

## MISCELLANEOUS

The Beatles sing this in an appearance at the end of the film *Yellow Submarine.*

## COMMENTS BY BEATLES

LENNON: "I enjoyed it when football crowds in the early days would sing 'All Together Now.' "   *Red Mole* (March 8-22, 1971) via *Own Words* and *Companion*

●

# "HEY BULLDOG"

**AUTHORSHIP** Lennon (.95) and McCartney (.05)

**RECORDED**
February 11, 1968, at Abbey Road
*Abbey* and *Day* and *Diary; Road* says mid-February; *Compleat*(b) says February.

This was the last song the Beatles recorded before leaving for India in early 1968. *A-Z*

This song was one of the most quickly recorded of the latter-day Beatles songs. It was completed in less than a day. *Road* and *Compleat*(b)

The Beatles were committed to being in the studio to make a promotional film for "Lady Madonna," and McCartney suggested that they might as well use the studio time to record a new song. He asked Lennon to write something, and Lennon brought in some lyrics he had at home. In the studio, the Beatles completed the lyrics. Lennon described how he wanted the song to go and the group played together and created a backing while they were being filmed.

The lyric "measured out in you" was supposed to be "measured out in news," but McCartney misread Lennon's handwriting and they agreed that the new line was better.

The title of the song was also changed during the session. It was originally called "Hey Bullfrog." *B-Lists* supports. Paul barked at the end of the song to make Lennon laugh; they kept the barking in and changed the title to "Hey Bulldog" even though a bulldog is never mentioned in the lyrics. A bullfrog is, however.

*Road; Compleat*(b) supports why name changed and that film crew worked around Beatles while they recorded this.

This recording session was the first Yoko Ono attended with Lennon. *A-Z* Lennon said later that he was embarrassed to be recording something as "lightweight" and "poppy" as this song during her first visit to the studio.

*Celebration;* supported by *Remembers*

**INSTRUMENTATION**

McCARTNEY: bass, harmony vocal
LENNON: piano, lead guitar, lead vocal

HARRISON: lead guitar, tambourine
STARR: drums

*Record; Road* agrees with McCartney's backing vocal but says McCartney probably played piano, not Lennon.

Although piano is heard on many Beatles recordings, its use on this song may have been a certainty because a piano was close at hand for the filming of the promo for the piano-based "Lady Madonna."

**MISCELLANEOUS**
This song was not used in the original U.S. version of the *Yellow Submarine* film.  A-Z

**COMMENTS BY BEATLES**
LENNON: "It's a good-sounding record that means nothing."
September 1980, *Playboy Interviews*

**COMMENTS BY OTHERS**
ERICH SEGAL, co-screenwriter of *Yellow Submarine* and author of the popular *Love Story,* claimed in the early 1970s that the Beatles wrote this song for him, titling it for the mascot of Yale, where he was a lecturer.
Washington *Post* (March 1987)

●

# "IT'S ALL TOO MUCH"

**AUTHORSHIP** Harrison (1.00)
HARRISON: " 'It's All Too Much' was written in a childlike manner from realizations that appeared during and after some LSD experiences and which were later confirmed in meditation."  *I Me Mine*

   This song was inspired by his wife, Patti Harrison. There is a reference to her in the lyrics: "With your long blond hair and your eyes of blue"— apparently taken from the song "Sorrow," a hit for the Merseys.
*A-Z; Record* agrees on "Sorrow" reference.

**RECORDED**
May 25, 1967, with overdubbing May 26 and June 2, all at De Lane Lea Music Recording Studios, London  *Abbey; Road* and *Day* say mid-June; *Diary* says June 22.

**INSTRUMENTATION**

McCARTNEY: bass, harmony vocal
LENNON: lead guitar, harmony vocal

HARRISON: lead guitar, organ, lead vocal (double-tracked)
STARR: drums, tambourine
Session musicians: two trumpets

*Record; Road* provides double-tracking information, agrees on Lennon and McCartney harmony vocals and brass, but adds assorted clapping.

**MISCELLANEOUS**
The version in the film includes an extra verse not on the album. *A-Z* and
*Record; Road* just says it's longer.

# "ALL YOU NEED IS LOVE"

(*See:* this song's entry as a single.)

# THE BEATLES
# (A.K.A. THE WHITE ALBUM)
### ALBUM

○

One of the great ironies of the Beatles' career is that the first album on which they didn't individually contribute much to the unit would be titled *The Beatles*. More commonly called the White Album because of its cover, it is essentially Lennon, McCartney, and Harrison taking turns recording their own songs and using the others as backing musicians. The Beatles later recognized this, and both Lennon and McCartney traced the bad feelings that led to the group's breakup to this album.

The White Album made a huge impact. People were starved for new Beatles songs—it had been three months since the last single (the group's biggest hit, "Hey Jude" b/w "Revolution") and nearly eighteen months since the last album proper, *Sgt. Pepper*. (The interim *Magical Mystery Tour* LP in the United States was half-filled with previously released singles, while in Britain it was an EP containing only the soundtrack songs.)

Buyers of the White Album also were excited by its sheer size—two discs, a total of almost ninety-four minutes—and its diversity, which ranged from hard rock to soft acoustic tunes, from the antimusic stance of "Revolution 9" to the overly lush "Good Night." But it lacked much of the experimentation that characterized previous Beatles releases.

## CHART ACTION
UNITED KINGDOM: Released November 22, 1968. It entered the *NME* album chart November 27 at No. 1, where it stayed for nine weeks. *Road*

UNITED STATES: Released November 25, 1968, with advance orders for 1.9 million copies. It entered the *Billboard* chart December 14 at No. 11 and rose to No. 1 two weeks later, where it stayed for nine weeks. *Road*

One month after release worldwide sales had reached more than 4 million copies. By the end of 1970 sales were estimated at 6.5 million, a phenomenal achievement for a double album. The White Album was the best-selling double album of all time, until the *Saturday Night Fever* soundtrack in 1977. *Road*

## RECORDED
Sessions began May 30, 1968, and continued through October 14. It was the longest time the Beatles ever took to record an album. *Abbey* and *ATN; Road* and Capitol say May 30 to October 17.

The tracks were recorded at Abbey Road, except for four done at

Trident Studios.  *Road* and *Abbey*  Mixing began October 14. Four days later, after the work was done, Lennon and Yoko Ono were arrested by the police and charged with possession of cannabis resin.  *Diary*

A lot of the work on songs was done by the band members alone—sometimes while work was being done by the others, separately, inside the other studios within the Abbey Road building.  *Musician* (July 1987)

Several songs were recorded during these sessions that never found their way onto a Beatles record, including Harrison's "Not Guilty" (rerecorded by him for a solo album in 1979), Lennon's "What's the New Mary Jane" (which had been recorded previously), and McCartney's "Jubilee" (rerecorded for his first solo album as "Junk").  *Road;* Capitol provided 1979 date.

Each released song took an average of thirty hours to record.  *Road*

Guest musicians included: Eric Clapton, Nicky Hopkins, Dave Mason, Coleman  and Jackie Lomax.  *Crawdaddy* (August 1975)

JACKIE LOMAX: "They would play [a song] in every kind of feel they could think of that would more or less suit that song. They would do it faster and slower and in 3/4 and 4/4 and 6/8. They'd try a whole bunch of things, drifting in and out of these with a lot of craziness in between. Weirdness. They gave the impression they were getting rid of a lot of nonsense, overplaying and stuff. They could do that because they had unlimited time."  *Crawdaddy* (August 1975)

George Martin went on vacation three months into the sessions and left engineer Chris Thomas in charge.

CHRIS THOMAS: "Actually, I thought the atmosphere was all right. Yet every day, in the middle of a song, they'd have to have a meeting about who to hire and fire at Apple. Yet when they started playing it was a really great atmosphere: they'd really rock out. And they were very funny: Paul was very quick, but John was out on his own. . . . But when I worked with Paul later, I realized how much he'd been leading the Beatles. He is staggeringly gifted—he can be so precise . . ."  Salewicz

► **RINGO QUITS**

*PETER BROWN, Beatles associate: "Most of the time [Ringo] spent in the studio he sat in a corner playing cards with Neil and Mal. It was a poorly kept secret among Beatle intimates that after Ringo left the studios, Paul would often dub in the drum tracks himself.*

*When Ringo returned to the studio the next day, he would pretend not to notice that it was not his playing."* Love

After one session in which McCartney criticized his drumming, Ringo quit—the first Beatle to do so. McCartney played drums on at least "Back in the U.S.S.R." Core

McCARTNEY: *"The real breakup in the Beatles was months ago. First Ringo left when we were doing the White Album, because he said he didn't think it was any fun playing with us anymore."* 1970, Own Words

STARR: *"... I felt I was playing like shit. And those three were really getting on. I had this feeling that nobody loved me; I felt horrible. So I said to myself, 'What am I doing here? Those three are getting along so well, and I'm not even playing well.' ... That was madness, so I went away on a holiday to sort things out. I don't know, maybe I was just paranoid. You know that to play in a band you have to trust each other."* Big Beat

McCARTNEY: *"But after two days of us telling him he was the greatest drummer in the world for the Beatles—which I believe—he came back."* 1970, Own Words

Ringo came back within a few days to find his drums smothered in flowers. Core; Compleat says a week; Abbey says he left August 22 and returned September 4.

STARR: *"... When I came back to work everything was all right again.... Paul is the greatest bass guitar player in the world. But he is also very determined; he goes on and on to see if he can get his own way. While that may be a virtue, it did mean that musical disagreements inevitably arose from time to time."* Core

HARRISON: "Paul would always help along when you'd done his ten songs —then when he got 'round to doing one of my songs, he would help. It was silly. It was very selfish, actually." Crawdaddy (February 1977)

McCartney's relationship with Lennon was also becoming strained. And Yoko Ono was present at every recording session Lennon attended.

RAY COLEMAN, Lennon biographer: "The other Beatles treated her shabbily and provocatively. . . . John broke a rigid, unwritten rule of the group: that their women would never be allowed in the studios. John perversely attended every session for the White Album with Yoko at his side. His message, unspoken, was obvious to all: they were inseparable. She sat on the speakers, offering suggestions and, incredibly, criticisms." Coleman

Yoko moved her bed into the studio. She followed John everywhere, even into the lavatory, according to a studio technician. Core


PETE SHOTTON: "At best, Yoko's presence tended to inhibit the other Beatles, and to stifle the extraordinary rapport that the four musicians had heretofore enjoyed; at worst, Paul or George would let their resentment boil to the surface, thus putting John on the defensive and exacerbating the tensions yet further. . . . During my many visits to Abbey Road during the summer and autumn of 1968, all the old fun, laughter, and camaraderie seemed conspicuous by their absence. The Beatles' recording sessions had turned into a very serious, dour operation—a far cry indeed from the festive atmosphere that had surrounded the creation of *Sgt. Pepper*." Shotton


McCARTNEY: "The White Album . . . was the tension album. We were all in the midst of the psychedelic thing, or just coming out of it. In any case, it was weird. Never before had we recorded with beds in the studio and people visiting for hours on end; business meetings and all that. There was a lot of friction. It was the weirdest experience because we were about to break up; that was tense in itself." *Musician* (February 1985)

Harrison agreed that the White Album was a tense period for the band. He blamed the Beatles' wives, mainly, for creating distance between them. *RS* (December 10, 1987)


Interestingly, Lennon later tried hard to persuade a court, while the dissolution of the group was being decided, that the group's relationships had not worsened during the White Album sessions or later. Core


LENNON, in a court affidavit: "We were no more openly critical of each other's music in 1968, or later, than we had always been. I do not agree [with Paul] that after the touring ceased we began to drift apart socially and that the drift became more marked after Brian Epstein's death." Lennon's comments in a *Rolling Stone* interview, however, were the opposite, and McCartney used them in one of his affidavits to refute Lennon's argument, which helped him to win court approval to dissolve the legal ties among the Beatles. Core

## ALBUM PACKAGE

The album has a white cover. On early copies the name *The Beatles* was embossed on its front; later it was simply printed in light-gray type.

The design was suggested by artist Richard Hamilton. He said the Beatles should make the cover design distinctive by having no "design" at all on it. But he thought the white cover should be defaced in some way and suggested that the albums be consecutively numbered as would a limited edition of a piece of art. The Beatles asked Gordon House to design the album package using Hamilton's ideas.

*Road;* Capitol supports the fact that Hamilton "conceived" the sleeve; *Celebration* says John Kosh designed the cover.

The album included color photos of each Beatle and a large poster-sized sheet with the songs' lyrics on one side and a photo collage on the other. Neil Aspinall and Mal Evans provided the photos, and Jeremy Banks coordinated the design. The English press created a controversy when it zeroed in on one small picture of McCartney in the nude.

*Road; Celebration* says Hamilton designed the photo collage.

Pete Shotton said it was McCartney's idea to stamp each copy of the album with an individual number. McCartney originally wanted to hold a lottery with those numbers; he thought it would be a strong marketing gimmick. But he came to the conclusion that it would make the Beatles seem cheap.

Shotton; *Love* supports the assertion that it was McCartney's idea and says he wanted numbers stamped as if the album were a fine lithograph.

"PAUL IS DEAD" HYSTERIA: A picture on the back of the lyric sheet showed McCartney in a bathtub with the back of his head unseen under water. Some thought that was a clue McCartney had been decapitated in the accident that caused his "death."

## MISCELLANEOUS

The album was recorded under the working title of *A Doll's House*. *B-Lists;* Capitol excludes the *A*.

This was the third album released on the Beatles' Apple Records label. It followed Harrison's *Wonderwall Music* and John and Yoko's *Unfinished Music No. 1: Two Virgins*. *ATN;* Capitol says it was the second after *Wonderwall.*

Most of the songs were composed during the Beatles' stay in India in early 1968. Many sources

Martin was not sure that all of the songs were good enough to merit releasing a double album. "I tried to plead with them to be selective and make it a really good single album, but they wouldn't have it." *Forever*

The Beatles insisted on a double album because they would then owe EMI one less album under their contract. *Forever* Also, Lennon loved the way the songs showed the development of the Beatles as individuals. *Coleman*

There is a snippet of a song between "Cry Baby Cry" and "Revolution 9." Sung by McCartney, the tune could be called "Can You Take Me Back." It's not listed with the album's song titles. The other Beatles apparently were not present when it was recorded. McCartney is presumed to have played all of the instruments: acoustic guitar, drums, maracas, and bongos. *Record*

## COMMENTS BY BEATLES
McCARTNEY, on why the album wasn't more experimental: "We felt it was time to step back because that is what we wanted to do. You can still make good music without going forward. Some people want us to go on until we vanish up our own B sides."    Probably around release date, *Forever*

LENNON: "I started simplifying my lyrics then, on the double album." *Own Words*

LENNON: "... It's like if you took each track off it and made it all mine and all George's. It's like I told you many times, it was just me and a backing group, Paul and a backing group, and I enjoyed it. We broke up then." *Own Words*

HARRISON: "I think in a way it was a mistake doing four sides, because it's just too big for most people to really get into. . . . I listen mainly to side one, which I like very much."    Late 1969, *Celebration*

STARR: "As a band member, I've always felt the White Album was better than *Sgt. Pepper* because by the end it was more like a real group again. There weren't so many overdubs like on *Pepper.* With all those orchestras and whatnot, we were virtually a session group on our own album." *Musician* (February 1982)

LENNON: "I keep saying that I always preferred the double album, because *my* music is better on the double album . . . because I'm being myself on it. . . . I don't like production so much."    Circa late 1970–early 1971, *Own Words*

## COMMENTS BY OTHERS
STEVEN SPIELBERG, movie producer and director: "I resented [the Beatles] at first because it wasn't a fad I discovered for myself. . . . I wasn't a Beatles fan until I listened to the White Album and became an instant convert." *Crawdaddy* (June 1978)

●

# "BACK IN THE U.S.S.R."

**AUTHORSHIP** McCartney (1.00)
LENNON: "Paul [wrote it]. Maybe I helped a bit, but I don't think so..."
*Hit Parader* (April 1972)

McCARTNEY: "I wrote that as a kind of Beach Boys parody. And 'Back in the U.S.A.' was a Chuck Berry song, so it kinda took off from there. I just liked the idea of Georgia girls and talking about places like the Ukraine as if they were California, you know?"   *Playboy* (December 1984)
   Chuck Berry's "Back in the U.S.A." is a tribute to our consumerist culture, with its skyscrapers, hamburgers, and freeways. McCartney's song mentions balalaikas, bugged telephones, and snow-peaked mountains.
   Mike Love, of the Beach Boys (who did their own pastiche of "Back in the U.S.A."), contributed the chorus while he was with McCartney in India in early 1968.   *Day*

McCARTNEY: "It was also hands across the water, which I'm still conscious of. 'Cause they like us out there, even though the bosses in the Kremlin may not. The kids do. And that to me is very important for the future of the race."   *Playboy* (December 1984)   McCartney would later record a solo album, with this as its title song, and release it only in the Soviet Union.
   The song's title came from the "I'm Backing Britain" campaign, which began in England in 1968. The title at one point was "I'm Backing the U.S.S.R."
*A-Z; Record* supports; *Forever* says Harrison said it started out as "I'm Backing the U.K."

## RECORDED
August 22, 1968, at Abbey Road, without Starr. Overdubs were added August 23.
*Abbey; Day* and *Diary* agree on date; *Road* says recording began on same date; *Record* says Starr participated.

## INSTRUMENTATION
McCARTNEY: lead guitar, piano, drums, lead and backing vocal
LENNON: 6-string bass (Bass VI), backing vocal
HARRISON: jazz bass, backing vocal

*Record* (except says Starr played drums); *Road* and *A-Z* support McCartney's guitar and drums, Lennon's bass, and Harrison's bass and vocal; *ATN* omits harmony; *Guitar* (November 1987) supports McCartney's guitar and drums and two basses and provides basses' names; *Musician* (July 1977) and *Abbey* say Starr did not play on session; *Transcriptions* supports McCartney's guitar, backing vocals, two basses, six-string.

McCARTNEY: "... I'm sure it pissed Ringo off when he couldn't quite get the drums to 'Back in the U.S.S.R.,' and I sat in. It's very weird to know that you can do a thing someone else is having trouble with. If you go down and do it, just bluff right through it, you think, 'What the hell—at least I'm helping.' Then the paranoia comes in: 'But I'm going to show him up!' I was very sensitive to that . . ." *Musician* (October 1986)

## MISCELLANEOUS
This originally was written for Twiggy to record. *A-Z*

The jet engine noise was overdubbed after the Beatles recorded the song. *Transcriptions*

Billy Joel performed this song as an encore to a Moscow concert in late July 1987 to thunderous applause and thousands in the audience singing along. AP (July 27, 1987)

## COMMENTS BY OTHERS
BRIAN WILSON, of the Beach Boys, on this song being a parody/tribute to his group: "I didn't even recognize that until someone said something. I thought that was really *adorable.*" *Crawdaddy* (July 1976)

●

# "DEAR PRUDENCE"

## AUTHORSHIP Lennon (1.00)
LENNON: "Written in India. A song about Mia Farrow's sister, who seemed to go slightly balmy, meditating too long, and couldn't come out of the little hut that we were livin' in. They selected me and George to try and bring her out because she would trust us."

September 1980, *Playboy Interviews; Road* supports the subject's identity.

## RECORDED
August 28, 1968, at Trident Studios, with overdubbing August 29 and 30

*Abbey; Day* and *Road* agree on August 28 and Trident; *Diary* agrees on August 28.

## INSTRUMENTATION
McCARTNEY: bass, piano, drums, flugelhorn, lead and backing vocal
LENNON: lead guitar (Epiphone), tambourine, lead and backing vocal

HARRISON: acoustic guitar, backing vocal
Mal Evans: tambourine

*Record* (except says Starr played drums); *Road* provides Epiphone and agrees on Lennon's instruments, McCartney's extra instruments, and Evans's tambourine, but says all Beatles sang backing vocals on chorus and says Evans, Jackie Lomax, and "John" provided clapping, "John" being a cousin of McCartney; *Diary* agrees on clappers, except that "John" was McCartney's nephew; *ATN* omits backing vocals, Lennon's guitar, clapping; *Crawdaddy* (August 1975) says Lomax sang background vocal; *Abbey* provides McCartney's drums.

Overdubbing of the guitar parts six or seven times helped create the rich sound.  *Forever*

## MISCELLANEOUS
A page containing the song's lyrics, with fourteen lines of verse and notes and doodles around the border, was sold for $19,500 to an unidentified investor June 27, 1987, at Sotheby's, New York.  New York *Times* news service

## COMMENTS BY OTHERS
This song is one of Julian Lennon's favorites.  Circa 1984, Coleman

●

# "GLASS ONION"

## AUTHORSHIP  Lennon (1.00)
LENNON: "That's me, just doing a throwaway song. . . . I threw the line in —'The walrus was Paul'—just to confuse everybody a bit more."
September 1980, *Playboy Interviews*

"PAUL IS DEAD" HYSTERIA: In some parts of Scandinavia, the walrus is an image of death.  *Diary*

LENNON: "That was a joke. The line was put in partly because I was feeling guilty because I was with Yoko and I was leaving Paul. I was trying—I don't know. It's a very perverse way of saying to Paul, you know, 'Here, have this crumb, this illusion, this stroke, because I'm leaving.' "  September 1980, *Playboy Interviews*

## RECORDED
September 11, 1968, at Abbey Road, with overdubbing September 12, 13, and 16 and October 10

*Abbey; Diary* agrees on September 11; *Day* agrees on September 11 but says recorded by Lennon and McCartney.

## INSTRUMENTATION
McCARTNEY: bass, piano, flute          HARRISON: lead guitar
LENNON: acoustic guitar (Gibson),    STARR: drums, tambourine
vocal (double-tracked)                Session musicians: orchestra

*Record; Road* provides Gibson and agrees on Lennon's acoustic, omits McCartney's instruments, but says McCartney sang backing vocal, Starr played double drum kit, and violins were added; *ATN* omits all but Lennon's vocals.

## MISCELLANEOUS
The lyrics allude to several previous Beatles songs, in order: "Strawberry Fields Forever," "I Am the Walrus," "Lady Madonna," "The Fool on the Hill," and "Fixing a Hole."

"Glass Onion" was originally what Lennon wanted to name the new Apple group that eventually called itself Badfinger. Shotton

## COMMENTS BY BEATLES
LENNON: "With 'Glass Onion' I was just having a laugh, because there had been so much gobbledegook written about *Sgt. Pepper.* People were saying, 'Play it backwards while standing on your head, and you'll get a secret message, etc.' Why, just the other day I saw Mel Torme on TV saying that several of my songs were written to promote the use of drugs, but really, none of them were at all. So this one was just my way of saying, 'You're all full of shit!' " *Celebration*

Harrison named this song as one of his favorites on the album. Late 1969, *Celebration*

●

## "OB-LA-DI, OB-LA-DA"

**AUTHORSHIP** McCartney (1.00)
LENNON: "I might've given him a couple of lyrics, but it's his song, his lyric." September 1980, *Playboy Interviews*

## RECORDED
July 3, 1968, at Abbey Road, with overdubbing July 4 and 5, a remake July 8, another remake July 9 (not used), and further overdubbing July 11 and 15 *Abbey; Day* and *Road* say recording began July 2.

The other Beatles became upset over doing so much work on this McCartney song.

RICHARD LUSH, second engineer: "After about four or five nights doing 'Ob-La-Di, Ob-La-Da' John Lennon came to the session really stoned, totally out of it on something or other, and he said, 'Alright, we're gonna do "Ob-La-Di, Ob-La-Da." ' He went straight to the piano and smashed the keys with an almighty amount of volume, twice the speed of how they'd done it before, and said, 'This is *it!* Come on!' He was really aggravated. That was the version they ended up using." *Abbey*

Pete Shotton was at the session in which McCartney recorded his lead vocal over and over again to get it perfect. Shotton described the scene:

*After finally turning in what sounded like a flawless performance, [Mc-Cartney] burst out laughing. "Oh shit!" he said. "We'll have to do it all over again!"*

*"Well, it sounded OK to me," John yawned.*

*"Yeah," George agreed. "It was perfect."*

*"But didn't you notice?" Paul demanded.*

*"Notice what?" said John.*

*"I just sang 'Desmond stays at home and does his pretty face'... I should've sung 'Molly'!"*

*The others refused to believe him—until George Martin played back the tape and proved Paul right.*

*"Oh, it sounds great anyway," Paul concluded. "Let's just leave it in—create a bit of confusion there. Everyone will wonder whether Desmond's a bisexual or a transvestite."* Shotton

## INSTRUMENTATION

McCARTNEY: bass, piano, lead vocal

LENNON: maracas, backing vocal

HARRISON: acoustic guitar, backing vocal

STARR: drums

Session musicians: brass

*Record; Road* agrees on McCartney's piano and backing vocal; *ATN* omits piano, backing vocals; Shotton says Pete Shotton played tambourine in the background; *Abbey* implies that Lennon played piano.

## MISCELLANEOUS

McCartney wanted to release this song as a single at about the time of the White Album's release, but Lennon and Harrison both voted against it; they thought it trite. *Record* and *A-Z*

Others, however, saw the catchy tune as a natural hit. Two groups—the Marmalade and the Bedrocks—rode the song into the U.K. charts during 1968. But the Beatles' version failed when it was released as a posthumous single in the U.S. by Capitol in November 1976; it rose to only No. 49 on the *Billboard* chart, becoming the first Beatles single on Capitol not to break into the U.S. Top 30. *Road*

The title was taken from a reggae band—Jimmy Scott and his Obla Di Obla Da Band. *A-Z* and *Record*

McCARTNEY: "A fella who used to hang around the clubs used to say [Jamaican accent], 'ob-la-di, ob-la-da, life goes on,' and he got annoyed when I did a song of it, 'cause he wanted a cut. I said, 'Come on, Jimmy, it's just an expression. If you'd written the song, you could have had the cut.' He also used to say, 'Nothin's too much, just outta sight.' He was just one of those guys who had great expressions, you know."

*Playboy* (December 1984); *Record* agrees with Jimmy Scott.

## COMMENTS BY BEATLES
Lennon hated this song. Fawcett and *Forever* (and others)

## COMMENTS BY OTHERS
In 1969, record producer Phil Spector called "Ob-La-Di, Ob-La-Da" a hit song. He said it would have been successful ten years before because it was a well-constructed song with a good hook and melody. *RS* (November 1, 1969)

STEWART COPELAND, composer and drummer for the Police, speaking on how drummers have to play in sympathy to the singer: "Articulation of the words really should determine the overall riff of the whole thing.... 'Ob-la-*di*' has an accent. 'ob-la-*da*' has an accent, 'life goes *on* ...' sort of leads you into that ska feel. There's a definite scansion to those lyrics, which is probably why they ended up playing a ska beat. In fact, that's one of the first examples of white reggae." *Musician* (June 1988)

●

# "WILD HONEY PIE"

## AUTHORSHIP McCartney (1.00)
The song came from a spontaneous sing-along at the Maharishi's camp in India. *A-Z* and *Record*

## RECORDED
August 20, 1968, at Abbey Road by McCartney. No other Beatles participated. *Abbey* and *Day* and *Road* and *Diary*

## INSTRUMENTATION
McCARTNEY: bass, electric and acoustic guitars, drums, vocals

*Record; Road* agrees McCartney played all instruments (omits bass, says guitar) and says double-tracked bass drum; *ATN* says guitar, bass, drums.

## MISCELLANEOUS
At 1:02, this is the album's shortest track. *Record*

## COMMENTS BY BEATLES
McCARTNEY: "This was just a fragment of an instrumental which we were not sure about, but Patti [Harrison] liked it very much so we decided to leave it on the album." *Own Words; Record* says Jane Asher was the one who liked it.

•

# "THE CONTINUING STORY OF BUNGALOW BILL"

**AUTHORSHIP** Lennon (1.00)
LENNON: "That was written about a guy in Maharishi's meditation camp who took a short break to go shoot a few poor tigers, and then came back to commune with God. There used to be a character called Jungle Jim, and I combined him with Buffalo Bill. It's a sort of teenage social-comment song and a bit of a joke." *September 1980, Playboy Interviews*

**RECORDED**
Between midnight and dawn on October 9, at Abbey Road. This was recorded immediately after "I'm So Tired."
*Abbey; Road* agrees (except it says October 10); *Day* and *Diary* say October 9.

**INSTRUMENTATION**
McCARTNEY: bass, backing vocal
LENNON: acoustic guitar, organ, lead vocal
HARRISON: acoustic guitar, backing vocal
STARR: drums, tambourine, backing vocal

Yoko Ono: backing and harmony vocal (chorus) and solo on "not when he looked so fierce"
Maureen Starkey: harmony vocal (chorus)
Chris Thomas (Beatles assistant): Mellotron

*Record; Road* agrees on Lennon's organ, Ono's vocal, and Thomas (but says he was the engineer); *ATN* omits Beatles backing vocals; *A-Z* agrees on Maureen.

This song was Yoko's singing debut on record. Capitol Her one-line vocal was the first for a female on a Beatles record. Abbey

•

# "WHILE MY GUITAR GENTLY WEEPS"

**AUTHORSHIP** Harrison (1.00)
HARRISON: "I had a copy of the I Ching—the [Chinese] Book of Changes, which seemed to me to be based on the Eastern concept that everything is relative to everything else, as opposed to the Western view that things are merely coincidental.

"This idea was in my head when I visited my parents' house in the North of England. I decided to write a song based on the first thing I saw upon opening any book—as it would be relative to that moment, at *that* time. I picked up a book at random, opened it—saw 'gently weeps'—then laid the book down again and started the song. Some of the words to the song were changed before I finally recorded it."

*I Me Mine*; Harrison quote (late 1969, *Celebration*) supports

## RECORDED

An acoustic version was recorded July 25, 1968, at Abbey Road. It was remade August 16 with an overdub September 3, and remade again September 5 with another overdub September 6.

*Abbey*; *Day* agrees recording began July 25 and says it was finished "much later"; *Road* agrees on beginning recording date; *Diary* says it was recorded July 25

HARRISON: "I worked on that song with John, Paul, and Ringo one day, and they were not interested in it at all. And I knew inside of me that it was a nice song. The next day I was with Eric [Clapton], and I was going into the session, and I said, 'We're going to do this song. Come on and play on it.' He said, 'Oh, no. I can't do that. Nobody ever plays on the Beatles' records.' I said, 'Look, it's my song, and I want you to play on it.'

"So Eric came in, and the other guys were as good as gold—because he was there. Also, it left me free to just play the rhythm and do the vocal. So Eric played that, and I thought it was really good. Then we listened to it back, and he said, 'Ah, there's a problem, though; it's not Beatley enough'— so we put it through the ADT [automatic double-tracker] to wobble it a bit." *Guitar* (November 1987)

HARRISON: ". . . When we laid that track down, I sang it with the acoustic guitar with Paul on piano, and Eric and Ringo—that's how we laid the track down. Later, Paul overdubbed the bass on it." *Guitar* (November 1987)

## INSTRUMENTATION

McCARTNEY: bass, piano, harmony vocal
LENNON: acoustic guitar, organ, harmony vocal
HARRISON: acoustic guitar, lead guitar, lead vocal (occasionally double-tracked)

STARR: drums, castanets, tambourine
Eric Clapton: lead guitar (Gibson Les Paul)

*Record*; *Road* provides double-tracking information, agrees on Lennon's and Harrison's acoustic guitars, Lennon's organ, and Clapton's lead guitar; *ATN* omits acoustic guitars, organ; *Diary* mentions Lennon's organ; Clapton's guitar from *Guitar* (November 1987)

## MISCELLANEOUS

"PAUL IS DEAD" HYSTERIA: At the end, Harrison sings what sounds like "Paul, Paul" as if he misses the "dead" Beatle. *Lists*

This was one of the few Beatles songs Harrison performed during his Dark Horse tour in late 1974.   Coleman

## COMMENTS BY BEATLES
HARRISON: "I love what Eric did on guitar for the original, but versions I did live are better in some respects. See, in the Beatles days, I never liked my singing. I *couldn't* sing very good. I was always very paranoid, very nervous, and that inhibited my singing."   *Musician* (November 1987)

●

# "HAPPINESS IS A WARM GUN"

**AUTHORSHIP** Lennon ( 1.00 )
LENNON: "A gun magazine was sitting around, and the cover was the picture of a smoking gun. The title of the article, which I never read, was 'Happiness Is a Warm Gun.' "   September 1980, *Playboy Interviews*

LENNON: "I thought, 'What a fantastic, insane thing to say.' A warm gun means that you've just shot something."   *Celebration*
    Lennon saw the American gun magazine a few days after Robert Kennedy's assassination.   *Forever;* Lennon said it was American in *Hit Parader* (April 1972)

LENNON: "It was put together from bits of about three different songs and just seemed to run the gamut of many types of rock music."   *Celebration*

## RECORDED
September 23, 1968, at Abbey Road, but none of the forty-five takes was deemed good enough. Of the twenty-five takes recorded September 24, one had a good first half and another had the best second half. They were edited together and overdubs were added September 25.
*Abbey; Day* and *Diary* say recorded September 23; *Road* says recording began September 23.

## INSTRUMENTATION
McCARTNEY: bass, backing vocal      HARRISON: lead guitar, backing
LENNON: lead guitar, tambourine,    vocal
lead and backing vocal              STARR: drums
*Record; Road* says harmony vocals; *ATN* omits backing vocals.
    The guitars are in 3/4 time and the drumming is in 4/4.   *Road*

## MISCELLANEOUS
This song was banned by the BBC because of its sexual symbolism.   *A-Z*

## COMMENTS BY BEATLES

LENNON: "I consider it one of my best. It's a beautiful song, and I really like all the things that are happening in it." *Celebration*

LENNON: "They all said it was about drugs but it was more about rock 'n' roll than drugs. It's sort of a history of rock 'n' roll. . . . I don't know why people said it was about the needle in heroin. I've only seen somebody do something with a needle once, and I don't like to see it at all."
*Hit Parader* (April 1972)

McCARTNEY: "I think this is my favorite on *The Beatles* album." *Own Words*
Harrison named this song as one of his favorites on the album.
Late 1969, *Celebration*

## COMMENTS BY OTHERS

RON REAGAN: "I remember once, when I was about thirteen, I borrowed the White Album from [my sister] Patti, and my mother got upset when she heard me listening to 'Happiness Is a Warm Gun.' It really bothered her a lot." *RS* (February 16, 1984)

●

# "MARTHA MY DEAR"

AUTHORSHIP  McCartney (1.00)

## RECORDED

October 4, 1968, with overdubs added October 5, at Trident Studios

*Abbey; Road* agrees on studio and says work began October 4; *Day* says "John Lennon" recorded the song October 4; *Diary* says McCartney recorded it October 4.

## INSTRUMENTATION

McCARTNEY: piano, vocal (double-tracked)
LENNON: bass

HARRISON: lead guitar
STARR: drums
Session musicians: strings, brass

*Record; Road* provides double-tracking and agrees on McCartney's piano and on brass and violins; *ATN* omits brass and violins.

## MISCELLANEOUS

This was written about McCartney's old sheepdog, Martha.

*Record* and *Road* and *Forever; Diary* and *Abbey* emphasize that it is not about his dog; *A-Z* says only that the title is a tribute to his dog and that the song is about a broken love affair.

●

# "I'M SO TIRED"

**AUTHORSHIP** Lennon (1.00)
LENNON: " 'I'm So Tired' was me, in India again. I couldn't sleep. I'm meditating all day and couldn't sleep at night." September 1980, *Playboy Interviews*

It was also a stressful time for Lennon in that he was trying to decide whether to leave his wife for Yoko. *A-Z*

**RECORDED**
October 8, 1968, at Abbey Road *Abbey; Day* and *Diary* and *Road* say October 9.

**INSTRUMENTATION**

McCARTNEY: bass, harmony vocal     HARRISON: lead and rhythm
LENNON: acoustic and lead guitars,     guitars
organ, lead vocal                                  STARR: drums

*Record; Road* and *ATN* just say Lennon sang vocals; *Diary* says Starr was absent from session.

**MISCELLANEOUS**
"PAUL IS DEAD" HYSTERIA: Between the end of "I'm So Tired" and the beginning of "Blackbird," Lennon utters some nonsense syllables. If played backward, they sound like: "Paul is dead, man, miss him, miss him."

*Forever* and *Record; Lists* omits "man" from quote; *Abbey* says Lennon mumbled "Monsieur, monsieur, how about another one?".

This song about insomnia is in interesting contrast to an earlier Lennon song, "I'm Only Sleeping," about not being able to get out of bed.

**COMMENTS BY BEATLES**
LENNON: "One of my favorite tracks. I just like the sound of it, and I sing it well." September 1980, *Playboy Interviews*

●

# "BLACKBIRD"

**AUTHORSHIP** McCartney (.95) and Lennon (.05)
McCartney was inspired while reading a newspaper account of U.S. race riots in mid-1968 and wrote this song as a metaphor of the struggle for black civil rights. *A-Z*

LENNON: "I gave him a line on that one."   September 1980, *Playboy Interviews*

## RECORDED

June 11, 1968, at Abbey Road, by McCartney   *Abbey* and *Day* and *Diary* and *Road*

Three microphones were used in recording the song: one each for McCartney's voice, his guitar, and his tapping foot. The chirping birds were overdubbed, the addition of which was "hotly debated."

*Crawdaddy* (August 1975) doesn't say who debated it.

## INSTRUMENTATION

McCARTNEY: acoustic guitar,                Blackbird: singing
percussion, vocal (occasionally
double-tracked)

*Record; Road* agrees on double-tracking, acoustic guitar, percussion (probably drumstick on table), and blackbird singing; *Abbey* says more than one blackbird.

## MISCELLANEOUS

This was one of five Beatles songs performed on McCartney's Wings over America tour in 1976.

McCartney said that one of his most cherished moments as a songwriter was when he woke one morning to the sound of a blackbird singing the tune of this song.   Capitol

McCartney was happy and sat on a windowsill playing an acoustic guitar and serenading the fans around his house by singing this song on the night Linda Eastman arrived from New York to live with him in late summer 1968.   Salewicz; *Shout* supports but says in summer.

●

# "PIGGIES"

AUTHORSHIP   Harrison (.85), Lennon (.1), and Louise Harrison (.05)
Harrison finished writing the song when he rediscovered it at his parents' home. He had started it in 1966. He finished it with his mother's help.   A-Z

HARRISON: " 'Piggies' is a social comment. I was stuck for one line in the middle until my mother came up with the lyric 'What they need is a damn good whacking!' which is a nice simple way of saying they need a good hiding. It needed to rhyme with 'backing,' 'lacking,' and had absolutely nothing to do with American policemen or Californian shagnasties!"
*I Me Mine*

LENNON: "I gave George a couple of lines about forks and knives and eating bacon." September 1980, *Playboy Interviews*

## RECORDED
September 19, 1968, at Abbey Road, with overdubbing September 20 and October 10  *Abbey; Day* and *Diary* and *Road* agree on starting date.

## INSTRUMENTATION
McCARTNEY: bass

LENNON: tape loops

HARRISON: acoustic guitar, vocal

STARR: tambourine

Chris Thomas (producer):
harpsichord

Session musicians: strings

*Record; Road* agrees on Starr's tambourine, Thomas's harpsichord, and Lennon's supplying tape loops but gives Lennon and McCartney credit for backing vocals; *ATN* omits backing vocals, tape loops; *Forever* says Lennon wasn't at the session.

Harrison's vocal was filtered in the second half of the song to create a nasal effect. *Road*

## MISCELLANEOUS
A concluding verse was written but not recorded. It read:

*Everywhere there's lots of piggies*
*Playing piggy pranks*
*You can see them on their trotters*
*At the piggy banks*
*Paying piggy thanks*
*To thee pig brother!* I Me Mine

Murderer Charles Manson interpreted this song as a description of the people who would be the victims in the black revolution he believed was imminent. *Forever*

●

# "ROCKY RACCOON"

**AUTHORSHIP** McCartney (1.00)

LENNON: "Paul [wrote it]. Couldn't you guess? Would I go to all that trouble about Gideon's Bible and all that stuff?" September 1980, *Playboy Interviews*

This Western cowboy song was written while McCartney was being exposed to Far Eastern culture in India.  *A-Z* and *Record*  He was assisted in its creation by Lennon and Donovan Leitch. The idea struck Paul while the three were playing their guitars on the roof of one of the buildings in the Maharishi's camp. *Road*

## RECORDED
August 15, 1968, at Abbey Road

*Abbey; Road* and *Diary* agree on date; *Day* says McCartney recorded this alone on the 15th with only Martin accompanying him on piano.

## INSTRUMENTATION

McCARTNEY: acoustic guitar, lead vocal
LENNON: harmonica, harmonium, backing vocal

HARRISON: bass, backing vocal
STARR: drums
George Martin: honky-tonk piano

*Record; Road* agrees on McCartney's "lead guitar," Harrison's bass, Lennon's harmonium, and Martin's honky-tonk piano; *ATN* omits bass; *A-Z* agrees on Lennon's harmonica.

## MISCELLANEOUS
The original name for the song was "Rocky Sassoon." *Road*

●

# "DON'T PASS ME BY"

**AUTHORSHIP** Starr (1.00)
Starr wrote this song in India. *Diary; Record* says he wrote it in 1963.
He had previously gotten a partial composing credit on "What Goes On" *(Rubber Soul)* and "Flying," an instrumental on *Magical Mystery Tour.* *Road*

STARR: "I'd write tunes that were already written and just change the lyrics, and the other three would have hysterics just tellin' me what I'd rewritten." *Forever*

## RECORDED
June 5, 1968, at Abbey Road, with overdubbing June 6 and July 12 and an edit piece (the tinkling piano intro) recorded July 22

*Abbey; Day* gives July 12 as date and says the song was recorded by Starr; *Road* says recording began July 12; *Diary* says recording began the week of May 30 and was completed July 12.

## INSTRUMENTATION

McCARTNEY: bass
LENNON: acoustic guitar, tambourine

HARRISON: violin
STARR: drums, piano, vocal

*Record; Road* agrees on Starr's piano but says a session musician played country fiddle.

**MISCELLANEOUS**

The original title for this song was "Some Kind of Friendly."

A-Z; *Diary* says "This Is Some Friendly."

"PAUL IS DEAD" HYSTERIA: This song contains lyrics about a car crash, which some people construed as alluding to McCartney's supposed fatal crash in which he was decapitated.

This was a No. 1 hit in Scandinavia, where it was released as a single.

*Forever*

•

# "WHY DON'T WE DO IT IN THE ROAD?"

**AUTHORSHIP** McCartney (1.00)

LENNON: "Paul [wrote it]—one of his best."   *Hit Parader* (April 1972)

**RECORDED**

October 9, 1968, at Abbey Road, with overdubs added October 10

*Abbey; Road* and *Day* and *Diary* say October 10; *A-Z* and *Record* says McCartney recorded it alone.

**INSTRUMENTATION**

McCARTNEY: bass, lead guitar, piano, drums, vocal (occasionally double-tracked)

*Record; Road* provides double-tracking information; *Road* and *ATN* agree McCartney played all instruments —guitar, piano, bass, drums; McCartney quote in *Beatles* says Ringo assisted; *Abbey* says Starr played drums.

**MISCELLANEOUS**

Lennon parodied this song during the later *Let It Be* sessions when he sang this one line between numbers: "Why don't you put it on the toast?"   Bootleg

**COMMENTS BY BEATLES:**

LENNON: "That's Paul. He even recorded it by himself in another room. That's how it was getting in those days. We came in, and he'd made the whole record. Him drumming. Him playing the piano. Him singing. . . . I can't speak for George, but I was always hurt when Paul would knock something off without involving us. But that's just the way it was then."

September 1980, *Playboy Interviews*

McCARTNEY: "There's only one incident I can think of which John has publicly mentioned [that hurt him]. It was when I went off with Ringo and did 'Why Don't We Do It in the Road?' It wasn't a deliberate thing. John and George were tied up finishing something, and me and Ringo were free, just hanging around, so I said to Ringo, 'Let's go and do this.'

"I did hear [John] some time later singing it. He liked the song, and I suppose he'd wanted to do it with me. It was a very John sort of song anyway. That's why he liked it, I suppose. It was very John, the idea of it, not me. I wrote it as a ricochet off John. . . .

"Anyway, he did the same with 'Revolution 9.' He went off and made that without me. No one ever says all that. John is now the nice guy, and I'm the bastard."    May 3, 1981, *Beatles*

●

# "I WILL"

**AUTHORSHIP** McCartney (1.00)

**RECORDED**
September 16, 1968, at Abbey Road. Sixty-seven takes were recorded, not all complete versions. The sixty-fifth was considered best, and more instruments and vocals were overdubbed on it September 17.

*Abbey; Day* and *Diary* say September 16; *Road* says recording began September 16

**INSTRUMENTATION**
McCARTNEY: bass, acoustic guitar,    STARR: drums, bongos, maracas
vocal (occasionally double-tracked)

*Record; Road* provides double-tracking information and agrees backing included bongos, but says Lennon played "skulls"; *ATN* omits instrumentation; *Day* says it was recorded "without Ringo."

**MISCELLANEOUS**
The tune is very similar to "I'll Follow the Sun," written by McCartney and performed on 1964's *Beatles for Sale.*    Forever

●

# "JULIA"

**AUTHORSHIP** Lennon (.75), Yoko Ono (.20), and Kahlil Gibran (.05)
LENNON: "Me [I wrote it]. Yoko helped me with this one."
*Hit Parader* (April 1972)

LENNON: "Julia was my mother. But it was sort of a combination of Yoko and my mother blended into one. That was written in India."

September 1980, *Playboy Interviews; A-Z* supports reference to his mother.

The line "oceanchild, calls me" refers to Yoko's letters to John in India. Coleman   In Japanese, Yoko means "ocean child."   Capitol and *Record*

The line "Julia, seashell eyes" was taken from poet Kahlil Gibran. *Forever; Compleat*(b) says lyrics were derived from Gibran's "Sand and Foam."

## RECORDED
October 13, 1968, at Abbey Road, by Lennon.

*Abbey* and *Day* and *Diary; Forever* agrees it was a Lennon solo.

## INSTRUMENTATION
LENNON: acoustic guitar (double-tracked), vocal (occasionally double-tracked)

*Record; Road* provides double-tracking information; *ATN* says *lead* acoustic guitar; *Forever* agrees no other Beatles played.

This was the only song Lennon recorded alone during his time with the Beatles.   *Abbey*

●

# "BIRTHDAY"

**AUTHORSHIP** McCartney (.7) and Lennon (.3)
LENNON: "Both of us [wrote it]."   *Hit Parader* (April 1972); *ATN* supports.

LENNON: " 'Birthday' was written in the studio. Just made up on the spot. I think Paul wanted to write a song like 'Happy Birthday Baby,' the old '50s hit."   September 1980, *Playboy Interviews; Road* supports that it was written in the studio.

But some sources say it was written for Patti Harrison, who celebrated her birthday while the Beatles were in India studying with the Maharishi.

*Record; A-Z* says written for Patti and another TM student.

## RECORDED
September 18, 1968, at Abbey Road   *Abbey* and *Day* and *Road* and *Diary*

CHRIS THOMAS, producer of the session: ". . . Paul was the first one in, and he was playing the 'Birthday' riff. Eventually the others arrived, by which time Paul had literally written the song, right there in the studio."   *Abbey*

Harrison wore a glove during the session to avoid getting more blisters.   *Road*

During a break in the session, the Beatles watched *The Girl Can't Help It* on television at McCartney's house. The 1956 film starred Jayne Mansfield and featured performances by Fats Domino, the Platters, Gene Vincent, and Little Richard.  *Diary*

**INSTRUMENTATION**

McCARTNEY: piano, lead vocal
LENNON: lead guitar, backing and occasional lead vocal
HARRISON: bass, tambourine

STARR: drums
Chorus singers include Yoko Ono and Patti Harrison

*Record* (but also says Harrison played lead guitar); *Road* agrees on double lead vocal, Harrison's tambourine, McCartney's piano, Yoko Ono and Patti Harrison in chorus but says Starr and Mal Evans provided hand-claps; *ATN* omits Lennon's vocal and any clapping; *A-Z* agrees on Yoko Ono and Patti Harrison; *Day* and *Diary* add Linda Eastman to chorus.

McCartney's piano was an upright that was prepared to sound like an electric harpsichord.  *Road*

**COMMENTS BY BEATLES**

LENNON: "It was a piece of garbage."    September 1980, *Playboy Interviews*

●

# "YER BLUES"

**AUTHORSHIP** Lennon (1.00)
LENNON: " 'Yer Blues' was written in India . . . up there trying to reach God and feeling suicidal."    September 1980, *Playboy Interviews*

**RECORDED**

August 13, 1968, at Abbey Road, with overdubbing August 14 and an edit piece (the count-in) added August 20

*Abbey; Diary* and *Road* agree on August 13 start; *Day* says "John Lennon" recorded it on this date.

**INSTRUMENTATION**

McCARTNEY: bass
LENNON: lead guitar, vocal

HARRISON: lead guitar
STARR: drums

*Record; Road* says Starr provides "two-three" count-in.

**MISCELLANEOUS**

This was the only Beatles song performed by Lennon at the Toronto Rock 'n' Roll Revival Concert (in mid-September 1969).  *Diary*

This song was performed in the Rolling Stones' legendary unreleased *Rock 'n' Roll Circus* film, shot on December 11, 1968. A bootleg album included a nine-minute version of the song, performed by Lennon, Yoko, Eric Clapton, Keith Richards, and Mitch Mitchell (the drummer in the Jimi Hendrix Experience).

*Diary; Forever* supports list of musicians and that it was performed; *Day* says song was performed for the film.

Lennon did not want to appear to be taking himself too seriously, so he opted for the lighter "Yer," instead of "Your," in the title, against McCartney's advice.    December 1970, *Remembers*

●

# "MOTHER NATURE'S SON"

**AUTHORSHIP** McCartney (1.00)
This was written during the Beatles' Indian sojourn.    *Road*

LENNON: "Paul [wrote this]. That was from a lecture of Maharishi where he was talking about nature, and *I* had a piece called 'I'm Just a Child of Nature,' which turned into 'Jealous Guy' years later. Both inspired from the same lecture of Maharishi."    September 1980, *Playboy Interviews*

**RECORDED**
McCartney recorded this song August 9, 1968, at Abbey Road, after the other Beatles had gone home. More instrumentation was overdubbed August 20.    *Abbey; Road* and *Day* agree on the date and that other Beatles had gone; *Diary* agrees on date.

ALAN BROWN, technical engineer: "Paul wanted an open effect on his drums [to give a bongo sound] and we ended up leaving the studio itself and putting the drums in the corridor, halfway down, with mikes at the far end. It wasn't carpeted then, and it gave an interesting staccato effect."
*Abbey*

KEN SCOTT, engineer: "Paul was downstairs going through the arrangement with George [Martin] and the brass players. Everything was great, everyone was in great spirits. It felt really good. Suddenly, halfway through, John and Ringo walked in and you could cut the atmosphere with a knife. An instant change. It was like that for ten minutes and then as soon as they left it felt great again. It was *very* bizarre."    *Abbey*

## INSTRUMENTATION

McCARTNEY: acoustic guitar,            Session musicians: horns
bongos, tympani, vocal
(occasionally double-tracked)

*Record; Road* provides double-tracking; *Road* and *ATN* agree on McCartney's guitar and that session musicians played horns and that no other Beatles are heard on the recording; *Abbey* indicates drums were used, not bongos.

●

# "EVERYBODY'S GOT SOMETHING TO HIDE EXCEPT ME AND MY MONKEY"

## AUTHORSHIP Lennon (1.00)

LENNON: "[The title] was just sort of a nice line that I made into a song. It was about me and Yoko. Everybody seemed to be paranoid except for us two, who were in the glow of love." September 1980, *Playboy Interviews*

## RECORDED

Rehearsed with the tape running June 26, 1968, at Abbey Road, then recorded June 27, with overdubbing July 1 and 23

*Abbey; Road* says work began July 31; *Day* and *Diary* say recorded on July 23.

## INSTRUMENTATION

McCARTNEY: bass, backing vocal       HARRISON: rhythm guitar, firebell
LENNON: lead guitar, maracas, lead   STARR: drums
vocal

*Record; Road* says McCartney and Harrison sang backing vocals; *ATN* omits backing vocal.

## MISCELLANEOUS

This song has the longest title of any Beatles song. Capitol

Its original title was "Come On, Come On" from the first line of the lyric. *Road* and *Diary*

LENNON: "Fats Domino did a great version of this one." *Hit Parader* (April 1972)

●

# "SEXY SADIE"

**AUTHORSHIP** Lennon (1.00)

LENNON: "That was inspired by Maharishi. I wrote it when we had our bags packed and we were leaving. . . . I was leaving Maharishi with a bad taste."   September 1980, *Playboy Interviews*

Lennon's original lyric was more directly pointed at the Maharishi and actually named him but Lennon decided to be more subtle when he recorded the song.   *List* and *Record*

## RECORDED

July 19, 1968, at Abbey Road, but remade July 24, remade again August 13, and overdubbed August 21

*Abbey; Day* and *Diary* say it was recorded July 19; *Road* says work began July 19.

## INSTRUMENTATION

McCARTNEY: bass, piano, backing vocal

LENNON: rhythm guitar, acoustic guitar (Gibson), organ, lead and backing vocal

HARRISON: lead guitar (Gibson Les Paul), backing vocal

STARR: drums, tambourine

*Record; Road* provides Lennon's acoustic guitar, McCartney's and Harrison's backing vocals (but *harmony*), Harrison's electric guitar, and McCartney's piano; *ATN* omits harmony vocals and Harrison's guitar; Harrison's guitar from *Road* and *Guitar* (November 1987)

## COMMENTS BY OTHERS

This song is one of Julian Lennon's favorites.   Circa 1984, Coleman

●

# "HELTER SKELTER"

**AUTHORSHIP** McCartney (1.00)

McCARTNEY, referring to a Pete Townshend interview in *Melody Maker*: "He said the Who had made some track that was the loudest, the most raucous rock 'n' roll, the dirtiest thing they'd ever done. It made me think, 'Right. Got to do it.' I like that kind of geeking up. And we decided to do the loudest, nastiest, sweatiest rock number we could. That was 'Helter Skelter.' "

*Musician* (February 1985); *Road* says McCartney had read a review of a record which said that that group had gone wild, but when he heard it, it wasn't like that at all, so he decided to record a song as wild as that suggested by the review.

## RECORDED

The first version, recorded July 18, 1968, at Abbey Road, was about twenty-five minutes long. *Road* (but says twenty-four minutes); *Day* and *Diary* and *Abbey* agree on date; *Record* and *A-Z* say twenty-five minutes; Capitol (Lewisohn) says twenty-seven minutes. The album version was recorded September 9 with an overdub added September 10. *Abbey; Day* says other versions were recorded throughout August; *Day* and *Diary* say final version was recorded September 1; *Road* says second week of September. This was recorded on an eight-track machine that EMI had just installed. *Road*

BRIAN GIBSON, technical engineer: "The version on the album was out of control. They were completely out of their heads that night. But, as usual, a blind eye was turned to what the Beatles did in the studio. Everyone knew what substances they were taking, but they were really a law unto themselves in the studio." *Abbey*

## INSTRUMENTATION

McCARTNEY: bass, lead guitar, lead vocal

LENNON: bass, lead guitar, saxophone, backing vocal

HARRISON: rhythm guitar, backing vocal

STARR: drums

Mal Evans: trumpet

*Record; Road* agrees on McCartney's lead vocal, Lennon's bass and sax, and Evans's trumpet, but says all Beatles sang harmony vocals; *ATN* omits harmony and Lennon's bass; *Guitar* (November 1987) supports Lennon's bass.

## MISCELLANEOUS

At the end of the song, Ringo screams, "I got blisters on my fingers!" *Road* and *A-Z* and *Record* and *Abbey*

A mono version was included on the U.S. *Rarities* LP. The mix is different: On the mono version, McCartney's vocals are more prominent, beeping sounds are heard, laughter is heard at the beginning, the drumming is different at the end, and there is no fadeout or exclamation about blisters by Ringo. *Road*

Convicted murderer Charles Manson took the title as the name for the race war and apocalypse he believed was destined to happen when the Black Panthers would rise up and kill the white "piggies." Manson had his group commit the Tate and LaBianca murders to show blacks how to "rise." In England the term helter skelter applies to an amusement-park slide. *Helter Skelter; Record* says Lennon supported slide meaning later in court.

Lennon found Manson's interpretation of "Helter Skelter" absurd. Manson's zealous reading of lyric signs and symbols was typical of Beatle fans, but—also typical, Lennon said—he came up with a message that simply did not exist in the song. December 1970, *Remembers*

●

# "LONG, LONG, LONG"

**AUTHORSHIP** Harrison (1.00)

**RECORDED**
October 7, 1968, at Abbey Road, with overdubbing October 8 and 9
*Abbey; Day* and *Diary* say recorded October 8; *Road* says recording began October 8.

HARRISON: "There was a bottle of Blue Nun wine on top of the Leslie speaker during the recording, and when our Paul hit some organ note the Leslie started vibrating and the bottle rattling. You can hear it on the record —at the very end."    *I Me Mine;* Capitol supports.

**INSTRUMENTATION**

McCARTNEY: bass, piano, Hammond organ

LENNON: acoustic guitar

HARRISON: acoustic guitar, vocal (double-tracked)

STARR: drums

*Record,* but also says Lennon played piano, not McCartney; *Road* agrees on double-tracking, Harrison's acoustic, McCartney's Hammond organ and bass, Starr's drums; *ATN* mentions only organ, acoustic guitar, and vocals; *Day* and *Diary* say Starr wasn't at session; *Forever* and *Abbey* say Lennon did not participate.

**COMMENTS BY BEATLES**
HARRISON: "The 'you' in 'Long, Long, Long' is God. I can't recall much about it except the chords, which I think were coming from [Bob Dylan's] 'Sad Eyed Lady of the Lowlands'—D to E minor, A, and D—those three chords and the way they moved."    *I Me Mine*

●

# "REVOLUTION 1"

(*See:* "Revolution" single entry above and "Revolution 9" entry below)

●

# "HONEY PIE"

**AUTHORSHIP** McCartney (1.00)

**RECORDED**
October 1, 1968, with overdubbing October 2 and 4, at Trident Studios
*Abbey; Day* and *Diary* say recorded October 1; *Road* says recording began October 1 at Trident.

**INSTRUMENTATION**

McCARTNEY: piano, vocal

LENNON: lead guitar (Sunburst Epiphone Casino)

HARRISON: bass

STARR: drums

Fifteen session musicians: brass backing

*Record* (but just says dance band backing); *Road* provides brass backing and agrees on piano, lead guitar, bass, fifteen musicians in brass backing; *ATN* agrees on piano, lead guitar, bass; *Guitar* (November 1987) agrees on bass and names Lennon's guitar; *Day* says Starr was not at session; *Abbey* says Starr played drums.

The brass arrangement was scored by George Martin.  *Road*

HARRISON: "John played a brilliant solo on 'Honey Pie' . . . sounded like Django Reinhardt or something. It was one of them where you just close your eyes and happen to hit all the right notes—sounded like a little jazz solo."  *Guitar* (November 1987)

**COMMENTS BY BEATLES**
LENNON, when asked about "Honey Pie": (laughing) "I don't even want to think about that."  September 1980, *Playboy Interviews*

●

# "SAVOY TRUFFLE"

**AUTHORSHIP** Harrison (.9) and Derek Taylor (.1)
HARRISON: " 'Savoy Truffle' is a funny one written whilst hanging out with Eric Clapton in the '60s. At that time he had a lot of cavities in his teeth and needed dental work. He always had [a] toothache but he ate a lot of chocolates—he couldn't resist them and once he saw a box he *had* to eat them all.

"He was over at my house, and I had a box of 'Good News' chocolates on the table and wrote the song from the names inside the lid."

The box shows the names creme tangerine, montelimart (contrary to the printed lyrics, the box includes the "r"), ginger sling, pineapple treat (not "heart"), coffee dessert, savoy truffle. There was no cherry cream but a toffee and cherry cup, no apple tart, and no coconut fudge but a coconut and caramel.

"I got stuck with the two bridges for a while and Derek Taylor wrote some of the words in the middle—'You know that what you eat you are.'"

*I Me Mine*

## RECORDED
October 3, 1968, at Trident Studios, with overdubbing October 5, 11, and 14 *Abbey; Day* and *Diary* say it was recorded October 3; *Road* says recording began October 3.

## INSTRUMENTATION
McCARTNEY: bass
LENNON: lead guitar
HARRISON: lead guitar, organ, vocal (double-tracked)

STARR: drums, tambourine
Session musicians: two baritone saxes, four tenor saxes

*Record* (except it just says brass); *Road* provides double-tracking and number and kind of saxes, agrees with session musicians playing, but says Lennon and McCartney sang backing vocals; *ATN* mentions only Harrison's lead vocals; *Day* says Starr was not at session; *Forever* says Lennon was not at session; *Abbey* says there is no evidence of Lennon participating.

## MISCELLANEOUS
The "beefy horns" that became a trademark for some of Harrison's solo work were first heard on this recording. *Forever*

●

# "CRY BABY CRY"

**AUTHORSHIP** Lennon (1.00)
Original lyrics: "Cry baby cry, make your mother buy." Lennon said, in about 1968, that he got the words from an advertisement.

*Beatles; A-Z* supports and adds "TV" to advertisement.

## RECORDED
Rehearsed July 15, 1968, at Abbey Road, then recorded July 16, with over-dubbing July 18

*Abbey; Diary* and *Day* say it was recorded July 15; *Road* says recording began July 15.

## INSTRUMENTATION

McCARTNEY: bass

LENNON: acoustic guitar, piano, organ, vocal

HARRISON: lead guitar (Gibson Les Paul)

STARR: drums, tambourine

George Martin: harmonium

*Record; Road* agrees on Lennon's piano and organ, Harrison's guitar, and Martin's harmonium, but says McCartney and Harrison sang backing vocals on choruses; *ATN* omits backing vocals but agrees on Lennon's guitar; *Diary* agrees on Martin's harmonium; Harrison's guitar from *Guitar* (November 1987)

## COMMENTS BY BEATLES

LENNON: "A piece of rubbish."    September 1980, *Playboy Interviews*

●

# "REVOLUTION 9"

**AUTHORSHIP** Lennon (.75) and Yoko Ono (.25)

This is completely different from the "Revolution" single and "Revolution 1." In fact, it's not a song at all but a musical montage, created by Lennon and Yoko Ono with no help from the other Beatles A-Z other than sounds of them on tape loops.  *Record*

LENNON: "It was somewhat under [Yoko's] influence, I suppose. Once I heard her stuff—not just the screeching and the howling but her sort of word pieces and talking and breathing and all this strange stuff—I thought, 'my God,' I got intrigued, so I wanted to do one."

September 1980, *Playboy Interviews*

## RECORDED

May 30, 1968, at Abbey Road, with effects added on June 6, 10, 11, 20, and 21  *Abbey; Diary* and *Road* agree work began May 30.

LENNON: "The slow version of 'Revolution' on the album went on and on and on, and I took the fadeout part . . . and just layered all this stuff over it. It has the basic rhythm of the original 'Revolution' going on with some twenty [tape] loops we put on, things from the archives of EMI. We were cutting up classical music and making different-size loops, and then I got an engineer tape on which some test engineer was saying, 'number nine, number nine, number nine.' All those different bits of sound and noises are all compiled. There were about ten machines with people holding pencils on the loops—some only inches long and some a yard long. I fed them all in and mixed them live. I did a few mixes until I got one I liked. Yoko was there for the whole thing and she made decisions about which loops to use."    September 1980, *Playboy Interviews; Road* says thirty tape loops.

George Martin and Lennon recorded tape loops on a two-track recorder from a sports sound-effects record. The sound of banging water glasses came from the first version of "Revolution." They also had a monologue by Yoko that had been recorded on a cassette tape recorder. Lennon made one vocal track at the console, phrasing it as he did it. All of these noises were transformed to sixteen tracks and, as Lennon directed, Martin orchestrated the piece in three hours.    *Crawdaddy* (August 1975)

Some of the noises were produced during an evening Lennon spent with Pete Shotton in May 1968.

SHOTTON: "We shared a piece of LSD, smoked a few joints, and idly amused ourselves with John's network of Brunell tape recorders.... We opened the windows to the spring air, and were shouting out whatever came into our heads at the uncomprehending trees while the tapes rolled in the room behind us. I, for one, had no inkling that this particular evening's lark was destined to be captured for posterity ... as part of 'Revolution 9.' "

Later, near dawn, Lennon told Shotton that he was Jesus Christ. After getting some sleep, Lennon summoned the other Beatles and insiders to Apple and told them. They agreed they needed time to consider this proclamation. That night, Lennon and Yoko got together and made love for the first time.    Shotton

## INSTRUMENTATION

McCARTNEY: piano (at beginning)    HARRISON: voice
LENNON: voice    STARR: voice

*Record; Road* says no instruments and no singing; *ATN* says Starr, Harrison, and Martin participated with Lennon and Yoko in mixing, editing, and providing most voices.

## MISCELLANEOUS

According to Gregg Jakobson, a witness against murderer Charles Manson: Charlie "spoke mostly of 'Revolution 9.' " He said "it was the Beatles' way of telling people what was going to happen [during 'Helter Skelter,' the black/white apocalypse]; it was their way of making prophecy; it directly paralleled the Bible's Revelation 9."    *Helter Skelter*

The sounds of "Revolution 9" detailed the chaos of the actual battle, Manson believed. He took the coincidental similarity of the name "Revolution 9" to "Revelation 9" as highly significant.    *Forever*

LENNON: "I thought I was painting in sound a picture of revolution, but I made a mistake, you know. The mistake was that it was antirevolution." *Red Mole* (March 8-22, 1971) via *Companion*

▶ **JOHN'S "9" OBSESSION**

*Although Lennon found the "number nine" soundcheck tapes by chance, the number nine was thought by John to be important.*

*RAY COLEMAN, Lennon biographer: "John was acutely aware of the fact that the number nine had dominated his life. He was born on October 9, 1940. Sean was born on October 9, 1975. Brian Epstein first saw John and the Beatles at Liverpool's Cavern on November 9, 1961, and he secured their record contract with EMI in London on May 9, 1962. The debut record, 'Love Me Do,' was on Parlophone R4949.*

*"John met Yoko Ono on November 9, 1966. John and Yoko's apartment was located on West 72nd Street, New York City (seven plus two making nine), and their main Dakota apartment number was also, at first, 72. The bus he traveled on as a student each morning from his home to Liverpool Art College had been the 72. John's songs included 'Revolution 9,' '#9 Dream,' and 'One After 909,' which he had written at his mother's home at 9 Newcastle [nine letters] Road, Wavertree [nine letters], Liverpool [nine letters]."* Coleman

"PAUL IS DEAD" HYSTERIA: Throughout much of the piece, a voice repeats "number nine, number nine." Supposedly, if you play this segment backward, it becomes "turn me on, dead man." Lennon said the "turn me on, dead man" revelation was a coincidence. *Lists*

At 8:15 this is the longest track ever released by the Beatles. Capitol and *B-Lists*

This was voted the most unpopular Beatles track in a *Village Voice* poll. *Forever*

**COMMENTS BY BEATLES**
LENNON: "*This* is the music of the future. You can forget all the rest of the shit we've done—this is *it! Everybody* will be making this stuff one day—you don't even have to know how to play a musical instrument to do it!" Said shortly after recording it, Shotton

HARRISON: ". . . 'Revolution 9' wasn't particularly like a Beatles number . . . [but it] worked quite well in the context of all those different songs. . . . I find it heavy to listen to myself—in fact, I don't, really."    Late 1969, *Celebration*

The other Beatles and George Martin tried to keep this off the album. *Compleat* and *A-Z* and *Record*    McCartney particularly disliked it.    *Forever*

●

# "GOOD NIGHT"

**AUTHORSHIP** Lennon ( 1.00 )
LENNON: " 'Good Night' was written for Julian the way 'Beautiful Boy' was written for Sean, but given to Ringo and possibly overlush."
September 1980, *Playboy Interviews; A-Z* agrees that Lennon wrote this.

**RECORDED**
June 28, 1968, at Abbey Road, with overdubbing July 2; then remade completely July 22    *Abbey; Road* says recording began June 11; *Day* and *Diary* say July 1.

**INSTRUMENTATION**
STARR: vocal                              Choir: four boys, four girls
Session musicians: thirty-piece
orchestra, harp

*Record* (except just "choir"); *Road* provides choir specifics, agrees on thirty-piece orchestra and harp, and says no other Beatles perform; Capitol agrees on thirty-piece; *ATN* omits choir.

The orchestration was scored by George Martin.    *Road*

LENNON: "I just said to George Martin: 'Arrange it like Hollywood. Yeah, corny.' "    *Forever*

**MISCELLANEOUS**
The placement of this song on the album, immediately after the "Revolution 9" sound collage, is undoubtedly the most jarring juxtaposition on any Beatles album.

Early versions of the song included a spoken introduction by Starr: "Come along children, it's time to toddle off to bed . . ."    Capitol

●

# "DON'T LET ME DOWN"

**CHART ACTION**
UNITED KINGDOM: Released as a single April 11, 1969, as the B side of "Get Back." *Road*

UNITED STATES: Released as a single May 5, 1969. It entered the Top 40 May 10, and spent three weeks there, climbing to No. 35. *Road* and *Billboard*

**AUTHORSHIP** Lennon (1.00)

**RECORDED**
January 28, 1969, at Apple Studios

*Abbey; Day* says January 30; *Road* and *ATN* say late January; *Day* also says a version was recorded "by John" in fall 1968.

When first rehearsing this song January 22, Lennon asked Starr to crash his cymbals loudly to "give me the courage to come screaming in." *Abbey*

**INSTRUMENTATION**

McCARTNEY: bass, harmony vocal          HARRISON: rhythm guitar
LENNON: lead guitar, lead vocal         STARR: drums
(double-tracked)                        Billy Preston: organ

*Record; Road* provides double-tracking and agrees with McCartney's "backing vocal," but says Preston played electric piano; *ATN* omits instruments.

**MISCELLANEOUS**
Performed in the film *Let It Be.*
    Lennon dedicated this to Yoko. *A-Z*

▲ ▼ ▲

# LET IT BE
## ALBUM

○

The *Let It Be* project was the nadir of the Beatles' career. Disagreements that had surfaced during the lengthy recording sessions for the White Album now blossomed into full-fledged fights. The Beatles could barely agree on anything except that their next album would be produced without the unending number of overdubs that had adorned all their tracks for the preceding several years (hence the original name for the album, *Get Back*).

After recording take after take of each song, none of the Beatles had the desire to go through the tapes to select the best versions. So the task was passed on to producer Glyn Johns and later to producer Phil Spector, and the album finally appeared more than a year later as *Let It Be,* after the group's demise.

**CHART ACTION**
UNITED KINGDOM: Released May 8, 1970, more than fifteen months after it was recorded. In a week, the album was No. 3 on the album chart. It hit No. 1 by June 3 and stayed in that position for three weeks, fell to No. 2 for two weeks, rose to No. 1 for one week, fell to No. 3, and then recaptured the top spot for two more weeks.  *Road*

UNITED STATES: Released May 18, 1970. Advance orders were huge: 3.7 million, the largest in the history of the U.S. recording industry. The album reached No. 2 in early June and the following week was at No. 1, where it stayed for four weeks.  *Road*

There was a big fight over the release date of this album. McCartney was asked to postpone the release of his first solo album to avoid its competing with *Let It Be.* McCartney refused. Starr was sent over to sort everything out, because only he still had a fairly good relationship with Paul.

STARR: "To my dismay, he went completely out of control, shouting at me, prodding his fingers toward my face, saying, 'I'll finish you all now' and 'you'll pay.' He told me to put my coat on and get out."  *Core*

McCartney got his way. His album was issued first, in April.  *Forever*  And with its release, McCartney announced he was leaving the Beatles.

**RECORDED**
Intensive recording sessions were held January 2 to 30, 1969. Sessions through January 16 were at Twickenham Film Studios, from January 20 to 30 at Apple Studios, and on January 30 live on the Apple rooftop.  *Road*

Some material was recorded in January 1970.   *Road; Digital* (December 1985) supports.

Originally, the early January 1969 sessions were to be rehearsals for a live performance to be filmed and shown worldwide on television. The rehearsals would be filmed for a separate documentary.  *Road*

MARTIN: "Right from the beginning everything about *Let It Be* seemed to be out of sync with what we had done before. It was not at all a happy recording experience. It was a time when relations between the Beatles were at their lowest ebb.

"The idea for *Let It Be* was a brilliant one, and I think it was Paul's. The original idea was that we should record an album of new material and rehearse it, then perform it before a live audience for the very first time— on record and film. In other words make a live album of new material, which no one had ever done before! . . . The trouble was that it was winter in England and, to get the kind of audience that the Beatles required, you needed a vast auditorium. And we simply didn't have one to use. At one point, we were even talking about doing a concert in the Tunisian desert! . . ."

*Digital* (December 1985); Lennon quote in *Celebration* supports the recollection that it was McCartney's idea.

LENNON: "Someone mentioned the Colosseum in Rome, and I think originally Paul might have even suggested a bloody boat in the middle of the ocean. As for me, I was rapidly warming up to the idea of an asylum!"
*Celebration*

MARTIN: "The thing that John had insisted upon from the start was that he didn't want any of the old recording rubbish [overdubs]. . . . And so, they rehearsed and we just recorded. Endless hours of recording. But we never got anything really spot on, as good as it should be, in spite of take after take. . . . We'd get up to sixty-two takes of one track alone."
*Digital* (December 1985)

"In order to get things together, Paul would try to get everybody organized and would be rather over-bossy, which the other boys would dislike. But it was the only way of getting together. John would go wafting away with Yoko. George would say he wouldn't be coming in the following day. It was just a general disintegration—disenchantment if you like."
*Compleat*

Finally on January 10, Harrison announced that he opposed the plan for the album and left the studio.  *Road; Diary* agrees on date.

Shortly before the sessions began, Harrison had returned from the United States where he had played with various musicians in a relaxed, cooperative atmosphere.

HARRISON: "This cooperation contrasted dramatically with the superior attitude which for years Paul had shown toward me musically. In normal circumstances, I had not let this attitude bother me and, to get a peaceful life, I had always let him have his own way, even when this meant that songs which I had composed were not being recorded.

"When I came back from the United States ... I was in a very happy frame of mind, but I quickly discovered that I was up against the same old Paul. ... In front of the cameras, as we were actually being filmed, Paul started to 'get at' me about the way I was playing." *Core*

"... There's a scene [in the film] where Paul and I are having an argument ... and we're trying to cover it up. Then the next scene I'm not there, and Yoko's just screaming, doing her screeching number. Well, that's where I'd left, and I went home and wrote 'Wah-Wah.' It'd given me a wah-wah, like I had such a headache with that whole argument, it was such a headache. ... " *Crawdaddy* (February 1977)

"Wah-Wah"—"Wah-wah—you've given me a wah-wah"—later appeared on Harrison's *All Things Must Pass.*

HARRISON: "... It was just weird vibes. You know, I found I was starting to be able to enjoy being a musician, but the moment I got back with the Beatles, it was just too difficult. There were just too many limitations based upon our being together for so long. Everybody was sort of pigeonholed. It was frustrating." *Crawdaddy* (February 1977)

STARR: "In the end he was in the most difficult position, because John and Paul even wanted to write his solos. Paul was very definite about how he wanted his solos, and George was very frustrated." *Musician* (February 1982)

Harrison stayed away for three days. *A-Z* He felt that McCartney treated him as more of a musical equal after the fight. *Core*

Since the original project could not progress with Harrison gone, the four Beatles then agreed that the sessions should continue but be used for an album instead, without the heavy overdubbing of previous albums, and that they continue to be filmed. *Road*

HARRISON: "... I pulled in Billy Preston on *Let It Be*—it helped because the others would have to control themselves a bit more. John and Paul mainly, because they had to, you know, act more handsomely."
*Crawdaddy* (February 1977)

LENNON: "[Paul] had the mistaken impression that he was going to rehearse us. Of course by that time we'd been playing together for about twenty years or something, and we just couldn't get into it. So anyway, we laid down a few tracks, but nobody was really into it at all. It was just such a very, very dreadful feeling being there in Twickenham Studios at eight o'clock in the morning with some old geezer pointing a camera up your nose expecting you to make good music with colored lights flashing on and off in your face all the time. To me the whole thing ended up looking and sounding like a goddamn bootleg version of an 8mm home movie, so I didn't want to know about it. None of us did." *Celebration*

## INSTRUMENTATION
McCARTNEY: Hofner bass, Martin D-28 guitar
LENNON: Sunburst Epiphone Casino, Martin D-28 guitars

HARRISON: Gibson Les Paul, Gibson J-200 acoustic, rosewood Fender Telecaster guitars
STARR: drums

Guitars from *Guitar* (November 1987)

About ninety-six hours of film and thirty hours of music were accumulated during the sessions. The music included many old rock standards. *Road*

STARR: "We *did* get back to being a band again on *Let It Be*. We were playing live on top of this building and that's what was being recorded. But it was getting too late then [to keep the Beatles together]."
*Musician* (February 1982)

## ALBUM PACKAGE
The black, almost funereal design of the album sleeve was by John Kosh. *Road*

The album was originally released in the United Kingdom as a boxed set with a paperback book called *The Beatles Get Back* (the original title of the album) that included stills and unused dialogue from the film. *Road*

The photograph originally intended for the cover of the album was taken at the same location as the cover shot for the Beatles' first album, *Please Please Me*. The photo was later used for the *1962–1966* and *1967–1970* compilation albums. *Road*

McCARTNEY: "There was a little bit of hype on the back of the sleeve for the first time ever on a Beatles album. At the time the Beatles were very strained with each other and it wasn't a happy time. It said it was a new-phase Beatles album and there was nothing further from the truth. That was the last Beatles album [that would be released] and everybody knew it."
Coleman

## MISCELLANEOUS
An album from the sessions was scheduled to be released in August 1969 with the title of *The Beatles Get Back*. The song list: "One After 909"

(rooftop version), "Save the Last Dance for Me," "Don't Let Me Down" (different from the single version), "Dig a Pony," "I've Got a Feeling," "Get Back," "For You Blue," "Teddy Boy" (later recorded by McCartney for his *McCartney* album), "Two of Us on Our Way Home," "Maggie Mae," "Dig It" (unedited), "Let It Be," and "The Long and Winding Road." But the album's release was held back at the last minute to coincide with that of the film. Because of the delay, the Beatles went back into the studio and recorded *Abbey Road.* *Road*

Lennon initially wanted to release *Let It Be* as it was, without studio trickery, to show the world how the band was falling apart.

December 1970, *Remembers*

Later, Lennon and Harrison decided to let Phil Spector re-produce and remix the tapes from the sessions. Instead of showing the Beatles without any studio sweetening, as originally intended by the group, Spector added a female choir and an orchestra to four tracks: "Across the Universe," "I Me Mine," "Let It Be," and "The Long and Winding Road." *Road*

MARTIN: "I thought the orchestral work on it was totally uncharacteristic. We had established a particular style of music over the years—generally overlaid music on most Beatles tracks—and I felt that what Phil Spector had done was not only uncharacteristic, but wrong. . . . I was totally disappointed with what happened to *Let It Be.*" *Digital* (December 1985)

## COMMENTS BY BEATLES

McCARTNEY: ". . . The best version of [the *Let It Be* album] was before anyone got hold of it: Glyn Johns's early mixes were great but they were very spartan; it would be one of the hippest records going if they brought it out. But before it had all its raw edges off it, that was one of the best Beatles albums because it was a bit avant-garde. I loved it." *Musician* (October 1986)

LENNON: "It was hell making the film *Let It Be.* . . . It was the most miserable session on earth." *Own Words*

McCARTNEY: "*Let It Be* was very sticky." *RS* (September 11, 1986)

HARRISON: "I couldn't stand it! I decided, this is it! It's just not fun anymore; as a matter of fact, it's very unhappy being in this band at all." *Celebration*

●

# "TWO OF US"

**AUTHORSHIP** McCartney (1.00)
McCartney wrote this about himself and his wife, Linda.  Coleman

**RECORDED**
January 31, 1969, at Apple Studios, after rehearsals January 24 and 25
*Abbey; Road* says late January.

**INSTRUMENTATION**

McCARTNEY: acoustic guitar (Martin D-28), lead vocal
LENNON: acoustic guitar, lead vocal

HARRISON: lead guitar
STARR: drums

*Record; Road* agrees on McCartney's guitar and on lack of bass but says Lennon sang harmony vocal; *ATN* omits instrumentation; guitar from *Guitar* (November 1987).

No bass was played on this recording, but Harrison played low notes on his guitar.  *Road*

**MISCELLANEOUS**
This song is performed twice in the film *Let It Be.* The first version is improvised and ad-libbed by McCartney and Lennon and is slightly faster. The second is the version heard on the album.  *A-Z* and *Record*

The original title was "On Our Way Home" and the song was recorded by Mortimer under that title in May 1969. Mortimer was a New York City trio that briefly recorded for Apple in 1969. McCartney produced the recording but it was never issued.  *Record* (provides time) and *Road; A-Z* supports.

●

# "DIG A PONY"

**AUTHORSHIP** Lennon (1.00)
With the refrain—"All I want is you"—the song is apparently about Yoko. Coleman

It was written by Lennon as two separate songs: "All I Want Is You" and "Dig a Pony." In fact, when the original song listing for the *Get Back* album was released this song was called "All I Want Is You."  *Record*

## RECORDED
January 30, 1969, on the Apple Studios rooftop, after rehearsals January 22 and 28   *Abbey; Road* says January 20.

## INSTRUMENTATION
McCARTNEY: bass, harmony vocal      STARR: drums
LENNON: lead guitar, lead vocal      Billy Preston: organ
HARRISON: rhythm guitar

*Record; Road* agrees on McCartney's harmony but says Preston played electric piano; *ATN* mentions only Lennon's vocals.

## MISCELLANEOUS
Performed in the film *Let It Be* during the live rooftop sequence.   *Day*
    This song was listed on the U.S. album sleeve as "I Dig a Pony."   *Record*

## COMMENTS BY BEATLES
LENNON: "Another piece of garbage."   September 1980, *Playboy Interviews*

•

# "ACROSS THE UNIVERSE"

## AUTHORSHIP  Lennon (1.00)
LENNON: "I was lying next to me first wife in bed, you know, and I was irritated. She must have been going on and on about something and she'd gone to sleep and I'd kept hearing these words over and over, flowing like an endless stream. I went downstairs and it turned into sort of a cosmic song rather than an irritated song. . . . It *drove* me out of bed. I didn't want to write it, I was just slightly irritable and I went downstairs and I couldn't get to sleep until I put it on paper. . . ."   September 1980, *Playboy Interviews*

    Others remember its creation differently. Some sources say Lennon wrote the lyrics to this song when he awoke one morning in 1967 at about seven o'clock thinking "Pools of sorrow, waves of joy." He wrote them down and added another nine lines or so.

*Road;* Coleman agrees on lyric; Shotton provides 1967.

## RECORDED
February 4, 1968, at Abbey Road, with overdubbing February 8. This recording then lay unused for several months until, in different forms, it appeared on a charity album for the World Wildlife Fund (released December 1969) and *Let It Be.* For the charity album, the original recording was speeded up and wildlife sound effects were added during the mixing pro-

cess on October 2, 1969. For *Let It Be,* producer Phil Spector removed some sounds from the original tape, slowed it down, and overdubbed an orchestra and choir.

*Abbey; Day* and *Diary* agree on the dates February 4 and 8; *Road* agrees work began February 4.

Lennon and McCartney decided during the February 4 session that they wanted falsetto harmonics on the song. McCartney went out to the fans gathered outside the studio, talked to them and invited two in for a try.

*Road* and *Abbey*

LENNON: "The original track was a real piece of shit. I was singing out of tune and instead of getting a decent choir, we got fans from outside . . . Apple Scruffs or whatever you call them. They came in and were singing all off-key. Nobody was interested in doing the tune originally."   Coleman

## INSTRUMENTATION

McCARTNEY: piano
LENNON: acoustic guitar, lead guitar, organ, vocal
HARRISON: sitar
STARR: maracas

George Martin: organ (with Lennon)
Session musicians: strings and choir (overdubbed)
Lizzie Bravo and Gayleen Pease: falsetto background vocals (on "Nothing's going to change my world"—not used on *Let It Be)*

*Record; ATN* says Lennon played lead guitar, McCartney played piano, and Lennon and George Martin played organ, agrees on names of the two girls; *Road* agrees with lack of drums and with the orchestra and choir, but says the band was also backed by acoustic guitars; *Road* says the two versions are two completely different recordings; *Record* implies both versions are the same recording and agrees on orchestra and lack of drums.

## MISCELLANEOUS

The first version of this song was originally meant to be the A side of the March 1968 single, but "Lady Madonna" replaced it at the last minute. *Record* and *Record2* Work on it began one day after "Lady Madonna" was recorded.   *Road* and *Diary*

The version provided to the World Wildlife Fund appeared on *No One's Gonna Change Our World,* a charity album featuring recordings of several artists, as well as on both the U.K. and U.S. versions of *Rarities* and the *Past Masters, Volume 2* compact disc.   *Road* and author

This song was performed in the film *Let It Be.*

David Bowie later recorded this song for his *Young Americans* LP with Lennon's guitar accompaniment.   *A-Z;* Coleman says only that Lennon backed

## COMMENTS BY BEATLES

LENNON: "This was one of my favorite songs . . ."   *Own Words*

"One of my best songs. Not one of the best recordings, but I like the lyrics."   *Hit Parader* (April 1972)

LENNON: ". . . The Beatles didn't make a good record of it. I think subconsciously sometimes we—I say 'we,' though I think Paul did it more than the rest of us; Paul would . . . sort of subconsciously try and destroy a great song . . . meaning that we'd play experimental games with my great pieces, like 'Strawberry Fields'—which I always felt was badly recorded. That song got away with it and it worked. But usually we'd spend hours doing little detailed cleaning-ups of Paul's songs; when it came to mine, especially if it was a great song like 'Strawberry Fields' or 'Across the Universe,' somehow this atmosphere of looseness and casualness and experimentation would creep in."    September 1980, *Playboy Interviews*

LENNON: "Phil [Spector] slowed the tape down, added the strings. . . . He did a really special job."    Coleman

•

## "I ME MINE"

**AUTHORSHIP** Harrison ( 1.00 )
Harrison based the music on a song he saw performed by an Austrian marching band on TV.    *RS* (July 9, 1970)

**RECORDED**
January 3, 1970, at Abbey Road, without Lennon. An orchestra and choir were overdubbed by producer Phil Spector April 1.

*Abbey; Road* and *ATN* and *Compleat*(b) and *Record* agree on date.

**INSTRUMENTATION**
McCARTNEY: piano, harmony vocal
HARRISON: acoustic guitar, lead electric guitar, lead vocal
STARR: drums

Billy Preston: organ
Session musicians: strings (overdubbed)

*Record,* but says Lennon played lead guitar and sang harmony vocal, and that no electric guitar was used; *Road* agrees on McCartney's harmony vocal.

**MISCELLANEOUS**
In the film *Let It Be,* Harrison auditions the song to Starr, accompanying himself with an acoustic guitar. He refers to the song as a "heavy waltz." Three of the Beatles perform the song while Lennon waltzes with Yoko Ono.    *Let It Be*

A year later, when rough cuts of the film showed that this song's rehearsal scenes would be included, the Beatles had to go into the studio and make a proper recording.    *Abbey*

## COMMENTS BY BEATLES

HARRISON: " 'I Me Mine' is the ego problem. . . . [After experiencing LSD] I looked around and everything I could see was relative to my ego—you know, like 'that's *my* piece of paper' and 'that's *my* flannel,' or 'give it to *me*' or '*I* am.' It drove me crackers; I hated everything about my ego—it was a flash of everything false and impermanent which I disliked.

"But later I learned from it: to realize that there is somebody else in here apart from old blabbermouth (that's what I felt like—I hadn't seen or heard or done anything in my life, and yet I hadn't stopped talking). Who am 'I' became the order of the day.

"Anyway, that's what came out of it: 'I Me Mine.' . . . Allen Klein thought it was an Italian song—you know, 'Cara Mia Mine'—but it's about the ego, the eternal problem. . . ." *I Me Mine*

•

# "DIG IT"

**AUTHORSHIP** Lennon (.25), McCartney (.25), Harrison (.25), and Starr (.25) CD and LP listings and *Road*

## RECORDED

Rehearsed with the tapes rolling January 24, 1969, at Apple Studios, then remade January 26 *Abbey; Road* says late January.

## INSTRUMENTATION

McCARTNEY: piano
LENNON: vocal
HARRISON: lead guitar

STARR: drums
Billy Preston: organ

*Record; Road* agrees on McCartney's piano but says Lennon played bass and Harrison acoustic guitar; *ATN* lists only Lennon's vocal.

## MISCELLANEOUS

The litany of celebrated personalities and institutions in the song was improvised by Lennon in the studio, as was the musical backing. *A-Z*

Among those named by Lennon were: Matt Busby (Manchester United soccer club manager), bluesman B. B. King, and actress Doris Day. Also included were various acronyms—the FBI, CIA, BBC.

The actual performance ran about five minutes and was originally intended to appear on the album at that length, but it was edited down to fifty-one seconds for release. *Road;* Coleman says forty-eight seconds; CD counter says fifty.

Performed in the film *Let It Be.*

•

# "LET IT BE"

## CHART ACTION
UNITED KINGDOM: Also released as a single March 6, 1970. It reached No. 9 on the chart on March 11 and peaked at No. 3 the following week. *Road*

UNITED STATES: Also released as a single March 11, 1970. It entered the Top 40 March 21, held the top spot for two weeks, and spent thirteen weeks in the Top 40. Sales reached 1 million within a month and later grew to more than 1.5 million.   *Road* and *Billboard*

## AUTHORSHIP McCartney (1.00)
McCARTNEY, on whether his mother is invoked in the song: "Yeah. I had a lot of bad times in the '60s. We used to lie in bed and wonder what was going on and feel quite paranoid. Probably all the drugs. I had a dream one night about my mother. She died when I was fourteen so I hadn't really heard from her in quite a while, and it was very good. It gave me some strength."   *Musician* (October 1986); his brother affirms in *Macs;* Salewicz supports.

## RECORDED
Began January 25, 1969, at Apple Studios. The recording that provided both the single and album versions was made January 31 with more overdubs on April 30, and again on January 4, 1970, at the last Beatles recording session (Lennon was absent).   *Abbey; Road* and *ATN* and *Day* say only late January 1969.

## INSTRUMENTATION
SINGLE VERSION

McCARTNEY: lead vocal, piano
LENNON: bass, harmony vocal
HARRISON: lead guitar, harmony vocal

STARR: drums
Billy Preston: organ
Produced by George Martin

*Road; Record* agrees with Preston's organ and McCartney's piano but says Harrison played bass and Lennon lead guitar; *ATN* omits harmony.

ALBUM VERSION
Same as the single version, except Harrison's guitar is a Lesley, which sounds like an organ at times, and Preston doesn't play. Orchestral backing dubbed in. Produced by George Martin and Phil Spector.

*Road; ATN* retains Preston organ; *A-Z* says Lennon played lead guitar.

Harrison plays different guitar solos in the two versions. The solo overdubbed on April 30, 1969, was used for the single; the January 4, 1970, overdub was used for the album version.  *Abbey*

## MISCELLANEOUS
Performed in the film *Let It Be* with soulful singing by McCartney.

McCartney performed this song at the Concert for the People of Kampuchea (December 29, 1979) with the Rockestra, which included many rock luminaries.  *Kampuchea;* date from *B-Lists*

The song was rerecorded March 14, 1987, to benefit the families of victims of the ferry disaster off the coast of Zeebrugge, Belgium. The new recording featured Boy George, Kim Wilde, Bananarama, the Alarm, and McCartney's original vocal.  *RS* (December 1987)

●

# "MAGGIE MAE"

**AUTHORSHIP** (Public Domain)

## RECORDED
January 24, 1969, at Apple Studios. It was recorded spontaneously between takes of "Two of Us."  *Abbey; Road* says late January.

## INSTRUMENTATION
McCARTNEY: acoustic guitar, harmony vocal
LENNON: acoustic guitar, lead vocal

HARRISON: bass, harmony vocal
STARR: drums

*Record; Road* says Lennon and McCartney sang vocals; *ATN* says Lennon sang vocals.

## MISCELLANEOUS
The Beatles had been playing this traditional song since before they were the Beatles. It was among the earliest songs performed by the Quarrymen. That group played it at the famous Woolton fete, after which Lennon met McCartney, July 6, 1957.  *Coleman and Live*  The Beatles would often use it, and other songs, to warm up at the beginning of recording sessions.  *Record*

This was the first non-Beatles composition released by the group since "Bad Boy" on a U.K. album in 1966.  *Road*

●

# "I'VE GOT A FEELING"

**AUTHORSHIP** Lennon (.5) and McCartney (.5)
McCartney wrote the first part—"I've got a feeling. . . ." Lennon wrote the
second part—"Everybody had a . . ."  *Road*

**RECORDED**
January 30, 1969, on the Apple Studios rooftop, after rehearsals held on
January 22, 24, 27, and 28  *Abbey; Road* says late January.

**INSTRUMENTATION**

| | |
|---|---|
| McCARTNEY: bass, lead vocal | STARR: drums |
| LENNON: lead guitar, lead vocal | Billy Preston: organ |
| HARRISON: rhythm guitar | |

*Record; Road* and *ATN* agree on double lead vocal.

**MISCELLANEOUS**
Performed in the film *Let It Be* during the rooftop sequence.

●

# "ONE AFTER 909"

**AUTHORSHIP** Lennon (1.00)
LENNON: "One of the first songs I ever wrote."  *Own Words*
    This was written by Lennon at one of the songwriting sessions with
Paul at Paul's house while cutting school.

Coleman, but later contradicts by saying written at Lennon's mother's house; *Road* and Coleman say both
Lennon and McCartney wrote this in 1959.

**RECORDED**
January 30, 1969, on the Apple Studios rooftop, after rehearsals January 28
and 29  *Abbey; Road* says late January.

**INSTRUMENTATION**

| | |
|---|---|
| McCARTNEY: bass, lead vocal | STARR: drums |
| LENNON: lead guitar, lead vocal | Billy Preston: organ |
| HARRISON: rhythm guitar | |

*Record; Road* agrees with double vocals, but says Preston played electric piano; *ATN* omits Preston's
contribution.

**MISCELLANEOUS**
This song was part of the Beatles' repertoire for concerts from the late 1950s to 1962. *Live*

It was performed twice in the film *Let It Be:* once in the studio and again during the concluding rooftop sequence.

The Beatles recorded versions of this song early on, in 1962 and 1963. Bootlegs

●

# "THE LONG AND WINDING ROAD"

**CHART ACTION**
UNITED STATES: Also released as a single May 11, 1970, a week before the album was issued in the United States. It entered the Top 40 May 23, climbed to No. 1, where it stayed for two weeks, and stayed in the Top 40 for ten weeks. *Road; A-Z* says different versions were used on LP and for single.

**AUTHORSHIP** McCartney (1.00)
McCARTNEY: "John never had any input on 'The Long and Winding Road.' "
*Musician* (February 1988)

**RECORDED**
January 31, 1969, at Apple Studios, after rehearsals held January 26. A massive orchestral and choir overdub was added April 1, 1970.
*Abbey; Road* says it was recorded in late January.

The song was recorded "live" for a warm sound. But producer Phil Spector, who was given the tapes a year later by Lennon, overdubbed orchestration. *Transcriptions*

PETE BENNETT, chief of U.S. promotion for Apple Records: "I was in London with them and the funny part of it was we worked on that record for hours and hours, day and night, editing for four days. I mean, there was times I forgot to eat. But Patti Harrison, George's wife, used to come in with carrots and celery and bananas. . . . So what happened was Phil Spector and myself used to sneak away from the recording studio at Abbey Road and we said we didn't feel well and we used to go and eat like human beings!" *Beatlefan* (August-September 1988)

**INSTRUMENTATION**
McCARTNEY: piano, vocal          Session musicians: choir, strings,
LENNON: bass                            harp, drums (overdubbed)
*Record; Road* agrees on McCartney's piano and Lennon's bass, agrees on violins, brass, and harp, but says there were no drums; *ATN* agrees drums were overdubbed.

**MISCELLANEOUS**
Performed in the film *Let It Be*. The film also contains a joke version of the song in samba style.

This song was one of five Beatles songs performed during McCartney's Wings over America tour in 1976.

**COMMENTS BY BEATLES**
McCartney was extremely upset with Spector's extensive overdubbing on this. *Core* and Salewicz and others  McCartney attempted to get the original, un-Spectorized version on the album, but wasn't able to either because his request was denied by Allen Klein  Salewicz  or because he waited too long before asking, as Lennon later claimed. *Core* Losing this battle may have been the final straw for Paul. He told Lennon shortly afterward he was quitting the Beatles.  Salewicz

●

# "FOR YOU BLUE"

**CHART ACTION**
UNITED STATES: Also released as a single May 11, 1970. It did not make the Top 40. *Road*

**AUTHORSHIP** Harrison (1.00)
The song was inspired by Patti Harrison. *A-Z*

**RECORDED**
January 25, 1969, at Apple Studios  *Abbey; Road* says late January.

**INSTRUMENTATION**

| | |
|---|---|
| McCARTNEY: bass, piano | HARRISON: acoustic guitar, vocal |
| LENNON: steel guitar | STARR: drums |

*Record; Road* and *ATN* agree on Harrison's acoustic, Lennon's slide steel guitar, McCartney's piano, and Starr's drums; *Guitar* (November 1987) agrees on Lennon's "lap steel."

**MISCELLANEOUS**
Performed in the film *Let It Be*.

Harrison performed this song during his Dark Horse tour in 1974.
Coleman

**COMMENTS BY BEATLES**
HARRISON: " 'For You Blue' is a simple twelve-bar song following all the normal twelve-bar principles, except it's happy-go-lucky!"  *I Me Mine*

●

# "GET BACK"

## CHART ACTION
Two disc jockeys played a version of the song before it was released. Hearing it convinced the Beatles that more remixing was needed. The song was remixed April 7, 1969, for the final version.  *Day* and *Abbey*

UNITED KINGDOM: Released as a single April 11, 1969. It entered the chart at No. 3 April 23. A week later it was No. 1, where it stayed for five weeks. Sales topped 530,000 copies.  *Road*

UNITED STATES: Released as a single May 5, 1969. It entered the Top 40 May 10 and climbed to No. 1 for five weeks, totaling twelve weeks in the Top 40. The single sold more than 2 million copies.  *Road*

The single was also a No. 1 hit around the world, including in Malaysia, Singapore, Australia, New Zealand, Canada, West Germany, France, Spain, Norway, Denmark, Holland, and Belgium.

Worldwide sales were estimated to have exceeded 4.5 million.  *Road*

## AUTHORSHIP McCartney (1.00)
Written in the studio and recorded immediately thereafter.  *Road*

The song apparently began as an ad-libbed comment on immigration in the United Kingdom. A bootlegged version of the song exists with lyrics that sound like this:

*Siddiatawher was a Pakistani living in another land*
*Always heard it all around*
*Don't dig no Pakistanis taking all the people's jobs . . .*

Some people have pointed to this early version of "Get Back" as a sign that McCartney is a racist. The key line above, which sounds like "Always heard it all around," would determine whether these are McCartney's sentiments or a reflection of what others believe. Unfortunately, that line is slurred and hard to decipher and may actually be different words with a different meaning from that presented here.

But it's doubtful that McCartney meant to attack Pakistanis with these lyrics. Immigration was a hot issue in England in January 1969.

McCARTNEY: ". . . When we were doing *Let It Be,* there were a couple of verses to 'Get Back' which were actually not racist at all—they were *anti*-racist. There were a lot of stories in the newspapers then about Pakistanis crowding out flats—you know, living sixteen to a room or whatever. So in one of the verses of 'Get Back,' which we were making up on the set of *Let*

*It Be* [the film], one of the outtakes has something about 'too many Paki-stanis living in a council flat'—that's the line. Which to me was actually talking out *against* overcrowding for Pakistanis.... If there was any group that was not racist, it was the Beatles. I mean, all our favorite people were always black. We were kind of the first people to open international eyes, in a way, to Motown."    *RS* (September 11, 1986)

The Beatles made at least two public gestures against racism: They consented to perform on September 11, 1964, in Jacksonville, Alabama, only after the promoters agreed to admit nonwhites to the show, and on July 29, 1966, they refused to sign a contract for a series of concerts in South Africa.    *Diary*

## RECORDED
January 27 (album) and 28 (single), 1969, at Apple Studios, after rehearsals in early January at Twickenham Film Studios and January 23 at Apple
*Abbey; Road* agrees the versions are different.

Billy Preston claims he created the piano lick used at the beginning of the song.    *Compleat*

## INSTRUMENTATION
### SINGLE VERSION
McCARTNEY: bass, lead vocal          STARR: drums
LENNON: lead guitar                  Billy Preston: electric piano
HARRISON: rhythm guitar              Produced by George Martin

*Road; ATN* and *Record* agree, except they say Preston played organ, not electric piano; *Record* says Lennon sang harmony vocal.

### ALBUM VERSION
Same instrumentation as on single version. Produced by George Martin and Phil Spector.    *Road*

## MISCELLANEOUS
Preston was the first guest artist to be credited on a Beatles single. The disc's credit reads: "The Beatles with Billy Preston."    *Road*

Apple took out a full-page ad in the May 17, 1969, issue of *Rolling Stone* for the "Get Back"/"Don't Let Me Down" single. It was headed: THE BEATLES AS NATURE INTENDED.    *RS* (May 17, 1969)

The song was performed twice in the film *Let It Be.* One version included an additional, ad-libbed verse by McCartney.    *A-Z* It was also per-formed by McCartney and many rock luminaries in the *Prince's Trust* film of 1986.

At the end of the version on the album, McCartney says "Thanks, Mo," referring to Maureen Starkey, Ringo's wife, who was clapping loudly.    *Road*

## COMMENTS BY BEATLES

McCARTNEY: "We were sitting in the studio and we made it up out of thin air . . . we started to write words there and then. . . . When we finished it, we recorded it at Apple Studios and made it into a song to rollercoast by."
*Own Words* and used in *RS* (May 17, 1969) ad.

LENNON: "That's a better version of 'Lady Madonna.' You know, a potboiler rewrite. . . . I think there's some underlying thing about Yoko in there. . . . You know, 'Get back to where you once belonged': Every time he sang the line in the studio, he'd look at Yoko."    September 1980, *Playboy Interviews*

# "THE BALLAD OF JOHN AND YOKO"

**CHART ACTION**
UNITED KINGDOM: Released as a single May 30, 1969. It climbed to No. 1 in three weeks and stayed there for two weeks. *Road*

UNITED STATES: Released as a single June 4, 1969. It entered the Top 40 June 21, rose to No. 8, and stayed on the chart for a total of eight weeks. *Road* and *Billboard*

The single's chart success was restricted by being banned by the BBC and most U.S. radio stations for the crucifixion refrain, which begins, "Christ, you know it ain't easy ..." (The formula determining chart position in the United States includes airplay and requests to radio stations.) *Road* and *Record;* supported by *Love.*

The single was a No. 1 hit in Holland, West Germany, Denmark, Malaysia, Austria, Norway, Spain, and Belgium. *Road*

**AUTHORSHIP** Lennon (1.00)
The song was written within days after Lennon married Yoko Ono on March 20, 1969. He wrote it about his marriage and their subsequent trips to Paris and Amsterdam. *Road; Diary* says written on wedding day.

**RECORDED**
April 14, 1969, at Abbey Road, by Lennon and McCartney
*Abbey; Road* and *ATN* say April 22.

Despite the animosity that had built up between Lennon and McCartney by this time, they came together for this session in good spirits and with affection.

They concentrated first on the basic rhythm track, recording eleven takes with Lennon playing acoustic guitar and singing and McCartney playing drums. Before take four, John said to Paul, "Go a bit faster, Ringo!" and McCartney replied, "Okay, George." After deciding on the best take, the two then overdubbed all the other instruments. They worked together so efficiently that the session ended one hour earlier than scheduled. *Abbey*

**INSTRUMENTATION**
McCARTNEY: bass, drums, piano, maracas, harmony vocal

LENNON: acoustic guitar, lead guitar, lead vocal

*Record; Road* and *ATN* agree on Lennon's guitar, McCartney's harmony vocal, drums, piano, and the fact that Harrison and Starr were not present; *Shout* says they were out of the country and that McCartney overdubbed drumming later; *A-Z* agrees on McCartney's bass; *Abbey* agrees on all except that Lennon played two lead guitars and provided percussion.

In return for McCartney's recording help, Lennon gave him coauthorship credit for "'Give Peace a Chance," which McCartney had nothing to do with. *Record*

## MISCELLANEOUS
This was the Beatles' first single to appear in stereo. *Road* And it was the last song recorded specifically as a single by the Beatles. *A-Z*

A promotional film clip was produced. *A-Z*

During the song, Lennon can be heard calling hello to Apple official Peter Brown, who was also best man at his and Yoko's wedding.

*Lists;* Lennon agreed in December 1970 *(Remembers)* that he called hello to Brown.

●

# "OLD BROWN SHOE"

## CHART ACTION
UNITED KINGDOM: Released as a single May 30, 1969, as the B side to "The Ballad of John and Yoko." *Road*

UNITED STATES: Released as a single June 4, 1969. It failed to crack the Top 40. *Road*

## AUTHORSHIP Harrison (1.00)
HARRISON: "I started the chord sequences on the piano (which I don't really play) and then began writing ideas for the words from various opposites. . . . Again it's the duality of things—yes-no, up-down, left-right, right-wrong, etc." *I Me Mine*

## RECORDED
A demo was taped by Harrison February 25, 1969, at Abbey Road, and the song was recorded April 16 with overdubs added April 18.

*Abbey; Road* says April; *Day* says it was "recorded by George" in March.

## INSTRUMENTATION
McCARTNEY: bass, piano, backing vocal
LENNON: backing vocal

HARRISON: lead guitar, lead vocal
STARR: drums
Billy Preston: organ

*Record; Road* agrees with Harrison's vocal and says piano used; *ATN* agrees on Lennon's and McCartney's backing vocals.

# ABBEY ROAD
*ALBUM*

○

*Abbey Road* was the Beatles' grand finale. Even though the rough *Let It Be* was released after it, the group's last complete recording sessions were for this album.

The personality clashes that had begun flaring during the White Album sessions and had worsened during *Let It Be* were even more bitter. Apple was still losing money and the fight to regain control of their song publishing was going poorly (they would admit defeat about two weeks after this album was released). McCartney was becoming more isolated from the other three due to their resentment of his treating them as his backup musicians, and, more recently, because of his lonely effort to bring in his new in-laws as the group's management, instead of Allen Klein, whom he mistrusted.

On *Abbey Road,* however, these problems are not apparent. The album is the Beatles' most polished, and the band sounds very much together— there is more three-part harmony singing than on any other effort. But it was a carefully crafted illusion: All four Beatles were rarely in the studio at the same time. In fact, a basic compromise was reached that side A would be as Lennon wanted it and side B (the suite) would be for McCartney.

The Beatles essentially broke up shortly after the album was recorded. During a meeting at Apple Lennon told McCartney that he wanted a "divorce." It was kept a secret at the time because Klein, as their new manager, was in the midst of negotiating a better contract with Capitol Records. McCartney finally went public the following spring, saying that he was leaving the group.

## CHART ACTION
UNITED KINGDOM: Released September 26, 1969. One week later it was No. 1 on the chart and it remained there for eighteen weeks. It stayed on the chart for thirty-six weeks. *Road*

UNITED STATES: Released October 1, 1969. It entered the album chart at No. 178, jumped to No. 4 one week later, and the following week was No. 1, where it stayed for eleven weeks. It was in the Top 30 for thirty-one weeks. *Road*

Estimated world sales: by the end of November, 4 million. By the end of 1969, 5 million. By 1980, 10 million. *Road*

## RECORDED
February 22 through August 19, 1969, at Abbey Road, Trident, and Olympic Sound Studios. *Abbey; Road* says April through August; *ATN* says early June through mid-August.

Versions of some songs were rehearsed during the *Let It Be* sessions. After the bad feelings of *Let It Be,* producer George Martin had had enough.

MARTIN: "I was really surprised when after we had finished that album Paul came to me and said, 'Let's get back and record like we used to—would you produce an album like you used to?' 'Well, if you'd allow me to, I will.' And that's how we made *Abbey Road.* It wasn't quite like the old days because they were still working on their own songs. And they would bring in the other people to work as kind of musicians for them rather than being a team." *Compleat*

The album was recorded more quickly than any Beatles LP since 1965. *Forever*

Much of the recording was done with only two or three Beatles present at a time. *Beatles Monthly* via *Datebook* (March 1970) Part of this was due to Lennon's auto accident on July 1, 1969, soon after the heaviest schedule of recording sessions began. *Day*

McCARTNEY: "By the time we made *Abbey Road,* John and I were openly critical of each other's music, and I felt John wasn't much interested in performing anything he hadn't written himself." *Life* (April 16, 1971)

Usually present when their husbands were recording were Yoko Ono and Linda Eastman, who was pregnant. *Salewicz*

McCARTNEY: "On *Abbey Road* I was beginning to get too producery for everyone. George Martin was the actual producer, and I was beginning to be too definite. George [Harrison] and Ringo turned around and said: 'Look, piss off! We're grown-ups and we can do it without you fine.' For people like me who don't realize when they're being very overbearing, it comes as a great surprise to be told. So I completely clammed up and backed off— 'right, okay, they're right, I'm a turd.'

"So a day or so went by and the session started to flag a bit and eventually Ringo turned 'round to me and said: 'Come on . . . *produce!*' You couldn't have it both ways. You either had to have me doing what I did, which, let's face it, I hadn't done too bad, or I was going to back off and become paranoid myself, which was what happened." *Musician* (October 1986)

One night during the album's recording, McCartney called Abbey Road to say he wouldn't be coming to the studio because it was the anniversary of his meeting Linda and they wanted to spend a romantic evening together. This infuriated Lennon, who ran over to McCartney's house at 7 Cavendish Avenue, rushed in, yelled at him for inconveniencing the others, and smashed a painting he had done and given to Paul. *Salewicz* McCartney denied this happened. NBC's *Today Show* (September 8, 1988) via *Beatlefan* (November 1988)

STARR, on the lack of studio embellishments: "It's more important that we play good together than to have lots of violins play good together."   *Forever*

## INSTRUMENTATION

McCARTNEY: Hofner bass, Martin D-28 guitar
LENNON: Sunburst Epiphone Casino, Martin D-28 guitars

HARRISON: Gibson Les Paul, Gibson J-200 acoustic, rosewood Fender Telecaster guitars
STARR: drums

Guitars from *Guitar* (November 1987)

MARTIN: "The one-inch, four-track system lasted right through *Pepper* up until *Abbey Road.* We experimented with eight-track in one case on the White Album at another studio, but Abbey Road [studios] didn't have eight-track until *Abbey Road* itself. EMI always tended to be a bit behind independent commercial studios."   *Musician* (July 1987)

## ALBUM PACKAGE

The photograph for the cover was taken on Abbey Road at 10 a.m. on August 8, 1969.   *Day* and Capitol

ANTHONY FAWCETT, assistant to Lennon: "Everybody was laughing about the fact that Paul had arrived with no shoes, and even though his house was just around the corner he said he couldn't be bothered to go get any. [Photographer Iain] McMillan set up his camera in the middle of Abbey Road, right outside the studios, and while the police stopped traffic the Beatles walked across the road three or four times. He kept shouting: 'Stop! Start again,' until he was confident that he had the right shot.

"Happy with the front cover, McMillan asked me to drive with him along Abbey Road to look for the best street sign to photograph for the back cover. It had to be one of the old-style tiled signs set into the bricks. The best one was at the far end of Abbey Road, and we set up the camera on the edge of the pavement. McMillan decided to take a series of shots and was angry when, in the middle of them, a girl in a blue dress walked by, oblivious to what was happening. But this turned out to be the most interesting shot, and the Beatles chose it for the back cover. Afterward, I joined John and Yoko at Paul's house in St. John's Wood, where everybody had gone for tea after the photo session."   Fawcett

"PAUL IS DEAD" HYSTERIA: The cover was alleged to portray a funeral procession, with Paul—because he's a corpse—out of step with the other Beatles. John was reputed to be the priest, Ringo the mortician, and George the gravedigger, because of their clothes. Paul also has no shoes on, which is the way the dead are buried in some societies. The impersonator pictured on the cover can't be Paul because he's holding his cigarette in his *right* hand; the real Paul is left-handed, of course. Also the Volkswagen's license plate reads "28IF," supposedly Paul's age if he had lived. (However, he was only twenty-seven when the album was released.)

McCARTNEY: "That Volkswagen has just recently been sold for a fortune. But it meant *nothing,* you know." *Musician* (February 1988)

The VW sold for £2,300 at a Sotheby's auction in 1986. *Abbey*

McCARTNEY: "It was a hot day in London, a really nice hot day.... Barefoot, nice warm day, I didn't feel like wearing shoes. So I went around to the photo session and showed me bare feet.... Turns out to be some old Mafia sign of death or something." Late 1973, *RS* (January 31, 1974)

## MISCELLANEOUS
Several songs on *Abbey Road* included bits from other compositions. Part of "Come Together" came from Chuck Berry, the lyrics of "Golden Slumbers" came from a four-hundred-year-old poem, and "Something" apparently got its crucial first line of lyric from a James Taylor song. *(See separate song entries.)*

McCARTNEY: ". . . We were the biggest nickers in town. Plagiarists extraordinaires." *Playboy* (December 1984)

HARRISON: "I used to have an experience when I was a kid which used to frighten me. I realized in meditation that I had the same experience, and it's something to do with always feeling really tiny.... I used to get that experience a lot when we were doing *Abbey Road,* recording. I'd go into this big empty studio and get into a soundbox inside of it and do my meditation inside of there, and I had a couple of indications of that same experience, which I realized was what I had when I was a kid." *Crawdaddy* (February 1977)

## COMMENTS BY BEATLES
McCARTNEY, on the medley on the album: "We did it this way because both John and I had a number of songs which were great as they were but which we'd never finished." *Own Words*

STARR: ". . . I love the second side of *Abbey Road,* where it's all connected and disconnected. No one wanted to finish those songs, so we put them all together and it worked. I think that piece of that album is some of our finest work." *Big Beat*

LENNON: "I liked the A side, but I never liked that sort of pop opera on the other side. I think it's just junk because it was just bits of songs thrown together." *Own Words*

LENNON: "It was a competent album, like *Rubber Soul.* It was together in that way, but *Abbey Road* had no life in it." *Own Words*

## COMMENTS BY OTHERS
George Martin considers this his favorite Beatles album. *Musician* (July 1987)

●

# "COME TOGETHER"

## CHART ACTION
UNITED KINGDOM: Also released as a single October 31, 1969, as the "second A side" to "Something." *Road*

UNITED STATES: Also released as a single October 6, 1969. It entered the Top 40 October 18, rose to No. 1, and stayed on the chart for sixteen weeks. *Road* and *Billboard*

## AUTHORSHIP Lennon (1.00)
Written after Lennon's car accident on July 1, 1969. *Road*

LENNON: " 'Come Together' is *me*—writing obscurely around an old Chuck Berry thing. I left the line in 'Here comes old flat-top.' It is *nothing* like the Chuck Berry song, but they took me to court because I admitted the influence once years ago. I could have changed it to 'Here comes old iron face,' but the song remains independent of Chuck Berry or anybody else on earth." September 1980, *Playboy Interviews*

Lennon was sued on grounds that he stole the opening melody and first two lines of the lyrics from Chuck Berry's "You Can't Catch Me." Several sources; *Forever* says most of the melody used. Lennon settled—while denying copying the song *Ballad* —in October 1973 by agreeing to record three songs published by Big Seven Music. *Love* They turned out to be Berry's "You Can't Catch Me" and "Sweet Little Sixteen," both on Lennon's *Rock 'n' Roll* album in 1975, and "Ya Ya," by Lee Dorsey and Morris Levy, on his *Walls and Bridges* album in 1974.

LENNON: "The thing was created in the studio. It's gobbledygook. 'Come Together' was an expression that Tim Leary had come up with for [possibly running for the governorship of California against Ronald Reagan], and he asked me to write a campaign song. I tried and I tried, but I couldn't come up with one. But I came up with *this*, 'Come Together,' which would've been no good to him—you couldn't have a campaign song like *that*, right?"

September 1980, *Playboy Interviews; Record* supports Leary connection but says idea for a campaign song was dropped only when Leary decided not to run.

## RECORDED

July 21, 1969, at Abbey Road, as Lennon resumed a regular recording schedule following recuperation from his auto accident. Overdubs were added July 22, 23, 25, 29, and 30.

*Abbey; Day* and *Diary* and *Road* agree that work began July 21.

Each exclamation of "shoot" one hears Lennon singing is actually "shoot me!" followed immediately by a handclap. *Abbey*

GEOFF EMERICK, engineer: "On the finished record you can really only hear the word 'shoot!' The bass guitar note falls where the 'me' is." *Abbey*

## INSTRUMENTATION

McCARTNEY: bass, harmony vocal     HARRISON: lead guitar
LENNON: lead guitar, electric     STARR: drums, maracas
piano, lead vocal

*Record; Road* agrees on vocals; *ATN* omits backing vocal; in *Playboy* (December 1984) McCartney said he played piano.

McCARTNEY: ". . . Whenever [John] did praise any of us, it was great praise, indeed, because he didn't dish it out much. If ever you got a speck of it, a crumb of it, you were quite grateful. With 'Come Together,' for instance, he wanted a piano lick to be very swampy and smoky, and I played it that way and he liked that a lot. I was quite pleased with that."

*Playboy* (December 1984)

## MISCELLANEOUS

This song was banned by the BBC because of the reference to Coca-Cola, which it deemed to be advertising. *Record*

## COMMENTS BY BEATLES

LENNON: "It was a funky record—it's one of my favorite Beatle tracks."

September 1980, *Playboy Interviews*

●

# "SOMETHING"

## CHART ACTION
UNITED KINGDOM: Also released as a single October 31, 1969. It, and its flip side, "Come Together," were the first British single tracks by the Beatles to be taken from an album that had already been released. The single entered the Top 30 at No. 17, the lowest entry position since "Love Me Do." It charted in the Top 10 for four weeks and the Top 30 for nine weeks. *Road*

UNITED STATES: Also released as a single October 6, 1969. It entered the Top 40 October 18, 1969, climbed to No. 3, and remained on the chart for sixteen weeks.  *Road* and *Billboard*

This was the only Harrison song released as an A side of a Beatles single.  *Road*

HARRISON: "They blessed me with a couple of B sides in the past. But this is the first time I've had an A side. Big deal!"  *Forever*

LENNON: " 'Something' was the first time he ever got an A side, because Paul and I always wrote both sides anyway. . . . Not because we were keeping him out, 'cause, simply, his material wasn't up to scratch."
September 1980, *Playboy Interviews*

"The song was released as a single at the insistence of Allen Klein to bring in some immediate cash," according to Lennon biographer Ray Coleman. The Beatles were losing a lot of money at Apple Records. This was the first time a Beatles single had been issued for the explicit and sole purpose of making money.  Coleman

## AUTHORSHIP Harrison (1.00)
HARRISON: " 'Something' was written on the piano while we were making the White Album. I had a break while Paul was doing some overdubbing so I went into an empty studio and began to write. That's really all there is to it, except the middle took some time to sort out! It didn't go on the White Album because we'd already finished all the tracks. I gave it to Joe Cocker a year before I did it."  *I Me Mine*

The song was inspired by Patti Harrison. She appeared with George and the other Beatles couples in a promo film clip for this song.  *A-Z*

Harrison apparently took the first line of the song from a composition by James Taylor called "Something in the Way She Moves" on Taylor's first LP. Taylor was an Apple recording artist at the time.  *A-Z* and *Forever*

## RECORDED

A demo was taped by Harrison February 25, 1969, at Abbey Road. The Beatles recorded it April 16. It was then remade May 2 with overdubbing May 5, July 11 and 16, and August 15.

*Abbey; Road* says it was originally recorded during January and February at Apple and remade May 2 with an orchestra. Harrison added his vocal July 12, and McCartney and Starr added their vocals and handclaps several days later; *Diary* agrees on the dates May 2 and July 12.

## INSTRUMENTATION

McCARTNEY: bass, handclaps, backing vocal

LENNON: lead guitar

HARRISON: lead guitar, organ, vocal (occasionally double-tracked)

STARR: drums, handclaps, backing vocal

Session musicians: strings

*Record,* except *Road* provides double-tracking information and McCartney's and Starr's backing vocals and handclaps.

## MISCELLANEOUS

"Something" is second only to "Yesterday" in the number of cover versions recorded.  *Forever*

HARRISON: "It's probably got a range of five notes which fits most singers' needs best. This I suppose is my most successful song with over 150 cover versions. My favorite version is the one by James Brown—that was excellent. When I wrote it, in my mind I heard Ray Charles singing it, and he did do it some years later. I like Smokey Robinson's version too."  *I Me Mine*

Harrison performed the song during his Dark Horse tour in late 1974. *Forever* and Coleman

This song, recorded by someone else, was used in a TV commercial to sell Chrysler LeBaron Coupes in late 1987 and early 1988.
Washington *Post* (November 26, 1987) supports.

McCARTNEY: "The other day I saw 'Something' . . . in a car ad, and I thought, 'Ewww, yuck! That's in bad taste.'"  *Musician* (February 1988)

## COMMENTS BY BEATLES

HARRISON: " 'Something' is a very nice song, I think. It's probably the nicest melody line I've ever written."  Late 1969, *Celebration*

Shortly after the album's release, Lennon said "Something" was the LP's best song.  *Forever*

**COMMENTS BY OTHERS**
FRANK SINATRA: ". . . The greatest love song of the past fifty years."  *Forever*

●

# "MAXWELL'S SILVER HAMMER"

**AUTHORSHIP** McCartney (1.00)
Written in mid-1968.  *Day*

McCARTNEY: "This epitomizes the downfalls in life. Just when everything is going smoothly, 'bang bang' down comes Maxwell's silver hammer and ruins everything."  *Own Words*
   According to McCartney, the term "pataphysical" (as in "He studied pataphysical") came from a Parisian club called the Pataphysical Society, which was actually a drinking club. ". . . But to be a professor of pataphysics sounds great."  *Musician* (February 1988)

**RECORDED**
The song was rehearsed during sessions for the *Let It Be* album in January 1969.  *Day*  At the session, McCartney referred to the song as "the corny one."  *Let It Be*  Recorded July 9, 1969, at Abbey Road, with overdubbing July 10 and 11 and August 6

*Abbey; Day* agrees with the dates July 9 and July 11; *Diary* says several versions were recorded July 9 to 11.

The July 9 session was the first for Lennon after his car crash.

PHIL McDONALD, balance engineer: "We were all waiting for him and Yoko to arrive. Paul, George, Ringo downstairs and us upstairs. They didn't know what state he would be in. There was a definite 'vibe'; they were almost afraid of Lennon before he arrived, because they didn't know what he would be like. I got the feeling that the three of them were a little bit scared of him. When he did come in it was a relief, and they got together fairly well."  *Abbey*

**INSTRUMENTATION**
JULY 9 SESSION
McCARTNEY: lead vocal, guitar,          STARR: anvil
piano
HARRISON: four-string guitar

JULY 11 SESSION
McCARTNEY: backing vocals
HARRISON: acoustic guitar, backing vocals

STARR: backing vocals
George Martin: organ

FINAL VERSION
McCARTNEY: bass, piano, lead and backing vocal
LENNON: lead guitar, harmony vocal

HARRISON: acoustic guitar, Moog synthesizer
STARR: drums, anvil

*Record; Road* and *Guitar* (November 1987) agree on Moog synthesizer being used; *Day* says Lennon was not at sessions.

## MISCELLANEOUS
Originally intended for the White Album but not recorded.   *Diary*

## COMMENTS BY BEATLES
LENNON: "The Beatles can go on appealing to a wide audience as long as they make . . . nice little folk songs like 'Maxwell's Silver Hammer' for the grannies to dig."   Shortly after release, *Forever*

HARRISON: " 'Maxwell's Silver Hammer' is just something of Paul's which we've been trying to record for ages. We spent a hell of a lot of time on it, and it's one of those instant, whistle-along tunes which some people hate and other people really like. It's quite like 'Honey Pie,' I suppose, a fun song, but it's pretty sick because Maxwell keeps on killing everyone."
Late 1969, *Celebration*

HARRISON: "Sometimes Paul would make us do these really fruity songs. I mean, my God, 'Maxwell's Silver Hammer' was so fruity. After a while we did a good job on it, but when Paul got an idea or an arrangement in his head. . . ."   *Crawdaddy* (February 1977)

LENNON: "I hate it. 'Cuz all I remember is the track—he made us do it a hundred million times. He did *everything* to make it into a single and it never was and it never could've been."   September 1980, *Playboy Interviews*

McCARTNEY: "So then we were doing *Abbey Road* and I got some grief on that because it took three days to do 'Maxwell's Silver Hammer.' You know how long Trevor Horn takes to do a mix for Frankie [Goes to Hollywood]? It takes two days to switch on the Fairlight [synthesizer]! I had a group in the other day, spent two days trying to find the ON switch!"
*Musician* (October 1986)

●

# "OH! DARLING"

**AUTHORSHIP** McCartney (1.00)

**RECORDED**
Rehearsed January 27, 1969, at Apple Studios, it was recorded April 20 at Abbey Road, with overdubbing April 26, July 23, and August 8 and 11.

*Abbey; Road* says it was recorded in July and completed July 18; *Diary* says it was recorded July 18.

McCARTNEY: "When we were recording this track, I came into the studios early every day for a week to sing it by myself because at first my voice was too clear. I wanted it to sound as though I'd been performing it on stage all week."    *Own Words; Record* supports.

ALAN PARSONS, second engineer: "He'd come in, sing it, and say, 'No, that's not it, I'll try it again tomorrow.' He only tried it once per day, I suppose he wanted to capture a certain rawness which could only be done once before the voice changed. I remember him saying, 'Five years ago I could have done this in a flash,' referring, I suppose, to the days of 'Long Tall Sally' and 'Kansas City.' "    *Abbey*

**INSTRUMENTATION**

McCARTNEY: bass, piano, lead and backing vocal
LENNON: backing vocal

HARRISON: lead guitar, synthesizer
STARR: drums

*Record; Road* says Lennon and Harrison shared harmony vocals; *Day* and *Diary* say Lennon was not at the session.

**MISCELLANEOUS**
An early version of this song was performed in the film *Let It Be.*

**COMMENTS BY BEATLES**
HARRISON: " 'Oh! Darling' is another of Paul's songs, which is a typical 1950-'60s-period song because of its chord structure.... This is really just Paul singing by himself. We do a few things in the background which you can barely hear, but it's mainly just Paul shouting."    Late 1969, *Celebration*

LENNON: " 'Oh! Darling' was a great one of Paul's that he didn't sing too well. I always thought that I could've done it better—it was more my style than his."    September 1980, *Playboy Interviews*

●

# "OCTOPUS'S GARDEN"

**AUTHORSHIP** Starr (1.00)

After Starr walked out on the Beatles during the White Album sessions, he took his family to Sardinia. A friend lent him a boat, and the captain served octopus for lunch. Ringo refused to eat it but got to talking with the captain. STARR: "He told me all about octopuses, how they go 'round the sea bed and pick up stones and shiny objects and build gardens. I thought, 'How fabulous!' 'cause at the time I just wanted to be under the sea, too. I wanted to get out of it for a while." *RS* (April 30, 1981)

Starr and Harrison worked on the song together during the *Let It Be* sessions in January 1969. In the film of the same name, there's a scene of them working on it at a piano. *Let It Be*

**RECORDED**

April 26, 1969, at Abbey Road, with overdubbing April 29 and July 17 and 18 *Abbey; Road* agrees on the dates April 26 and July 17; *Day* says April; *Diary* says July 17.

**INSTRUMENTATION**

McCARTNEY: bass, piano, backing vocal

LENNON: lead guitar, backing vocal

HARRISON: lead guitar, synthesizer

STARR: drums, lead vocal

*Record; Road* agrees on McCartney's piano, Harrison's guitar, and Lennon's guitar but says Harrison provided backing vocal.

Starr created the water sounds by blowing bubbles in a glass of water. The backing vocals halfway through the song were altered by special amplifiers, to provide an underwater effect. *Road*

**COMMENTS BY BEATLES**

HARRISON: " 'Octopus's Garden' is Ringo's song. It's only the second song Ringo has written, mind you, and it's lovely. Ringo gets bored with just playing drums all the time, so at home he sometimes plays a bit of piano, but unfortunately he only knows about three chords. He knows about the same on guitar, too. This song gets very deep into your consciousness, though, because it's so peaceful. I suppose Ringo is writing cosmic songs these days without even noticing it." Late 1969, *Celebration*

Harrison specifically praised the phrase "warm below the storm." *Forever*

●

# "I WANT YOU (SHE'S SO HEAVY)"

**AUTHORSHIP** Lennon (1.00)

LENNON: "On *24 Hours* [a BBC-TV program] they just sardonically read the 'I Want You' lyrics: 'I want you. She's so heavy.' That's all it says, but to me that's a damn sight better than 'Walrus' or 'Eleanor Rigby' lyric-wise because it's a progression to me. If I want to write songs with no words or one word, then maybe that's Yoko's influence...."   *Own Words*

## RECORDED

Rehearsed with the tapes running January 29, 1969, at Apple Studios. Recorded February 22, at Trident, as the first *Abbey Road* song seriously committed to tape. Overdubbing was added April 18 and 20 and August 8 and 11, at Abbey Road. It was the final song to be mixed for the album, on August 20, the last time all four Beatles were in the studio together.

*Abbey; Day* says it was recorded in mid-July.

Guitars were overdubbed during the April 18 session.

JEFF JARRATT, engineer: "John and George went into the far left-hand corner of number two [studio] to overdub those guitars. They wanted a *massive* sound so they kept tracking and tracking, over and over."   *Abbey*

## INSTRUMENTATION

McCARTNEY: bass, harmony vocal
LENNON: lead guitar, organ, lead vocal

HARRISON: rhythm guitar, synthesizer, white-noise maker (at end)
STARR: drums

*Record; Road* agrees on Lennon's lead guitar and McCartney's vocal but says that Harrison sang backing vocal, there was an unidentified organ player, and various tape loops were used near the end.

## MISCELLANEOUS

This song is probably the closest the Beatles ever came to what is now known as "heavy metal."   *Forever*

This is the longest Beatles *song* at 7:49, although the "Revolution 9" track is longer.   *B-Lists* and record label

## COMMENTS BY BEATLES

HARRISON: "... It *is* very heavy. John plays lead guitar and sings, and it's just basically an old blues riff he's doing, but again, it's a very original John-type song as well.... It's a very good chord sequence he used on this particular one."   Late 1969, *Celebration*

●

# "HERE COMES THE SUN"

**AUTHORSHIP** Harrison (1.00)
HARRISON: "[This] was written at the time [early 1969] when Apple was getting like school, where we had to go and be businessmen, all this signing accounts, and 'sign this' and 'sign that.' Anyway, it seems as if winter in England goes on forever; by the time spring comes you really deserve it. So one day I decided—I'm going to 'sag off' Apple—and I went over to Eric [Clapton]'s house. I was walking in his garden. The relief of not having to go and see all those dopey accountants was wonderful, and I was walking around the garden with one of Eric's acoustic guitars and wrote 'Here Comes the Sun.'" *I Me Mine; Celebration* and *Forever* support.

## RECORDED
July 7, 1969, at Abbey Road, with overdubbing added July 8 and 16 and August 6, 11, 15, and 19

*Abbey; Diary* says work began July 24 on this and "Sun King" as one combined song; *Day* says work began July 24; *Road* says work began in early July.

    Lennon was absent during the original recording session but participated in the overdubbing. *Road*

## INSTRUMENTATION
McCARTNEY: bass, harmony vocal, handclaps
LENNON: acoustic guitar, harmony vocal, handclaps

HARRISON: acoustic guitar, Moog synthesizer, lead vocal, handclaps
STARR: drums, handclaps
Session musicians: strings

*Record* (but says *backing* vocals); *Road* provides Moog for synthesizer, and handclaps, says the vocals are harmony, and agrees on Harrison's acoustic; *Guitar* (November 1987) agrees on use of Moog; *Transcriptions* agrees on Harrison's, McCartney's, and Starr's instruments but says only Lennon was singing backing vocals and clapping.

●

# "BECAUSE"

**AUTHORSHIP** Lennon (1.00)
LENNON: "I was lying on the sofa in our house, listening to Yoko play Beethoven's 'Moonlight Sonata' on the piano. Suddenly, I said, 'Can you play those chords backward?' She did, and I wrote 'Because' around them. The song sounds like 'Moonlight Sonata,' too. The lyrics are clear, no bullshit, no imagery, no obscure references." September 1980, *Playboy* (January 1981)

## RECORDED

August 1, 1969, at Abbey Road, with overdubbing August 4 and 5   *Abbey; Day*
says it was recorded in mid-July.

The intricate harmony singing was thoroughly rehearsed before recording began.   *Road*

MARTIN: "Having done the backing track, John, Paul, and George sang the song in harmony. Then we overlaid it twice more, making nine-part harmony altogether, three voices recorded three times."   *Abbey*

## INSTRUMENTATION

McCARTNEY: bass, harmony lead vocal

LENNON: lead guitar, harpsichord, harmony lead vocal

HARRISON: Moog synthesizer, harmony lead vocal

*Record* (except for Harrison's vocal); *Road* and *ATN* say all three sing harmony lead vocals; in *Celebration* Harrison says he sang; *Road* provides Moog for synthesizer.

The first Moog overdubs on a Beatles recording were made on this song, August 5.   *Abbey*

## MISCELLANEOUS

A piece of this music was first heard on John and Yoko's *Wedding Album.*
*A-Z.*

## COMMENTS BY BEATLES

LENNON: "This is a terrible arrangement, a bit like Beethoven's Fifth backwards."   *Hit Parader* (April 1972)

McCartney and Harrison said this was their favorite song on the album. *Forever*   Harrison thought this contained the best Beatles harmonies ever. *A-Z*

HARRISON: ". . . A bit like 'If I Needed Someone'—you know, the basic riff going through it is somewhat the same, but it's actually quite a simple tune. It's a three-part harmony thing which John, Paul, and myself all sing together. . . . I think this is possibly my favorite one on the album because it's so damn simple. The lyrics are uncomplicated, but the harmony was actually pretty difficult to sing. We had to really learn it, but I think it's one of the tunes that will definitely impress most people."   Late 1969, *Celebration*

●

# "YOU NEVER GIVE ME YOUR MONEY"

**AUTHORSHIP** McCartney (1.00)
The song was apparently inspired by the money hassles McCartney, the Beatles, and Apple were going through. Apple was losing money through badly thought-out projects and outright theft by employees, and Lennon and McCartney were fighting a losing battle to own their song publishing.

**RECORDED**
May 6, 1969, at Olympic Sound Studios, with overdubbing added July 1, 11, 15, 30, and 31 and August 5, at Abbey Road
*Abbey; Day* and *Road* and *Diary* say work began July 15.

**INSTRUMENTATION**
McCARTNEY: bass, piano, lead and backing vocal
LENNON: lead guitar, backing vocal

HARRISON: rhythm guitar
STARR: drums, tambourine

*Record; Road* agrees on McCartney's piano and Lennon's backing vocal but says Harrison sang the harmony vocal at end; *ATN* omits all except McCartney's vocal.

**COMMENTS BY BEATLES**
HARRISON: "... It does two verses of one tune, and then the bridge is almost like a different song altogether, so it's quite melodic."  Late 1969, *Celebration*

●

# "SUN KING"

**AUTHORSHIP** Lennon (1.00)
Lennon said this song came to him in a dream.  *Record*

**RECORDED**
"Sun King" and "Mean Mr. Mustard" were recorded as one song July 24, 1969, at Abbey Road. Overdubbing was added July 25 and 29.
*Abbey; Day* and *Road* and *Diary* say work on "Sun King" began July 24.

HARRISON: "At the time, [Fleetwood Mac's] 'Albatross' was out, with all the reverb on guitar. So we said, 'Let's be Fleetwood Mac doing "Albatross," ' just to get going. It never really sounded like Fleetwood Mac ... but [it was] the point of origin." *Musician* (November 1987)

## INSTRUMENTATION

McCARTNEY: bass, harmonium    HARRISON: lead guitar
LENNON: lead guitar, maracas,    STARR: drums, bongos
multi-tracked vocal    George Martin: organ

*Record; Road* says Lennon, McCartney, and Harrison share harmony vocals and agrees on Lennon's maracas, McCartney's harmonium, Starr's bongos, and Martin's organ.

Several acoustic guitars were added, as were various nature noises.

*Road*

## MISCELLANEOUS
The original title was "Los Paranoias."

*Celebration* and *A-Z* and *Record; Abbey* says it was originally recorded as "Here Comes the Sun-King."

## COMMENTS BY BEATLES
LENNON: "That's a piece of garbage I had around."

September 1980, *Playboy Interviews*

●

# "MEAN MR. MUSTARD"

**AUTHORSHIP** Lennon (1.00)
LENNON: "This was just one of those written in India" in early 1968.

*Own Words;* a Harrison quote in *Celebration* corroborated that it was written in India.

LENNON: "That's me, writing a piece of garbage. I'd read somewhere in the newspaper about this mean guy who hid five-pound notes, not up his nose but somewhere else. No, it had nothing to do with cocaine."

September 1980, *Playboy Interviews*

## RECORDED
"Sun King" and "Mean Mr. Mustard" were recorded as one song July 24, 1969, at Abbey Road. Overdubbing was added July 25 and 29.

*Abbey; Day* and *Road* and *Diary* say work on "Mean Mr. Mustard" began July 24.

This song was rehearsed during the *Let It Be* sessions in January 1969. The lyrics were essentially the same then, except Mr. Mustard's sister was named Shirley, not Pam.    Bootlegs

## INSTRUMENTATION

McCARTNEY: fuzz bass, harmony vocal
LENNON: piano, lead vocal

HARRISON: lead guitar
STARR: drums, tambourine

*Record; Road* says Harrison sang backing vocal and McCartney played piano, and corroborates that tambourine was used.

●

# "POLYTHENE PAM"

**AUTHORSHIP** Lennon (1.00)
Written in India in early 1968, according to Lennon and Harrison.
*Own Words* and *Celebration*

LENNON: "That was me, remembering a little event with a woman in Jersey, and a man who was England's answer to Allen Ginsberg, who gave us our first exposure. . . . I met him when we were on tour and he took me back to his apartment, and I had a girl and he had one he wanted me to meet. He said she dressed up in polythene, which she *did*. She didn't wear jackboots and kilts, I just sort of elaborated. Perverted sex in a polythene bag. Just looking for something to write about."   September 1980, *Playboy Interviews*

## RECORDED

"Polythene Pam" and "She Came in Through the Bathroom Window" were recorded as one song July 25, 1969, at Abbey Road. Overdubbing was added July 28 and 30.

*Abbey; Day* and *Diary* say "Polythene Pam" was recorded July 28; *Road* says work began July 28.

LENNON: ". . . When I recorded it, I used a thick Liverpool accent because it was supposed to be about a mythical Liverpool scrubber dressed up in her jackboots and kilt." *Own Words*

## INSTRUMENTATION

McCARTNEY: bass, lead guitar, harmony vocal
LENNON: acoustic guitar, lead guitar, lead vocal

HARRISON: rhythm guitar, tambourine
STARR: drums, maracas

*Record; Road* says Lennon played maracas and McCartney cowbells and piano, while Harrison contributed backing vocals and tambourine.

## MISCELLANEOUS

Originally intended for the White Album but not recorded. *Diary* and *Road*

●

# "SHE CAME IN THROUGH THE BATHROOM WINDOW"

**AUTHORSHIP** McCartney (1.00)
Written May 13, 1968, in New York. *Diary*

According to one source, McCartney said this song was inspired by an incident in which a fan entered his house uninvited. A-Z  That may not be true. Intrusions and break-ins became a problem after Paul's marriage to Linda Eastman in March 1969—McCartney even had to negotiate for the return of a photo of his father  Salewicz  —but the song was rehearsed during the *Let It Be* sessions in January.  Bootlegs

LENNON: "[Paul] wrote that when we were in New York announcing Apple [spring 1968], and we first met Linda. Maybe she's the one that came in the window."  September 1980, *Playboy Interviews*  McCartney had actually met Linda at least twice before.  *Love*

## RECORDED

The song was rehearsed January 22, 1969, at Apple Studios, during the *Let It Be* sessions.  *Abbey; Road* says January 13.  For one version, which has appeared on bootleg albums, *Lennon* sings the lead vocal.  Bootlegs  "Polythene Pam" and "She Came in Through the Bathroom Window" were recorded as one song July 25, 1969, at Abbey Road. Overdubbing was added July 28 and 30.

*Abbey; Diary* says "She Came in Through the Bathroom Window" was recorded July 25; *Day* and *Road* say work began July 25.

## INSTRUMENTATION

McCARTNEY: lead guitar, lead and backing vocal
LENNON: acoustic guitar, backing vocal

HARRISON: bass, tambourine
STARR: drums, maracas

*Record; Road* says McCartney played piano and Lennon and Harrison provided backing vocals; *ATN* gives only McCartney's lead vocal.

## MISCELLANEOUS

This song's original title was "Bathroom Window."  *Day*

McCartney originally wanted to have Joe Cocker record the song. Cocker did so after the release of the Beatles' version.  A-Z

## COMMENTS BY BEATLES

HARRISON: "... A very strange song of Paul's with terrific lyrics, but it's hard to explain what they're all about!"  Late 1969, *Celebration*

●

# "GOLDEN SLUMBERS"

**AUTHORSHIP** McCartney (.7) and Thomas Dekker (.3)
McCARTNEY: "I was at my father's house in Cheshire messing about on the piano and I came across the traditional tune 'Golden Slumbers' in a songbook of Ruth's [his step-sister]. And I thought it would be nice to write my own 'Golden Slumbers.' " *Own Words*

"I can't read music and I couldn't remember the old tune, so I started playing my tune to it, and I liked the words so I just kept that." *Forever*

The original "Golden Slumbers" was a four-hundred-year-old poem by Thomas Dekker. *A-Z; List* and *Forever* agree on Dekker and age of poem.

McCartney changed the lyrics slightly. The original lines, as written by Dekker:

*Golden slumbers kiss your eyes;*
*smiles awake you when you rise.*
*Sleep pretty wantons do not cry,*
*and I will sing a lullaby.*
*Rock them, rock them, lullaby.* *Forever*

McCartney wrote the rest of the song's lyrics. *Road*

## RECORDED
"Golden Slumbers" and "Carry That Weight" were recorded as one song July 2, 1969, at Abbey Road. Overdubbing was added July 3, 4, 30, and 31 and August 15.

*Abbey; Day* and *A-Z* and *Diary* and *Road* say "Golden Slumbers" was recorded July 31; *A-Z* says it was the last song the Beatles recorded together.

## INSTRUMENTATION
McCARTNEY: bass, piano, vocal      Session musicians: strings
STARR: drums

*Record; Road* agrees on McCartney's piano and orchestral backing.

## COMMENTS BY BEATLES
HARRISON: ". . . Another very melodic tune of Paul's which is also quite nice." Late 1969, *Celebration*

## COMMENTS BY OTHERS
BOB ZEMECKIS, film director: "The first 8mm films I made when I was thirteen had Beatles music on the soundtracks. Even my first 16mm film at USC used 'Golden Slumbers' on the track." *Crawdaddy* (June 1978)

# "CARRY THAT WEIGHT"

**AUTHORSHIP** McCartney (1.00)
In this song McCartney shows his feelings on carrying the burden to keep the Beatles together during 1969—a hard year full of conflicts.  *A-Z; Record* supports.

**RECORDED**
"Golden Slumbers" and "Carry That Weight" were recorded as one song July 2, 1969, at Abbey Road. Overdubbing was added July 3, 4, 30, and 31 and August 15.  *Abbey; Day* and *Diary* say "Carry That Weight" was recorded July 31.

**INSTRUMENTATION**
McCARTNEY: piano, lead and chorus vocal
LENNON: bass, chorus vocal
HARRISON: lead guitar, chorus vocal

STARR: drums, chorus vocal
Session musicians: strings, brass

*Record; Road* agrees on group singing on chorus and orchestral backing.

All four Beatles sing the "Carry that weight" chorus. All but Starr sing the "I never give you my pillow" verse.  *Road*

# "THE END"

**AUTHORSHIP** McCartney (1.00)
LENNON: "That's Paul again, the unfinished song, right? . . . He had a line in it—'The love you take is equal to the love you make'—which is a very cosmic, philosophical line. Which again proves that if he wants to, he can think."  September 1980, *Playboy Interviews* (corrected lyric)

**RECORDED**
July 23, 1969, at Abbey Road, with overdubbing added August 5, 7, 8, 15, and 18  *Abbey; Day* and *Diary* say it was recorded July 31.

## INSTRUMENTATION

McCARTNEY: bass, piano, lead and backing vocal
LENNON: lead guitar, backing vocal
HARRISON: rhythm guitar, backing vocal

STARR: drums
Session musicians: strings

*Record; Road* agrees on orchestral backing.

McCartney, Harrison, and Lennon take turns on lead guitar, in that order and one bar at a time, during the solo.

*Forever; Guitar* (November 1987) agrees on order.

The song includes the only recorded drum solo by Starr as a Beatle.

*Forever* and *Guitar* (November 1987)

McCARTNEY: "We could never persuade Ringo to do a solo. The only thing we ever persuaded him to do was that rumble in 'The End' on *Abbey Road*. He said, 'I hate solos.' " *Musician* (February 1988)

## MISCELLANEOUS

Appropriately, this was the last significant song at the end of the last album recorded by the Beatles.

●

# "HER MAJESTY"

**AUTHORSHIP** McCartney (1.00)
Written as a tribute to the Queen of England. *Road*

## RECORDED

July 2, 1969, at Abbey Road, by McCartney

*Abbey; Diary* agrees on date; *Day* says recorded July 2 to 4.

McCartney, as usual, was the first Beatle in the studio and recorded this song quickly—in three takes—before the others arrived. *Abbey*

## INSTRUMENTATION

McCARTNEY: acoustic guitar, vocal

*Record; Road* agrees with McCartney's guitar and vocal and that other Beatles were not in the studio.

## MISCELLANEOUS

At 23 seconds, this is the shortest recorded Beatles song. *Road*

"Her Majesty" was originally meant to be placed in the middle of the album's medley, between "Mean Mr. Mustard" and "Polythene Pam." When a rough edit of the medley was put together July 30, McCartney changed his mind.

JOHN KURLANDER, second engineer: "We did all the remixes and cross-fades to overlap the songs, Paul was there, and we heard it together for the first time. He said, 'I don't like "Her Majesty," throw it away,' so I cut it out —but I accidentally left in the last note. He said, 'It's only a rough mix, it doesn't matter,' in other words, don't bother about making a clean edit because it's only a rough mix. . . .

"I'd been told never to throw anything away, so after he left I picked it up off the floor, put about twenty seconds of red leader tape before it and stuck it onto the end of the edit tape. The next day, down at Apple, Malcolm Davies cut a playback lacquer of the whole sequence and, even though I'd written on the box that 'Her Majesty' was unwanted, he too thought, 'Well, mustn't throw anything away, I'll put it on at the end.'

"I'm only assuming this, but when Paul got that lacquer he must have *liked* hearing 'Her Majesty' tacked on the end. . . . We never remixed 'Her Majesty' again, that was the mix which ended up on the finished LP." *Abbey*

This is why "Her Majesty" doesn't have a final guitar chord—it lays, unheard, at the beginning of "Polythene Pam." And the jarring electric guitar chord that begins "Her Majesty" is actually from the end of the original "Mean Mr. Mustard." *Abbey*

"Her Majesty" was not originally listed on the album package. *Forever*

▲ ▼ ▲

# "YOU KNOW MY NAME
# (LOOK UP THE NUMBER)"

**CHART ACTION**
UNITED KINGDOM: Released as a single March 6, 1970, as the B side to
"Let It Be." *Road*

UNITED STATES: Released as a single March 11, 1970. It failed to chart.
*Road*

**AUTHORSHIP** Lennon (1.00)

**RECORDED**
This was recorded as an instrumental in five parts May 17 and June 7 and
8, and combined June 9, 1967, shortly after the release of *Sgt. Pepper*.
Lennon and McCartney added vocals and sound effects April 30, 1969,
assisted by Mal Evans. Three different mono mixes were then made. Lennon
edited the best mix down from about six minutes to its final length on
November 26, 1969, in anticipation of issuing it as a Plastic Ono Band
single. The idea was dropped at the last minute. All work was done at Abbey
Road.

*Abbey; Road* says original sessions were in early 1967; *Day* says May 1967; *Record* says it was recorded
during the White Album sessions.

**INSTRUMENTATION**
McCARTNEY: piano, double bass,
lead vocal
LENNON: maracas, lead vocal
HARRISON: xylophone, backing
vocal

STARR: drums, bongos, lead vocal
Brian Jones of the Rolling Stones:
saxophone (taped June 8, 1967)
Mal Evans: backing vocal

*Record; Road* agrees on Evans's vocal; *Road* and Lennon quote in *Playboy Interviews* and *Abbey* confirm
Jones of Stones on sax; Coleman says it was *not* the Stones' Brian Jones but a session musician.

**COMMENTS BY BEATLES**
LENNON: "That was a piece of unfinished music that I turned into a comedy
record with Paul. I was waiting for him in his house, and I saw the phone
book was on the piano with the words, 'You know the name, look up the
number.' That was like a logo, and I just changed it. It was going to be a
Four Tops kind of song—the chord changes are like that—but it never
developed, and we made a joke of it." September 1980, *Playboy Interviews*

McCARTNEY: "... Probably my favorite Beatles track.... Just because it's so insane. All the memories ... I mean, what would you do if a guy like John Lennon turned up at the studio and said, 'I've got a new song.' I said, 'What's the words?' and he replied, 'You know my name look up the number.' I asked, 'What's the rest of it?' 'No, no other words, those are the words. And I wanna do it like a mantra!' ...

"We had these endless, crazy fun sessions.... And it was just hilarious to put that record together. It's not a great melody or anything, it's just unique." *Abbey*

▲ ▼ ▲

# APPENDIX 1
## THE GREAT SONGWRITING CONTEST

○

STARR: "The priority was always the song. The song is what remains. It's not how you've done it. I honestly believe in the song more than the music. It's the song people whistle. You don't whistle my drum part. And John and Paul wrote some amazing songs." *Big Beat*

McCARTNEY: "We were always in competition. I wrote 'Penny Lane,' so he wrote 'Strawberry Fields.' That was how it was." May 3, 1981, *Beatles*

MARTIN: "They did love each other very much throughout the time I knew them in the studio. But the tension was there mostly because they never really collaborated. They were never Rodgers and Hart. They were always songwriters who helped each other with little bits and pieces. One would have most of a song finished, play it to the other, and he'd say: 'Well, why don't you do this?' That was just about the way their collaboration worked.'" Coleman

LENNON: "You could say that [Paul] provided a lightness, an optimism, while I would always go for the sadness, the discords, a certain bluesy edge. . . . I'd be the one to figure out where to go with a song—a story that Paul would start. In a lot of the songs, my stuff is the middle-eight, the bridge." September 1980, *Playboy Interviews*

The Lennon/McCartney songwriting credit obscured the true author of most of the songs the Beatles recorded. Generally, the lead vocalist was the author, with the exception of most songs Ringo Starr sang and early lead vocals by Harrison. Beyond that it gets much trickier. Lennon and McCartney would often help each other with little bits of lyric, assistance that became known only because they sometimes mentioned specific examples in interviews. Those comments are collected in this book.

The specific credit breakdowns for each song are noted in each song entry, along with information to indicate how the credits were determined.

Some examples:

"Paperback Writer": McCartney .8; Lennon .2

"Penny Lane": McCartney .8; Lennon .2

"Norwegian Wood": McCartney .2; Lennon .8

"The Word": McCartney .4; Lennon .6
"Michelle": McCartney .7; Lennon .3
"What Goes On": McCartney .2; Lennon .6; Starr .2
"Revolution 9": Lennon .75; Yoko Ono .25
"Golden Slumbers": McCartney .7; Thomas Dekker .3

For some titles, in which separate songs by Lennon and McCartney were combined—such as "Baby You're a Rich Man" and "I've Got a Feeling"—and for songs Lennon and/or McCartney simply acknowledged were written together, one-half credit is given to each.

Only compositions that appear on a record label of an official release are counted. That leaves out the short unlisted McCartney tune that precedes "Revolution 9" on the White Album but includes his twenty-three-second "Her Majesty" on *Abbey Road*. Duplications, such as the single and album versions of "Revolution," though they are in vastly different tempos, are counted only once.

Following are the number of songs—recorded and officially released by the Beatles—written by various songwriters.

And the winner is:

LENNON: 84.55
McCARTNEY: 73.65
HARRISON: 22.15
Carl Perkins: 3
Larry Williams: 3
STARR: 2.7
Chuck Berry: 2
Arthur Alexander: 1
Bert Berns (Medley/Russell): 1
Bradford and Gordy: 1
David, Williams, and Bacharach: 1
Dixon and Farrell: 1
Garret, Bateman, Dobbins, Holland, and Gorman: 1
Richard P. Drapkin: 1
Goffin and King: 1
Buddy Holly: 1
Roy Lee Jackson: 1
Marlow and Scott: 1
Smokey Robinson: 1
Russell and Morrison: 1
Meredith Willson: 1
(Public Domain): 1
Richard Penniman (Little Richard): 0.83
Johnson and Blackwell: 0.67

Leiber and Stoller: 0.5
Yoko Ono: 0.45
Thomas Dekker: 0.3
Derek Taylor: 0.1
Louise Harrison: 0.05
Kahlil Gibran: 0.05
TOTAL: 209

How did Lennon write the most songs for the Beatles? There was a general understanding during the Beatles' existence that he and McCartney would equally split the songwriting presented on each album (other than Harrison's contributions). And that generally held true, except for a short period in early 1964.

While the Beatles were conquering the United States, and the pressure was on to produce more recordings and consolidate their gains, Lennon wrote a lot of songs, and for some reason McCartney's productivity fell off.

Chart 1 below clearly shows that Lennon firmly took the lead with the *Hard Day's Night* album and the singles released immediately before it. His margin during that period was 12.95 songs to 3.05. Singles and tracks off EPs are included in the total for the album that followed.

Chart 2 shows the songwriting totals of Lennon and McCartney album to album. It shows that Lennon slightly outwrote McCartney for each of the first two albums, by about ten songs during the *Hard Day's Night* period, and by a mere two-tenths of a song on *For Sale*. They tied during the *Help!* period and Lennon outwrote McCartney by almost two songs around *Rubber Soul*. Lennon led 42.9 to 27.9 at that point.

Then McCartney outwrote Lennon until the White Album. Lennon had a slight edge for the remainder of the group's life. McCartney's prolific songwriting during the Beatles' middle years was not enough to make up for Lennon's overwhelming dominance during the *Hard Day's Night* period.

It should be noted that Lennon's total was helped by his many interviews in which he noted his contributions in writing parts of songs. McCartney has been less revealing (more modest?) and many of his contributions to Lennon's songs are not known.

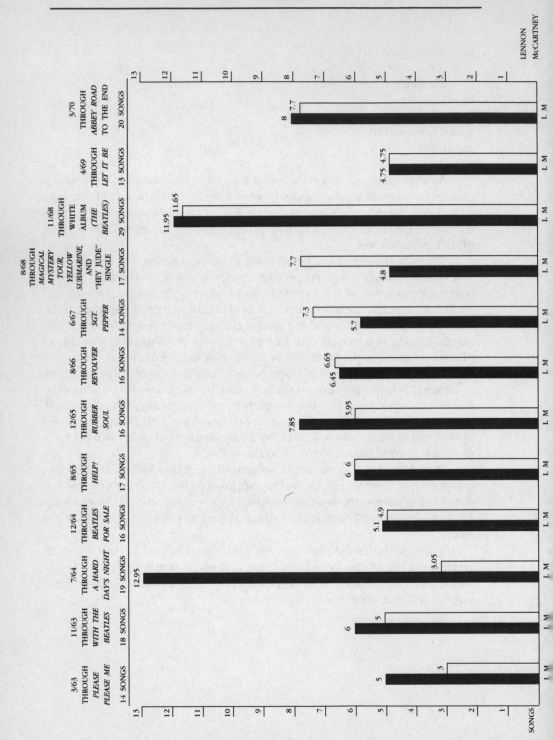

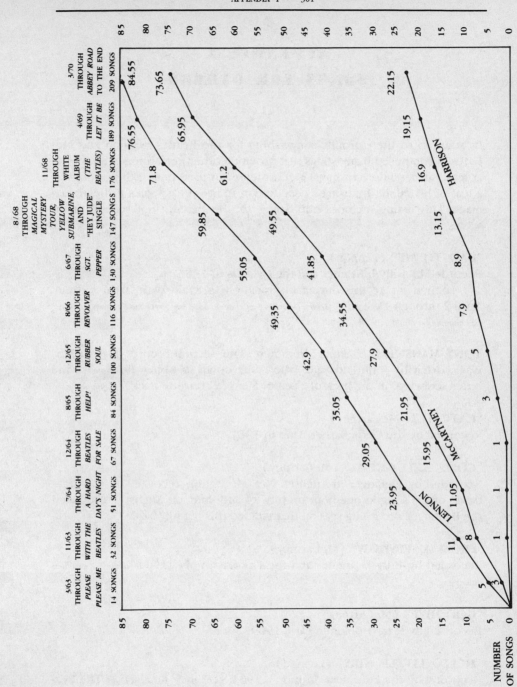

# APPENDIX 2
# SONGS FOR OTHERS

○

In addition to their prolific songwriting for the Beatles, Lennon and Mc-Cartney composed many songs that provided other performers with hits or at least successful recordings. McCartney even used one of these songs as a test of his talent, by using a pseudonym to avoid easy sales to Beatlemaniacs. This listing includes only songs the Beatles did not release themselves.

**"BAD TO ME"** (Lennon)
Recorded by Billy J. Kramer and the Dakotas in 1963.
    Lennon wrote this during his vacation in Spain with Brian Epstein, April 2 through 11, 1963. *Diary; Day* says Beatles recorded a version of this February 11, 1963; other sources say in March.

TONY MANSFIELD, Dakotas drummer: "Our second record, 'Bad to Me,' was written by John and Paul, who came down to Abbey Road with the lyrics scrawled on the back of a Senior Service cigarette pack." *Celebration*

**"CATCALL"** (McCartney)
Recorded by the Chris Barber Band in 1967. *Road*

**"COME AND GET IT"** (McCartney)
Recorded by Badfinger in August 1969. McCartney recorded an elaborate demo of the song in one hour on July 24 and then, on August 2, produced the Badfinger recording session that yielded this big hit. *Abbey*

**"FROM A WINDOW"** (McCartney)
Recorded by Billy J. Kramer and the Dakotas in May 1964. *Day; A-Z* provides only the year.

**"GOODBYE"** (McCartney)
Recorded by Mary Hopkin in early 1969. *Road*

**"HELLO LITTLE GIRL"** (Lennon)
Recorded by the Fourmost on July 3, 1963, at Abbey Road. *Day* The Beatles recorded versions in 1962 and 1964. Both were unreleased. *Day* This was one of the songs the Beatles performed during their unsuccessful audition for Decca in 1962. *A-Z*

LENNON: "This was one of the first songs I ever finished. I was then about eighteen and we gave it to the Fourmost. I think it was the first song of my own that I ever attempted to do with the group." *Own Words*

**"I DON'T WANT TO SEE YOU AGAIN"** (McCartney)
Recorded by Peter and Gordon in early August 1964 at Abbey Road. *Day*

**"I'LL BE ON MY WAY"** (McCartney)
Recorded by Billy J. Kramer and the Dakotas in March 1963. Performed by the Beatles on BBC radio in fall 1962. *Day*

LENNON: "That's Paul, through and through. Doesn't it sound like him? Tra la la la la [laughs]." September 1980, *Playboy Interviews*

**"I'LL KEEP YOU SATISFIED"** (McCartney)
Recorded by Billy J. Kramer and the Dakotas on July 22, 1963. *Day*

**"I'M IN LOVE"** (Lennon)
Recorded by the Fourmost in October 1963 at Abbey Road. *Day*

**"IT'S FOR YOU"** (McCartney)
Recorded by Cilla Black in early 1964. *Road*

**"LIKE DREAMERS DO"** (McCartney)
Recorded by the Applejacks in April 1964. *Day* This was one of the songs the Beatles performed during their unsuccessful audition for Decca in 1962. *A-Z*

**"LOVE OF THE LOVED"** (McCartney)
Recorded by Cilla Black in July 1963. The Beatles recorded an unreleased version in 1963. *Day* This was one of the songs performed by the Beatles during their unsuccessful audition for Decca. *A-Z*

LENNON: "One of his very early songs, but I think he changed the words later for Cilla." *Hit Parader* (April 1972)

**"NOBODY I KNOW"** (McCartney)
Recorded by Peter and Gordon in April 1964 at Abbey Road. *Day*

**"ONE AND ONE IS TWO"** (McCartney)
Recorded by Mike Shannon with the Strangers in March 1964. *Day; A-Z* says the Strangers with Mike Shannon in 1964. The Beatles recorded an unreleased version in 1964. *Day*

LENNON: "That was a terrible one."  *Hit Parader* (April 1972)
　　This song never made the charts.  *A-Z*

**"SOUR MILK SEA"** (Harrison)
Recorded by Jackie Lomax in 1968. Harrison produced the session.  *Road*

**"STEP INSIDE LOVE"** (McCartney)
Recorded by Cilla Black in early 1968. It was written as the theme for
Black's BBC television series.  *Road*

**"THAT MEANS A LOT"** (McCartney)
Recorded by P. J. Proby in 1965.  *Road*

**"THINGUMYBOB"** (McCartney)
Recorded by the John Foster and Sons Ltd. Black Dyke Mills Band in 1968.
It was written as the theme for the BBC television series "Thingumybob."
*Road*

**"TIP OF MY TONGUE"** (McCartney)
Recorded by Tommy Quickly in June 1963.  *Day; A-Z says 1963.*  The Beatles
recorded an unreleased version in March 1963 at Abbey Road.  *Day* and *Road*

**"WOMAN"** (McCartney, under the pseudonym of Bernard Webb)
Recorded by Peter and Gordon in late 1965.  *Road*

**"A WORLD WITHOUT LOVE"** (McCartney)
Recorded by Peter and Gordon on January 21, 1964.  *Day*

LENNON: "An early one he wrote when he was about sixteen or seventeen.
I think he changed the words later for the record by Peter and Garfunkel
or something."  *Hit Parader* (April 1972)
　　Lennon derisively thought the lyrics of this song were hilarious, particularly the line "Please lock me away."  *Coleman*

●

# APPENDIX 3
# UNRELEASED RECORDINGS

○

HARRISON: "What never came out was stuff that wasn't supposed to be a record. That is to say if we were rehearsing things and someone happened to leave the tape running. It's not supposed to represent the Beatles or their music. But people want to scrape the barrel for anything they can find."
Denver *Post* (October 18, 1987)

NORMAN SMITH, Beatles' engineer through *Rubber Soul:* "We always had a lot of fun together [in the studio]. We recorded a lot of strange remarks, jokes, imitations, and craziness. It's all still in the EMI archives; someday they'll use it as a piece of pop history."   Diary

Following are some of the recordings by the Beatles that were not officially released. It is, by necessity, an incomplete list.

### RECORDED FALL 1960
"Fever"
"Summertime"
"September Song"
These were the first recordings by the Beatles. They backed bassist/vocalist Lu Walters from Rory Storm and the Hurricanes. Recorded at Akustik Studios, Hamburg, West Germany, for £10. A 78 rpm disk was produced, of which four copies were made. Performing were Lennon, McCartney, Harrison, Stu Sutcliffe, and Ringo Starr (subbing for Pete Best).
*Day; Live* says only "Summertime" was recorded.

### RECORDED MAY (OR APRIL) 1961
"Kansas City"
"Hey, Hey, Hey, Hey"
"What'd I Say"
Versions of these were recorded by Tony Sheridan and the Beat Bros. (Beatles) in Hamburg for Polydor Records.   *Day*  A later medley of "Kansas City/Hey, Hey, Hey, Hey" appeared on *Beatles for Sale.*

### RECORDED JANUARY 1, 1962
"Like Dreamers Do" (McCartney) (McCartney: lead vocal)
"Money (That's What I Want)" (Lennon: lead vocal)
"September in the Rain" (McCartney: lead vocal)

These are among the songs recorded during the Beatles' unsuccessful audition for Decca Records.  *A-Z* and *Road*

## RECORDED IN EARLY TO MID-1962

"Catswalk," later known as "Catcall" (instrumental)
"I Lost My Little Girl"
"Looking Glass"
"Thinking of Linking"
"The Years Roll Along"
"Winston's Walk" (Lennon: lead vocal)
"Keep Looking That Way"
Recorded for a demonstration tape for Decca Records. "Catcall" was later recorded by the Chris Barber Band in 1967.  *Day* and *Road*

## RECORDED (MAYBE) JUNE 1962

"Besame Mucho" (McCartney: lead vocal)
Apparently recorded at the Parlophone audition.

## RECORDED AUGUST 18, 1962

"Some Other Guy"
A live recording made at the Cavern Club the same night as Starr's first session as a group member.  *Day*

## RECORDED SEPTEMBER 11, 1962

"Please Please Me"
The original slow version recorded at the same session as the first single. A speeded-up version of this song became the Beatles' second single and their first big hit.  *Day*

## RECORDED NOVEMBER 26, 1962

"How Do You Do It" (Mitch Murray) (Lennon: lead vocal)
Recorded for Parlophone. The Beatles at first refused George Martin's recommendation that they record and release this song as their second single. Martin compromised: If they would record this, he would allow them to record the reworked "Please Please Me" and "Ask Me Why." The group unenthusiastically played "How Do You Do It" and then put all their energy into "Please Please Me," which convinced Martin that that should be the single. After a tea break, the group recorded "Ask Me Why." "How Do You Do It" was later the first hit single by Gerry and the Pacemakers.
*Diary*

## RECORDED IN LATE 1962
"I Forgot to Remember to Forget"
"Lucille"
"Dizzy Miss Lizzy"
   A later version of the last appeared on *Help!*  Road

## RECORDED FEBRUARY 11, 1963
"Hold Me Tight" (an early version)
"Keep Your Hands off My Baby"
   These were recorded during the *Please Please Me* session. The Beatles
did release a remake of "Hold Me Tight" nine months later.

*Day* and *Road*; *Abbey* says "Keep Your Hands off My Baby" was not recorded.

## RECORDED MARCH 1963
"Tip of My Tongue"  Road

## RECORDED (MAYBE) MARCH 1963
"One After 909"
   Slightly slower than the version on the *Let It Be* LP.  Bootlegs

## RECORDED PROBABLY IN 1963
"Carol" (Chuck Berry) (Lennon: lead vocal)
"Clarabella" (Frank Pingatore) (a hard rocker with McCartney: lead
vocal)
"Don't Ever Change" (Goffin/King)
"Hippy Hippy Shake" (Chan Romero) (a hard rocker with McCartney:
lead vocal)
"I Got a Woman" (Ray Charles) (Lennon: lead vocal)
"Lend Me Your Comb" (Kay Twomey/Fred Wise/Ben Wiseman [or Weis-
man]) (harmony vocals with McCartney lead on middle-eight)
"Lonesome Tears in My Eyes" (Burnette/Burnette/Burlison/Mortimer)
(C&W with Lennon: lead vocal)
"Memphis" (Chuck Berry) (Harrison: lead vocal)
"Nothin' Shakin' (but the Leaves on the Trees)" (Colacrai/Fontaine/Lam-
pert/Cleveland) (Harrison: lead vocal)
"A Shot of Rhythm and Blues" (A. Alexander OR Terry Thompson)
"So How Come (No One Loves Me)" (Felice Bryant/Boudleaux Bryant)
(Harrison: lead vocal)
"Soldier of Love" (Buzz Cason/Tony Moon) (Lennon: lead vocal, with full
harmonies by band)
   Songs recorded for various BBC broadcasts, apparently bootlegged off
the air. Some of these match the performance quality of the Beatles' early
releases.  Bootlegs

## RECORDED IN 1964

"Woman" (McCartney: lead vocal)  *Day*
"One and One Is Two"
"Hello Little Girl" (apparently the second version)
"Home"
"Moonglow"
"Raunchy"
"You Are My Sunshine"
"Shout" (from a BBC-TV special taped April 27 and 28; each Beatle takes a turn as lead vocalist)  *Diary*

## RECORDED AUGUST 14, 1964

"Leave My Kitten Alone" (Turner/McDougall)
A rampaging rocker with a strong, rocking Lennon lead vocal. This is one of the best of the unreleased.  *Abbey* and bootlegs

## RECORDED SEPTEMBER 21/OCTOBER 8, 1964

"You'll Know What to Do"
"Always and Only"
Versions cut during sessions for *Beatles for Sale*.  *Day; Road* supports.

## RECORDED MAY OR JUNE 1965

"Keep Your Hands off My Baby"
Recorded by Lennon either with or without the band.  *Road*

## RECORDED OCTOBER 12/EARLY NOVEMBER 1965

"If You've Got Troubles"
Recorded during *Rubber Soul* sessions.  *Road*

## RECORDED IN MID-1966

"Pink Litmus Paper Shirt," recorded by Harrison
"Colliding Circles" (Lennon: lead vocal)  *Road*

## RECORDED MAY-JUNE 1967:

"Not Unknown" (Harrison)
"Anything" (Harrison)
"India" (Harrison)
"Annie" (McCartney)
"What's the New Mary Jane" (Lennon) (first version) (also known as "What's the News Mary Jane" or "What a Shame Mary Jane Had a Pain at the Party") (probably recorded without McCartney)
"Peace of Mind" (Lennon)
Recorded during the same period as "All You Need Is Love."  *Road*

**RECORDED (PROBABLY) IN SEPTEMBER 1967**
   "Jessie's Dream"
   "Shirley's Wild Accordion"
      Written by the Beatles and performed by accordionist Shirley Evans, these were recorded for the *Magical Mystery Tour* BBC-TV special.   *Day*

**RECORDED NOVEMBER 28, 1967**
   "Christmas Time (Is Here Again)"
      Recorded for the Beatles' Christmas album for fans. Instrumentation: Lennon: tympani; McCartney: piano; Harrison: guitar; Starr: drums. Sung by them, George Martin, and actor Victor Spinetti.   *Abbey*

**RECORDED IN 1968**
   "Step Inside Love"
   "Goodbye"
      Both primarily McCartney recordings, "Step Inside Love" was written as the theme music for the Cilla Black BBC-TV series. "Goodbye" was later recorded by Mary Hopkin, on March 1 and 2, 1969, with McCartney producing; it was a big hit.   *Road* and bootlegs

**RECORDED MARCH 15, 1968**
   "Indian Ropetrick/Happy Birthday Mike Love"
      Recorded in Rishikesh, India, without Starr.   *Day*

**RECORDED AUGUST 7, 1968**
   "Not Guilty"
      Written by Harrison. Eric Clapton added a guitar track to it. Harrison said he wrote it before the White Album and "it seems to be about that period: Paul-John-Apple-Rishikesh-Indian friends, etc."   Bootlegs
      A version of the song was later used on the *George Harrison* LP (1979).   *Diary* agrees on date.

**RECORDED AUGUST 14, 1968**
   "What's the New Mary Jane" (Lennon)   *Diary* and *Abbey*

**RECORDED JANUARY 1969**
   "All Shook Up"
   "All Things Must Pass" (Harrison: lead vocal)
   "Be-Bop-A-Lula"
   "Blowin' in the Wind"
   "Blue Suede Shoes"
   "Commonwealth" (political song ad-libbed by McCartney)
   "Domino" (McCartney: lead vocal)

"Don't Be Cruel"

"Good Rockin' Tonight"

"Hare Krishna" (mock version by McCartney who sang about Harold Pinsker, Apple's chief financial advisor)

"Hi Ho Silver"

"Hitch Hike"

"The House of the Rising Sun"

"I Threw It All Away" (Dylan) (Harrison: lead vocal)

"Little Queenie"

"Love Me Do"

"Lucille"

"Mailman, Bring Me No More Blues" (Lennon: lead vocal)

"Mean Mr. Mustard"

"Michael Row the Boat Ashore"

"Midnight Special"

"Penina" (McCartney: lead vocal)

"Save the Last Dance"

"Shaking in the Sixties" (Lennon: lead vocal)

"She Came in Through the Bathroom Window" (Lennon: lead vocal at beginning)

"Short Fat Fanny"

"Stand by Me"

"Suzy Parker" (improvised)

"Teddy Boy" (McCartney later recorded for solo LP)

"Tennessee"

"Third Man Theme"

"Watching Rainbows" (Lennon: lead vocal)

"When Irish Eyes Are Smiling"

"White Power/Winston, Richard and John" (McCartney ad-libs vocal, calling out names)

"Whole Lotta Shakin' Going On"

"You Win Again"

These are among the many songs recorded during the *Let It Be* LP sessions. Most of the songs were just fragments. It's estimated that more than one hundred songs recorded during the month were officially unreleased. Of that total, some fifty-seven tracks have never shown up anywhere, including on bootleg albums.   *Day* and bootlegs

## RECORDED EARLY MARCH 1969

"What's the New Mary Jane" (another version) (Lennon)

"Jubilee" (later known as "Junk" on *McCartney* LP. Written in India.)

"Not Guilty" (another version) (Harrison)

"I Should Like to Live up a Tree" (Starr: lead vocals)

Lennon almost released ". . . Mary Jane" as a single in December 1969. It was slated for release on Apple for December 5, 1969, b/w "You Know My Name (Look Up the Number)," and then pulled back. "You Know My Name" later appeared as the B side of "Let It Be." *Day*

## RECORDED SUMMER 1969
"Bad Penny Blues"
"Four Nights in Moscow"
"Just Dancing Around"
"Little Eddie"
"My Kind of Girl"
"Portraits of My Love"
"Proud as You Are"
"Suicide"
"Swinging Days"
"When Everybody Comes to Town" or "When I Come to Town"
"Zero Is Just Another Number"   *Day*

## UNKNOWN TIME
"Lullaby for a Lazy Day"

A tape of this song was found among Lennon's personal possessions after his death. It's supposedly a finished performance. Lennon's voice is ethereal and high-pitched over a slow tempo. Backing vocals consist of wordless falsetto voices.   *Musician* (April 1988)

# BIBLIOGRAPHY

○

**BOOK SOURCE KEY**

***Abbey*** ***The Beatles: Recording Sessions.*** 1988. Mark Lewisohn. Harmony Books, New York. © EMI Records Ltd. Excerpts appear as liner notes on the *Sgt. Pepper's Lonely Hearts Club Band* and *Past Masters* compact discs. Fascinating information from notes and tapes made at all the Beatles' recording sessions. Highly recommended.

***ATN*** *All Together Now.* 1976. Harry Castleman and Walter J. Podrazik. Ballantine Books, New York. A lot of dates and session information, but some omissions in this discography.

***A-Z*** *The Beatles A to Z.* 1980. Friede/Titone/Weiner. Methuen, New York. A fun browse.

***Ballad*** *The Ballad of John and Yoko.* 1982. The editors of *Rolling Stone.* Rolling Stone Press, Garden City, New York. An interesting "greatest hits" package of *Rolling Stone*'s coverage of Lennon and a lot of new material written after his murder.

***Beatles*** *The Beatles* (second revised edition, 1985). Hunter Davies. McGraw-Hill, New York. An occasionally fascinating firsthand account of the Beatles' activities in 1967–68. Particularly interesting are the accounts of three songwriting sessions.

***Beatles Book*** *The Beatles Book.* 1968. Edited by Edward E. Davis. Cowles Education Corp., New York. A collection of essays on the Beatles, by authors ranging from Timothy Leary to William F. Buckley, Jr.

***Big Beat*** *The Big Beat: Conversations with Rock's Great Drummers.* 1984. Max Weinberg with Robert Santelli. Contemporary Books, Chicago. Drummer Weinberg interviewed Ringo Starr, among others.

***Billboard*** *The Billboard Book of Top 40 Hits.* 1983. Joel Whitburn. Billboard Publications, New York. An authoritative argument settler and a key aid when putting together nostalgia hit audio tapes.

***B-Lists*** *The Book of Beatles Lists.* 1985. Charles Reinhart. Contemporary Books, Chicago. Various, mostly trivial, lists relating to the Beatles.

***Celebration*** *The Beatles: A Celebration.* 1986. Geoffrey Giuliano. Methuen, Toronto. Distributed by St. Martin's Press, New York. Lots of beautiful new photos and some interviews, mainly with the Beatles' outer circle.

**Coleman** *Lennon.* 1985. Ray Coleman. McGraw-Hill, New York. Probably the authoritative biography on John Lennon.

***Companion*** *The Lennon Companion: Twenty-five Years of Comment.* 1987. Edited by Elizabeth Thomson and David Gutman. Schirmer

Books, New York. A collection of newspaper and magazine articles about John Lennon.

**Compleat(b)**   *The Compleat Beatles,* Vols. 1 and 2. 1981. Various authors. Delilah Communications/ATV Music Publications, New York. Primarily the Beatles' arrangements of their songs. Also has reprints of some interesting articles.

**Core**   *Apple to the Core.* 1972. Peter McCabe and Robert D. Schonfeld. Pocket Books, New York. Exhaustingly details the financial tangles of Apple and the Beatles near the end.

**Day**   *A Day in the Life: The Beatles Day by Day, 1960-1970.* 1980. Compiled and edited by Tom Schultheiss. Pierian Press, Ann Arbor, Michigan. A meticulous diary-style reconstruction of the Beatles' daily activities. A good job despite mistakes and contradictions.

**Diary**   *The Beatles: An Illustrated Diary.* 1982. H. V. Fulpen. Perigee Books, New York. Similar to *Day* (above) but more readable. Also has various feature articles.

**Ears**   *All You Need Is Ears.* 1979. George Martin with Jeremy Hornsby. St. Martin's Press, New York. It's good to know what Martin, the Beatles' producer, thinks about the history he shared with the Moptops. Several pages of technical information on how he recorded the Beatles would have been nice.

**Edie**   *Edie: An American Biography.* 1982. Jean Stein. Edited with George Plimpton. Alfred A. Knopf, New York. Interesting tale of Edie Sedgwick, '60s "youthquaker" and a member of Andy Warhol's circle. Fascinating chapter on the speed/acid doctor who apparently was the subject of the Beatles' "Dr. Robert."

**Fawcett**   *John Lennon: One Day at a Time.* 1976. Anthony Fawcett. Grove Press, New York.

**Forever**   *The Beatles Forever.* 1978. Nicholas Schaffner. McGraw-Hill, New York. One of the best general reference books on the Beatles.

**Helter Skelter**   *Helter Skelter.* 1975. Vincent Bugliosi and Curt Gentry. Bantam Books, New York. Includes Charles Manson's interpretation of the Beatles song "Helter Skelter."

**I Me Mine**   *I Me Mine.* 1980. George Harrison with Derek Taylor. Simon and Schuster, New York. A slim, barely coherent narrative of Harrison's memories and philosophies combined with lyrics of his songs with and notes on their composition. Taylor's contributions help.

**Lists**   *The Book of Rock Lists.* 1981. Dave Marsh and Kevin Stein. Dell/Rolling Stone Press, New York. A quick read filled with interesting trivia on pop music.

**Live**   *The Beatles Live!* 1986. Mark Lewisohn. Henry Holt and Co., New York. Painstakingly thorough on the Beatles' more than 1,400 live performances.

**Love**    *The Love You Make.* 1983. Peter Brown and Steven Gaines. Signet/ New American Library, New York. An interesting insider's account of the Beatles' career.

**Macs**    *The Macs: Mike McCartney's Family Album.* 1981. Michael McCartney. Delilah Books, New York. Eccentric and humorous remembrances from Paul's brother.

**No Direction**    *No Direction Home: The Life and Music of Bob Dylan.* 1986. Robert Shelton. Beech Tree Books/William Morrow, New York. Not much on the Beatles, but Dylan was the *other* light during the sixties. The book overintellectualizes everything but has its moments.

**Own Words**    *Beatles in Their Own Words.* 1978. Compiled by Miles. Delilah/Putnam, New York. Interesting but with several flaws. It blends quotes together without indicating some words are missing, doesn't credit its sources, and doesn't disclose when things were said (so there's little perspective).

**Paperback**    *The Beatles, Vol. 3: Paperback Writers: The History of the Beatles in Print.* 1984. Bill Harry. Avon Books, New York. A remarkably complete run-through on books, fanzines, magazines, etc., on the Beatles.

**Playboy Interviews**    *The Playboy Interviews with John Lennon and Yoko Ono.* 1981. Interviews by David Sheff. Berkley Books, New York. A lengthy interview conducted in September 1980, some of which was published in *Playboy* magazine.

**Record**    *The Beatles on Record.* 1982. J. P. Russell. Charles Scribner's Sons, New York. A book that goes through the Beatles' catalog, song by song, providing instrumentation credits and a very subjective description of the way the songs sound.

**Record2**    *The Beatles on Record.* 1982. Mark Wallgren. Fireside, New York. Focuses on the chart-topping accomplishments of the Beatles.

**Remembers**    *Lennon Remembers: The Rolling Stone Interviews.* 1971. Jann Wenner. Straight Arrow Books, San Francisco. The most famous, and revealing, interview any of the Beatles ever gave.

**Road**    *The Long and Winding Road: A History of the Beatles on Record.* 1984. Neville Stannard. Avon Books, New York. A motherlode of information on recording sessions, plus a section on bootlegs, and the best information on the Beatles' Christmas albums.

**Salewicz**    *McCartney.* 1986. Chris Salewicz. St. Martin's Press, New York. A light biography with some interesting information.

**Shotton**    *John Lennon In My Life.* 1984. Pete Shotton with Nicholas Schaffner. Stein and Day, New York. A fun account of Shotton's long friendship with John Lennon. He adds a lot of new, insider information to the public knowledge.

**Shout**    *Shout! The Beatles in Their Generation.* 1982. Philip Norman.

Warner Books, New York. Very thorough biography, especially on the early years. McCartney hates this book because of what he considers inaccuracies.

*Transcriptions*   *Complete Beatles Transcriptions.* (No credits.) Hal Leonard Publishing Corp., Winona, Minnesota. Good information along with music/lyric sheets for some of the Beatles' songs.

*20 Years*   *It Was Twenty Years Ago Today.* 1987. Derek Taylor. Fireside, New York. Informative but rambling remembrances of the making of *Sgt. Pepper* and the Summer of Love.

*Yesterday*   *George Harrison: Yesterday and Today.* 1977. Ross Michaels. Flash Books, New York, London. A slight book, obviously put together in a hurry, with occasionally interesting graphics.

## ARTICLE SOURCE KEY

Included but not listed are articles from various newspapers. They are identified at the end of specific items.

**AP**   Associated Press. Various wire-service articles.

*Beatlefan*   *Beatlefan* magazine.

*Crawdaddy*   *Crawdaddy* magazine.

*Digital*   *Digital Audio* magazine.

**ENS**   Entertainment News Service.

**Fulton**   Series of syndicated articles by David Fulton.

*Guitar*   *Guitar Player* magazine, particularly the November 1987 issue.

*Hit Parader*   *Hit Parader* magazine. Lennon attributed authorship to songs in the April 1972 issue.

*Innersleeve*   *Innersleeve* (a Capitol Records promotional publication). Interview with McCartney about the time his solo album *London Town* was released in early 1978.

*Jamming!*   *Jamming!,* London, England. McCartney interview.

*Life*   *Life* magazine.

*Musician*   *Musician* magazine. Various interviews with solo Beatles and others.

*Newsweek*   *Newsweek* magazine.

*Now*   *Now* magazine story by Ray Coleman. Syndicated in St. Louis *Post-Dispatch,* June 17, 1980.

*People*   *People Weekly* magazine, particularly March 7, 1988, issue.

*Playboy*   *Playboy* magazine. Various interviews.

*Rock Express*   *Rock Express* magazine. November/December 1986 issue.

**RS**   *Rolling Stone.* Various issues.

## FILM SOURCE KEY

*Compleat*   *The Compleat Beatles* documentary, 1982.

*Let It Be*   *Let It Be.* 1970.

*Prince's*   *The Prince's Trust* concert. 1986.
*Kampuchea*   *Rock for Kampuchea.* Filmed December 29, 1979.

**MISCELLANEOUS**
**Bootlegs**   Various bootleg recordings.
**Capitol**   Capitol Records promotional material.
**CD**   Compact disc liner notes.

# SONG INDEX

The entries for the Beatles' songs are arranged chronologically by album (for those listening while reading) and as separate singles. Use this index to find a particular song or album. Page numbers for major entries are boldfaced; an incidental mention is distinguished with lightface type.